FROM SLAVERY TO THE STARS
A PERSONAL JOURNEY

ANDREEA KINDRYD

Published in Australia by Andreea Kindryd

First published in Australia 2023
This edition published 2023

Copyright © Andreea Kindryd 2023

Typesetting: Luke Harris, WorkingType (www.workingtype.com.au)
Cover design: Tim Kliendist, Alphabet Studio
Author photo and collages: Zak Campbell, NPZR Media

The right of Andreea Kindryd to be identified as the
Author of the Work has been asserted in accordance with the
Copyright, Designs and Patents Act 1988.

All rights reserved. No part of this publication may be reproduced, stored in a retrieval system, or transmitted, in any form or by any means without the prior written permission of the publisher, nor be otherwise circulated in any form of binding or cover other than that in which it is published and without a similar condition being imposed on the subsequent purchaser.

ISBN: 978-0-6455382-2-9

This book is my Granny responsibility.

My California grandkids inspired this book. They have families and AJ wanted to know where he came from who his people were. Chris asked how I met Malcolm X, Janina queried if I worked on *Star Trek* why had they never seen me? Writing the answers was too lonely. Talking about it was easier, and the answers became a solo show, *From Slavery to Star Trek*.

I premiered the show at the Adelaide Fringe Festival and it got invited to the very important Edinburgh Fringe Festival. It was well received and Sydney, Auckland and Los Angeles followed. The Covid 19 lockdown birthed the book. Many thanks and gratitude to all of you who worked in some way to keep us safe during that time.

Warning: The voices in this book all come from my head — some faint, some indelibly imprinted. Sometimes I'm looking back, and sometimes I feel there, in that moment ... It may be a bumpy read. I couldn't afford a ghost writer!

We are only two, and yet our howling can
Encircle the world's end.
Frightened, you are my only friend.
And frightened, we are everyone.
Someone must make a stand.
Coward, take my coward's hand.
(from Eve Merriam, "The Coward")

PART I
I'M HERE BECAUSE THEY WERE

1

For Jim Shankle the Mississippi wasn't just a river. That raging river was an almost impossible impediment separating him from Winny, the woman he loved. She had been stolen from him and was somewhere on the other side. He was determined, willing to risk everything, to get across that river to find her.

Jim couldn't just catch a ferry. He was a runaway slave. If he was caught, it would guarantee at least a whipping. At the extreme, if an example was needed, his feet could be amputated. Slave catchers, like some law enforcers today, did what they liked. They encouraged a reputation so fearsome it would even stop thoughts about freedom.

Winny and Jim had been enslaved on different plantations in Mississippi, and they'd met at church. The Catholic Pope had used 'saving African souls' as the justification for ripping them from their families and homeland; stealing these potential artists and innovators.

Slaves were allowed Sunday off to worship and to form community. Church wasn't Christian kindness. It was control. Religion offered rewards payable after death in the sweet by-and-by that required obedience in the here-and-now. The word of God was explicit: "Slaves, accept the authority of your masters with all deference, not only those who are kind and gentle but also those who are harsh." And, "Slaves, obey your earthly masters in everything you do. Try to please them all the time, not just when they are watching you". "Serve them sincerely because of your reverent fear of the Lord."[1] That fear was shared, encoded, and passed on to the next generation.

I'm sure Winny and Jim made their lives as good as they could without having control of it. But, when Winny and her three children were sent to a plantation in Texas, there was no way Jim would be without her. Jim was a planner, intelligent and determined. One night he slipped off into the darkness, leaving home to find the woman he loved. Jim became a runaway, slave-catcher prey.

Winny and the children had travelled downriver to the Gulf of Mexico and then by river up into Texas. Jim had to travel entirely by land—and at night, foraging in the dark wherever he could, eating whatever he found, and always aware that the slave catchers were out there. Their only job: to find him and take him back to his owner. Or maybe sell him to somebody else and make a bit more money. OK, a lot more money. Jim had skills. He was prime merchandise—Jim's original owner had named him specifically in his will to be given to an heir.

On the Mississippi riverbank, faced with the fact that he had no safe transport across, Jim had to come up with a solution, or he'd never see Winny again. He wasn't just smart; he was also brave. Nothing was going to keep Jim from Winny.

---

1   Ephesians 6:5-9 and Peter 2: 18-24

1

So he swam the Mississippi, and later, another river, the Sabine River, which would eventually defeat several Union attempts to invade Texas during the Civil War.

In East Texas he focused his search. Cautiously approaching other blacks, comparing what he learned from them with what he knew. One place he chose for a closer look was a plantation with fairly recent arrivals. The woman and her three children sounded very like Winny. What was lucky for Jim was that this woman was allowed to go alone every night to fill the water jugs at the spring. Jim found the spring and that evening the slow trickle of water wasn't all Winny got. She heard Jim's call. He was there, waiting, hoping, praying that it would be her. It was Winny! He found home in her arms!

★ ★ ★

Winny Brush was my grandmother's grandmother. She was born in Tennessee in 1814. The first stories I heard about Winny were from when she was resident on the Rollins plantation in Mississippi. She had three children. Based on the color of their skin and their last name, they had most likely been visited upon her by her owners. They were Wash Rollins and Mary Rollins and Tobe Perkins, whose father had provided the British Isles in my DNA. A perfect example of the slave owner replenishing his own stock. Breeding his inventory.

The Newton County plantation was owned by Rev. David Ford, a Methodist minister. He was not a slave owner, and his family never had been. Winny and her children had come to the plantation as a wedding gift to his wife, Courtney

Carraway, who was from a wealthy Mississippi family and was accustomed to having slaves.

Winny had been allowed to roam freely around the plantation without an overseer, so she was able to feed Jim and keep him hidden; but there was punishment for sheltering a runaway. Even a white, found to be sheltering a runaway could be killed, probably hung. For what she was doing, Winny could've been beaten, her kids sold. Jim would've been returned, and made an example of to make other slaves think twice about running away. Even if they'd chopped off his feet, he'd still have to work. No work, no value, no life—just feed him to the pigs.

To the north was the Kansas free territory. To the west, just on the other side of the New Mexico territory, California was a free state. Jim could be free, but without Winny. No way was she leaving her kids. No way could her kids go with them.

Winny trusted David Ford. She had faith that he was a good person. Plus he believed in the sanctity of slave marriages. The majority of the Methodists were against slavery. It was dangerous, but she'd told Rev Ford that Jim had come to be with her.

Winny and Jim had presented a good case. Rev Ford appreciated how special Jim was. He agreed to buy him, and the owner agreed to sell, and Jim voluntarily went back into slavery to be with the woman he loved.

Slaves were free to mate but not marry; encouraged to breed but not to bond. Winny and Jim publicly declared their intention in front of their community by "Jumping the

1

Broom"—a marriage ritual that has been reclaimed. "Jim and Winny jumped the broom and started having children."[2]

★ ★ ★

June 19, 1865. When Union soldiers arrived in Galveston, Texas, with the news that the war was over and slavery abolished, the news was two years old in that part of the nation. I imagine slave owners made sure word about it got around and was enforced in a way they could get a couple more crops out of the help before they were forced to give them their freedom.

Winny and Jim had worked hard on the plantation. Now they worked hard for themselves. They had added more children and were now a big family. And a close one. "After July 1865 they and others found land in the bottoms. The Freedman's Bureau was established to give newly freed slaves any unclaimed land. But angry white Texans bought all the unclaimed property. Stephen McBride was married to Winny's daughter Mary Rollins and partnered with Winny and Jim in buying land. They "had unusual financial resources that they initially used to purchase land early on."[3] "Jim Shankle saved either $200 or $400 dollars to buy land about 5-6 years later he bought it along with an ex-slave Steven McBride."[4] Like LeBron James today, Jim, Winny, and Stephen shared their

---

2   From a letter from the family genealogist Pam Scourton Thomas https://youtube/R-3L6UjkKcQ

3   https://en.m.wikipedia.org/wiki/Shankleville,_Texas

4   From a letter from the family genealogist Pam Scourton Thomas https://youtu.be/R-3L6UjkKcQ

resources which fostered the development of the community." My guess would be they had been able to charge for their skills and saved while still enslaved—or somehow used Steven McBride's ability to pass for white.

They established Shankleville, Texas in 1867, one of ten Freedman's Colonies established in Newton County. These colonies were communities where blacks lived on their own land, free of the economic enslavement that had replaced the physical. And together they were safer amidst growing resentment of their change in status.

Not all slaves were freed. But Shankleville welcomed all who came. They invited the arrivals to live and create businesses and to build homes with timber from their own sawmill. As Shankleville grew, there were more mills and businesses and work in the community.

Landowners had a different focus from the poor blacks and whites who were sharecroppers, and they made much of a short-lived opportunity. Commerce and churches flourished. And *education*! McBride College was inspired and built by an astute black businessman who hadn't been allowed to learn to read or write but valued education. The Shankleville educational facility provided a meeting and learning center for the area.

The 13th Amendment (*mostly*) abolished slavery. The 14th Amendment gave citizenship rights and equal protection under the law, and the 15th Amendment gave men the right to vote regardless of race, color, or previous condition of servitude. Voter registration records in the area show that Jim Shankle registered and voted.

Enthusiastically, black citizens registered and voted and were elected to office. There was a black governor of Louisiana.

The black section of Tulsa was called "Black Wall Street" because of its affluence. Black people stayed close together, creating their own separate "Freedom Colonies," where they focused on serving the black community, not on initiating contact with the whites.

During Reconstruction, the ten-year period after the Civil War, being black was still dangerous. It was unsafe to think that the Reconstruction amendments had actually made you an equal citizen. And when you were prosperous, able, and confident, it was easy to "forget your place."

Some white people couldn't stand impartial and just treatment of blacks. The pushback started. The South swore they had a change of thinking and were different. And as they placed their hand on the Bible, they built crosses to burn and uncoiled their lynching ropes. The Compromise of 1877, an unwritten, informally arranged deal, resulted in the Federal Government pulling troops out of the South and ending the Reconstruction Era. The politically motivated deal promised to protect civil and political rights. It didn't. We lost the vote and lives, and Jim Crow laws[5] came into force. The good white citizens crossed their hearts, burned the crosses, and hung the ropes—and people—from trees.

There were three Reconstruction periods followed by three pushbacks. Gutting the Voting Rights Act threatens to allow the new Jim Crow. The vote was taken from black people in 1876 and 2012 and is attempting to do it again in 2020s.

★ ★ ★

---

5   Laws that took away rights and promoted discrimination and unequal justice.

I walked on the land and I drank from the spring.

Jim and Winnie are buried in the Jim Shankle Cemetery. Winnie's son, Tobe Perkins, and his wife, Jane Harris, my grandmother's parents, are also buried there.

The Perkins and The Bookers

1. *The State of Texas historical place marker at Shankleville, Texas.*
2. *Aunt Regina Perkins who started her family member's move to California.*
3. *Grandad's brother Ulysses Booker, the eldest in his family and Grandma's sister Olivia Perkins who raised her and married him.*
4. *Grandads brother CJ Booker and my Grandma Gertha Perkins, the youngest of the Perkins children.*
5. *Grandma's brother Leroy Perkins and his students. He was the eldest and the only brother, who took over care of his sisters when their parents died.*

2
Tobe and Jane Perkins — My Great Grand Parents (around 1880)

TOBE PERKINS WAS BORN IN 1848. His full name was Noah Wesley Perkins. On our side of the family, he was always just called Tobe. I was told that he was handsome and smooth, a railroad man who knew how to look after people. He was a sleeping car porter, and that was a good job for Negros. The porters would form the first black union to be part of the American Federation of Labor. A powerful enough union to confront FDR[6] over employment discrimination. Early photos of railway porters show that the complexion that allowed entry into non-manual labor-oriented work was usually the ability to pass the "paper bag test"—a gauge of skin color. Most likely Tobe showed the heritage he inherited from his owner-father. He would have been light, bright, and damn-near white.

Tobe was looking for a wife when he was introduced to Ann Harris. She also had connections to the railroad: a railroad

---

6   Franklin Delano Roosevelt. Only three times elected President of the United States. Supported, arts, infrastructure and integration. One influence may have been his black 'Kitchen Cabinet', the black brain trust who advised him.

conductor. The conductors were white, while the porters black. The conductors could afford a second family on the "other side of town." Sometimes, like Ann, a black woman was "set down," kept, looked after by a white man of means. Tobe courted Ann, and she probably thought "Oh, I got me this," and felt the satisfaction of feeling the attraction. Then Tobe ran off with Jane, her youngest daughter. Whatever she'd felt, Ann never spoke to her daughter again. And, to their sadness, had nothing to do with the grandchildren. I know little about Jane, only my mother's story of once seeing a photo of her, and that she was beautiful. Jane didn't live long enough for my grandmother to know her. She died when my grandmother was only eight months old, and her raising was delegated to her sisters, especially her sister Olivia.

Tobe and Jane had eight children. LeRoy, the only boy and the oldest, and seven girls: Eula, Jenny, Regina, Olivia, Ola, Sisley Ann, and my grandmother, Gertha. There were other women in Tobe's life—a wife before Jane and another after.

Before my grandmother was eight years old, Tobe died. Her brother LeRoy, although he was only a teenager, stepped up. He managed the family and made sure that every sister had an education—every one of them went to Teachers College, and every one of them knew how to handle a shotgun. He'd raised them well. He'd disliked the farm so much, as soon as he could he moved into town to work and then to train as a teacher himself. When he'd qualified as a teacher, he'd left Shankleville. LeRoy never left Texas but named a daughter New Zealand. Why? What was he thinking of, dreaming of?

With federal troops gone and Jim Crow laws in place, things got worse for blacks. When D. W. Griffith's *Birth of a*

Nation was screened at the White House on February 18, 1915, it became the first film shown inside the White House, and black people needed to take note. The film demonized black-painted white men as lascivious beasts lusting after white women, heinously putting at risk Lilian Gish, the most loved actress of the day. It became the first-ever blockbuster movie.

Black filmmaker Oscar Micheaux's[7] response must have been witheringly effective because his film *Within Our Gates* was banned for fear of causing a riot. Any response that refutes racist lies gets buried under denial, counterattack and pushback.

The Ku Klux Klan peaked with as many as six million members by 1925. In 1926 twenty-three black men were lynched. At least it was down from 134 in 1894, after Reconstruction when the Troops left and the 1877 Compromise proved a sham.

Great Aunt Regina was visited by some white men on her first night of a teaching assignment in a small Texas town. before her arrival she had heard from a friend that a group of hooded men were killing off light-skinned blacks. Regina had a friend whose fair-skinned father had been dragged from the house while his family watched. It was as though they were trying to erase signs of the sins they had committed.

Aunt Regina had light skin, but the men weren't wearing hoods. And a "good-time woman," a prostitute, had lived in the house previously. Regina didn't know if the men in her front yard were there for sex or slaughter. Maybe they hadn't known who she was. She went to the doorway and called out

---

7   Early black filmmaker, 1884-1951.

that she was the new schoolteacher, she had just moved in and didn't want any problems. She secured the door, hoping they would just go away. They didn't.

What they made clear was that they didn't care what or who she was. They only gave her two choices: "You better open up this door, or we're going to kick it down." What could she do? Black woman, white men? It would seem obvious who was the most powerful. Her brother had raised her well, and she politely responded back to them, "If you kick my door in it will be the last thing that you do." Well, they did, and it was. Her shotgun killed one, and blew a leg off of another. That night Aunt Regina became the first of our family to migrate to California.

3
Gertha and Jesse Booker – My Grandparents

WHEN MY GRANDMOTHER GERTHA met Jesse Booker, she knew he was *the one*. They say he was tall like pine, black like crow, and talked more shit than a radio. At thirteen she'd fallen in love with him, and as soon as she turned eighteen, they married. Jesse was a graduate of Prairie View A&M, a small college in Texas where his father had taught. Gertha had attended Teacher's College in Shankleville.

With a shrinking population and businesses closing, opportunities in the Shankleville area were limited. Not only were opportunities limited, there were also resentments. The rifle slung across Grandad's saddle had caused local whites to say, "That Jesse Booker's a crazy nigah." So, if you had ability and didn't like hanging around a diminishing town or hanging from trees, it was time to get out of the South.

Grandad had a college friend in Watts, a suburb of Los Angeles. There were job opportunities there. My grandparents were part of a migration that started after WWI in 1918. The war had exposed many black men to more than bullets and mustard gas. Europeans had treated them differently. For some internalized shackles broke. The trickle out of the south became a flood. Around 1921 Aunt Regina was joined in California by the two of her sisters who were married to brothers—my Gramma Gertha and Aunt Olivia. Aunt Olivia, who had looked after Gramma as she'd grown up, was married to Ulysses Grant Booker, Grandad Jesse's older brother also known as Uncle Bud.

The families moved to Watts, a lovely little market garden suburb in south Los Angeles which produced fruit and vegetables. Residents, mom had said, were mostly Mexicans, Blacks and immigrants like Watts Tower's creator Simon Rodia[8], who'd built the towers out of broken ceramics, plates, and bottles mixed in with seashells and scrap metal. Mom told me she used to occasionally break a dish to have something to give him as he rolled his pushcart past her house, searching the street for material for his art.

Grandad got a job working at Goode's shoes in downtown Los Angeles as a stock clerk and elevator operator. Uncommon in those days for a black man, he wore a suit and tie to work every day. Luckily, he was the same size as the owner and recipient of his passed-on quality suits. From 103rd Street Granddad caught the Red Car, the fearsome fast train that went into downtown, occasionally running over someone who thought they were faster. In 1920 it was the largest electric railway system in the world; but it wasn't able to withstand the petroleum, automobile and tire lobby and support for freeways.

There were thriving black business and professionals

---

8   A collection of 17 interconnected structures, two of which reach heights of over 99 feet (30 m). https://www.atlasobscura.com/places/watts-towers

on Central Avenue, spreading from the city near Olivera Street down towards Watts. Blacks who worked in non-black businesses were generally restricted to service and manual labor jobs. One job I remember mom talking about was those black men who carried "the hod," a kind of tray with a pole handle that was filled with the construction material. Hod carriers were the hardest workers on the construction site with the lowest rate of pay.

Grandma's Texas teaching credentials weren't accepted in California, so she became a Madam C.J. Walker[9] hair consultant—a hairdresser. Madam Walker, a black woman, was America's first self-made female millionaire from creating products and a program to equip other black women to create businesses looking after other women. Doing hair gave them a way to earn their own income and reduce their dependence. Grandma mainly used it so that her little girls could always look good. She also learned how to sew. Her girls had to look good. It was a family requirement. How you looked said who you were.

Like Shankleville, contribution to their community was also important to this generation. Gramma and Grandad were partners in their community efforts. Every Sunday people that needed help would drop by after church. Some needing help to read and write, others wanted their rights explained, especially how to deal with bureaucrats and not be intimidated, and new business owners who were looking for support and advice.

When Grandad helped open the first Democratic Party

---

9   https://www.womenshistory.org/education-resources/biographies/madam-cj-walker

office in Watts, Gramma gained secretarial skills to assist him. The branch nurtured fellow Democrats. Two were men my mom called Uncle Gus and Uncle Gil. Augustus Hawkins, the first African American from California in the US Congress in 1962, and Gilbert Lindsey, LA's first black city councilman in 1963. Hawkins was the first black representative elected west of the Mississippi, and Lindsey, without Hawkins's University education, started as a janitor at City Hall.

In Grandad's day, Blacks largely voted Republican—the party of Lincoln, but Grandad said, "Uh-uh, the Democrats are the only ones who have a candidate who has come out against lynching." Well, that's the story passed down. I have to question if Grandad supported President Woodrow Wilson, a Democrat and an out-and-out racist. Not only did he premiere *Birth of a Nation* at his White House, he also resegregated the Federal Government, creating separate lunchrooms and bathrooms. W.E.B. du Bois, the Father of Pan Africanism, had supported Wilson in the 1912 election, but Wilson became too racist, which might have turned du Bois toward a more militant path.

My grandparents were "perfect." Perfectly human! Gramma Booker wasn't a hugger; I think it was not having had a mother and being raised by sisters. But Gramma was quick with a sense of humor and an equally quick temper. Grandad thought he'd made a date with a woman but he'd called home by mistake. Fast-thinking Gramma disguised her voice and set up the meet. He got a *big* surprise, and she whacked Grandad with her umbrella all the way home. I understand he walked quickly and tried to hold onto a bit of dignity. Except for that misstep, Grandad moved smoothly between work and politics, black and white, home and outside.

Their small community continued to prosper. If you've seen *Watchmen*,[10] the destruction of an all-black town, you'll understand thriving black businesses and communities created jealousies and fear with their success. The backlash came. In Oklahoma there were only two airports in the entire state but six black families in Tulsa owned their own planes. These accomplishments were an incitement to suppress and destroy. There were others[11]; but in Watts, no one was ostentatiously rich. They were workers and strivers for a better life and mostly got along with each other.

My mother Olivia, named for the aunt who raised her mother, grew up bilingual, picking up Spanish from the next-door neighbors, the Bonitos, and sharing food and recipes with an individual touch: oxtail tacos, *nopales*, and okra on Mexican rice. The Bonitos owned a small grocery store on Wilmington at 109th where we did our shopping. I think Mr. Bonito was the one that told Grandad that the tall weed growing in the back yard was healthy. It was good for catarrh if you dried it and smoked it. It was known where he came from as *marihuana*. Grandad evidently spent lots of time in the backyard. Grandmother didn't approve.

As was the practice, the two Booker families temporarily merged, sharing one house and working to gain the down payment for another. The house Aunt Olivia and Uncle Bud bought was just four blocks north on 105th.

In January of 1930, Granddad Jesse had come home from

---

10 HBO TV Series, 2019. Nine Episodes.
11 Tulsa was destroyed in 1921; other towns destroyed were Springfield, Illinois, 1908; East St Louis, Illinois, 1917; Rosewood, Florida, 1923; Wilmington, North Carolina, 1898.

work ill. He hadn't been feeling well and had a pain in his gut on the right side. He'd kept going because he'd been given a chance to design a shoe at the store. He wouldn't let some pain stop him. But when he'd gone to bed, he didn't get up again. The doctor said his appendix had burst, and there was nothing that could be done. As he lingered for several days, a white woman, a co-worker, visited and spent hours sitting by his bed, holding his hand. It was obvious they'd had more than a work relationship. The woman gave money to Gramma Booker "to help out." Gramma didn't say anything, just accepted her presence and her money. It was recognized that men were just like that.

Before he'd died Jesse asked Olivia, my mom, to take care of the family, to "look after Kiddo," his pet name for Gramma Booker. He was concerned Gramma wouldn't be able to cope. She couldn't. The depression that ran through our family sent her to bed.

In recognition of his Democratic Party work, the state governor sent his representative to the funeral, and Uncle Gil and Uncle Gus helped carry the coffin. My mom Olivia, at fourteen, stood tall, held back her tears, and got a job as a mother's helper to support her family.

By the time mom was eighteen, she was working as a live in for a wealthy family, and it looked as though that would be her life. Until her employer said she couldn't have a friend visit. The restriction was unacceptable to her. The Booker independence streak came out, and she quit. By now the whole country was in a depression. Gramma got up, picked up her hairdressing bag, and went to work. Even in a depression, a black woman would find fifty cents to "get they hair did."

Gramma married again. Mr. Thompson was the richest man on the street and had a big black Packard car. It didn't last. She married one last time in the 40s to Dan Lewis; but that didn't last either. Gramma spent her time from then on in the company of men but not in a relationship. She became licensed as a master barber, which every barber shop was required to have. Many shop owners didn't have that qualification, so she was much in demand.

Mom's dream of being a doctor had been shoved aside to support the family. Now she felt she was too old to resume her studies at Jordan High. Because she wanted to be her own boss, she chose to become a hairdresser. She enrolled at Frank Wiggins Beauty School, part of Los Angeles's Trade Tech College.

With only one uniform, she washed, starched, and hung it to dry every evening, washing the shoe strings and whitening her shoes. Everything was white. Spotless—she made sure. In the morning she ironed the dress and hot combed her hair, making sure there were no naps. She felt she had to be exceptionally groomed because to do less would bring discredit on her and her race. Also, she was a little vain.

She was often told that she was "pretty for a dark girl." She would self-disparagingly turn the half-assed compliment away, but I know she was flattered. (The compliments continued into her 80s). Mom excelled at beauty school, graduated, accepted a sheepskin-covered diploma, and started making plans for her own shop.

The Watts my generation knew was our "old country'"—the place where my family used to live before. We moved north to the West side, the Home of Sugar Hill, where rich black people lived in Berkeley Square on a wide boulevard in storied mansions with ballrooms. The city put the freeway through Berkeley Square and called it urban renewal. We called it what it was: negro removal[12]. Housing: segregation of, covenants on, redlining of. The resulting problems were at the root of my getting the job on *Star Trek* when Watts exploded, and I found myself in a burning building with my arms full of children's clothing.

---

12 https://www.berkeleysquarelosangeles.com

4
Olivia and Sidney White, My Parents 1937-38

My mom, Olivia Booker was hugely disappointed in love. The man of her dreams, the love of her life, was unable to keep his penis in his pants. While mom was waiting until after the wedding, he impregnated a girl, and being honorable, married her.

My dad, Sidney William White, got lucky. His best friend was dating mom's best friend, and they talked her into a double-date. She was so pissed off with losing the man she loved that she married "Big Red." She even signed the documents agreeing to raise all children in the Catholic Church, even though she was raised in the African Methodist Episcopal Church, the first independent Protestant denomination to be founded by black people.

The code she lived by for most of her life:

(1) "You can't have hair that's too straight" was a biggie. There was no excuse other than sudden, unexpected moisture reverting the straightened hair.
(2) "The worse you feel the better you make yourself look."

You are what you look like, and don't show your feelings was one she rigorously practiced, which I rebelled against.

(3) "Bookers are haters that always get you back, and they hold onto resentment" is the one I'm still working on getting rid of.

(4) "Never let them see you cry." She never did; I saw her close to tears once. Mom didn't do tears. She started withholding them early when her father died, and she was ordered not to cry at his funeral. She did learn to hug. Got rid of the A-frame hug with back patting for hugs with real feeling.

(5) "Find a man who can set you down." This was the only kind you wanted, she insisted. A woman should make the home, be social and do good works.

(6) "You have to be the best." She instructed, "It doesn't matter if you're a dishwasher; just be the **best in** *the world*." But worse for me was my interpretation. There were so many things I didn't even try because there wasn't a chance, I'd be the best in the world. Instantly and immediately, of course! The nasty part was that I was, unconsciously, in undeclared competition with everyone, even my best friends. Comparison can be malevolent and self-destructive.

Dad was her opposite. Easy going, knew everyone, everywhere. Dad was born in Arkadelphia, Arkansas, one of three boys from three fathers. As a child he watched the body of a black man who had been lynched being dragged through the black neighborhood of the small town. The move west had freed him of intense racial restrictions and changed his life.

Dad was a people-person who could sell anything to anyone. He'd broken Ernest and Julio's heart when he quit selling their Gallo wines, but that "I can help you; I know what you need" confident sales manager faded with the memory as he related how the lynched man's body had looked, how it had moved as the grinning occupants of the car slowly paraded up one street and down the other again and again.

His mother, my Gram Percilla, was a single mother and a born leader. No ... she was a ruler. Her word was law. She was the first in her family to move to California. Percilla chose the smaller San Diego and began bringing her dozen brothers and sisters over from the segregated South. Gram Percilla was a live-in with a room behind the kitchen. She was the only servant for a retired doctor, Mary O'Donnell, another serious Catholic like herself and both members of the Catholic Daughters of America. Gram Percilla had a side hustle. She hosted regular card games and bingo nights at her home on Commercial and took a house cut.

Mom was pregnant when she left Los Angles and moved with her husband to his mother's house. It wasn't what she was used to—plus she had no friends; just a lot of new relatives, many of whom lived on the same block with freight train tracks down the middle of the street. Mom suffered cravings. She told me how intensely that she craved ice cream, was desperate for it. Freezers hadn't been invented yet, and the closest ice cream was in town. Dad couldn't be bothered; he was busy hanging out with his best buddy Scooter Marshall. Dad was a charmer who got away with everything while giving little but a wink and a smile. His mother would step in and fix things for him. But Percilla was across the bay in Pt. Loma,

4

so she arranged to have her mother make the trips into town for ice cream. Her mother, Maggie—called Mama White or Aunt Mag—kept her eye on everything. Everyone watched their behavior when she was around. She was a Witherspoon before she married Sam Green White. She would have been born a slave, and by family legend, Sam was from the Creek Nation, but that's not supported by my DNA test, to my huge disappointment.

5

I was born prematurely on February 19, 1939 at 12:07am, on two astrological cusps, Aquarius/Pisces and Tiger/Rabbit. To be certain mom had waited until she was married, I had checked the marriage certificate date, the birth certificate said premature birth. My birth was an early indication of my impatience and haste and then overthinking. I was two months early but had to be delivered by forceps when I couldn't make up my mind about coming out. Overthinking was probably the first negative pattern I developed.

Being stubborn showed up in a few years when mom insisted on giving me curls like Shirley Temple, the child star of the day. I preferred the smooth, upswept pompadour style she wore. I refused to wear the curls and defiantly cut them off. She whipped my butt. But I was a Booker like her. I followed her code #5: resentment and revenge. "The Hair War," that I passively aggressively fought with my mother, the ice queen, didn't end for decades.

The whipping I got was fierce, but it was honest. As I approached my teens she switched to a "you will be spanked at 2pm on Sunday if you accrue more than 20 demerits" style of sentencing and execution each week. I fought back.

Always covertly. She was scary. I would do anything to avoid a confrontation. I was such a disappointment to her, just like my dad.

Mom had held onto resentment of Dad's indifference to her pregnancy craving for ice cream. There's a saying, "You can eat at my house as long as you don't break your plate." If you break your plate, you can't eat there no more... Well Dad had broken his plate. The marriage didn't last, but mom kept her marriage agreement, and I was baptized at Christ the King Catholic Church: Andra (later Andreea) Cecilia (Patron Saint of Music) White. Yes, I was born White. But I was called colored, then we became negro, and after a fight to add dignity, got a capital: *Negro*

Mom's next husband was Woodworth Smith. Woody was from Bay City, Texas and was driving for a family on elite Coronado Island when they'd met. With the country's entry into WWII, he joined the navy and after discharge, worked at the Coronado Naval Shipyard.

★ ★ ★

My war went unnoticed, though it lasted for decades because there was a world war on, and San Diego was a major naval base. I remember looking down Broadway, masses of sailors on leave, their "Dixie cup" hats creating white-capped waves, rippling up the street. They owned the town. In our living room, I was quietly playing with my paper dolls, unnoticed by the adults who discussed a woman being raped by sailors in a dark area of the train station courtyard. A Red Cap at the station, JW, Woody's nephew, related the story. The women in the room made serious disapproval sounds, and I waited to hear more when mom called attention to my presence and the conversation quickly wrapped up with, "We let her use the bathroom to clean herself up after they left." Which seemed to be all that was necessary to be done.

With all the war effort, babysitters were hard to find, and one of the people who looked after me before I started school was only four or five years older. I was around six when she spread me out on the bed, took off my panties, and licked between my legs. I liked it just fine. Then she said that it was my turn. I had to do it to her. Okay, but I needed to examine the situation first. My conclusion was that I was about to lick the place where the wee comes from, and I needed to make sure it would taste good.

She was older, and though I was intimidated, I was stubborn. I would do it to her only if I made sure it would taste good. She agreed, and I grabbed something I knew from experience would taste good in my mouth: tooth powder. She laid back on the bed and opened her legs. I crawled between them and curiously opened the sparsely haired lips. I shook in a goodly amount of the tooth powder. In fact it looked like the snow scene in the glass ball I'd gotten for Christmas that year. She cannoned off the bed, screaming, shoving me aside to get to the bath room and the cold water. That minty cool flavor must have burned like hell.

The next time, she became an observer rather than participant. Putting some distance between her and the tooth powder, she sweet-talked the little Italian boy next door over to play. She told us to take off all our clothes and draped a bath towel around my neck and told me I was the Queen of the Naked Jungle. She showed us what we were supposed to do and briefly took us in hand to demonstrate how our parts were to meet. She handed his little wiggly thing to me. It was soft and smooth with interesting folds. I fell in love with my first penis. Soon I was coaxing another little boy into a vacant shed at the back of the apartments so I could see his. I enjoyed the delicious terror of potential discovery and the pleasure of playing with his penis.

Then Gramma Percilla got me transferred to Our Lady of Angels Catholic school. Misery started. The classroom was in a basement, the windows too high to see out, and I had to repeat first grade. I could read but was unable to recite the alphabet in order. Piled on top of that humiliation, I had to disclose to all in my class that my mother worshiped at a place called a church, but it wasn't Catholic, therefor not a "real" church. I was frustrated at the things I was learning about God. No one could help me understand why He would make a baby that died at birth go to purgatory instead of heaven and why I had to write JMJ at the top of each page. "Just do it because they say so," was all mom said.

6

After the war ended, my step-dad Woody returned from the Navy and got a job working at North Island Naval Station, and we moved to the suburbs, to Linda Vista and I went to an all-white Catholic School.

I was an awkward, lonely, spoiled only-child who didn't play well with others, living in an area where kids went to the local public school, all the mothers stayed home, every family had two or more kids, and the mothers had the same last name as their kids. When they got home from school their mother made them a sandwich to hold them 'til dinner. My mother's last name was different, I had a house key around my neck, and when I got home, I made my own sandwich because I didn't know what time my mom would finish working. Food had started to be important. My sandwich would be a pound of bacon, half a dozen eggs, and lots of bread, and I would eat it on the porch. An audience of drooling kids would gather around. They made me feel powerful; I could select who would be my favorite to share with that day. Food became my salve, salvation, and my go-to to feel good.

6

Nye, the street we lived on, curved sharply away from the base of the football field at Kearny High School. Manning, the street behind it dropped off into the canyons where we went to catch snakes or to hold secret meetings in the small caves. Then Manning curved around to join Nye St. briefly black before the street abruptly turned white. Only white families lived on it from there on. The racial change started at the same exact point on both sides of the Nye St. at the Wilson's house on one side and the Taylor's house on the other side of the street. We were segregated—not the kind that's advertised but impossible to be accidental.

Linda Vista was a planned community for servicemen and war industries workers. It had the first mall, one that was designed around a grassy open space. It had a cinema with a separate "crying room" that was sound proofed, with seats for mothers with babies and smokers who watched the movie through a huge window and a speaker. Everything in Linda Vista looked integrated, except the churches. Although the Black Catholics went to church locally, the Methodists, Baptists, and the rest of the Black church members had to go into town to the black part which clustered around Imperial Avenue.

Mom had influence on Nye St., especially with the teens. In her work clothes, or dressed up, she was stunningly beautiful and covertly copied. One of the teens, Evangeline Wilson, would marry James Edwards, the brilliant, defiant black actor, and one of the Harris girls would marry Redd Foxx, the equally brilliant, and hysterically funny role model for generations of comics. I think Redd later took me under his wing because of my connection to Linda Vista. James

Edwards's role in *Home of the Brave*[13] inspired my desire to speak out, to tell stories, to howl. He was my movie hero.

Mom's business, Olivia's Beauty Shop, was the birthplace of a powerful image I grew up with, where I learnt about the hidden power of the Rich White Lady, the RWL. While I read my favorite comic or discovered new words in the latest *Reader's Digest*, I would hear tales starting with "a rich white lady..."

They could be about money: a RWL who bestowed some gift or gratuity, as in a RWL bought, paid, gave, or withheld it. Or employment and education: she works for a RWL; or learned how from a RWL. The RWL was the employer of many of mom's clients, and a RWL gave it, sold it, took it, helped, and hurt. A RWL was mythic being of subtle but effective power. I pictured her as the image of Wonder Woman. Somehow, I knew if I grew up to be a rich white lady, I would be forever safe and happy and loved. I also knew there was no way I could.

★ ★ ★

At Gram Percilla's work there was a huge glass-fronted bookcase in her room filled with books left over from her employer's daughter, the only child who had grown up there. I started on *The Bobbsey Twins*, an extremely popular, unconsciously racist book series: seventy-two volumes of fun adventures and life lessons I took on board. In one I learned "two black women don't make a white." Twice as much wasn't half as good.

---

13 *Home of the Brave* 1949 film based on 1945 play, "a powerful indictment of racism for its time." Speech that starts this book.

6

I loved reading. The Linda Vista library was my refuge. It was the only place I belonged. Until I tried to return some books the same day. "You couldn't have read those books that fast; stop lying." I had no defense but truth, that I did read that fast. The librarian's stern face looked just like the ones that I saw each day wearing nun's habits. The ones that made the rules each day at school and were to be obeyed.

My school was St. Agnes and it was across town, in an exclusive suburb where Gram Percilla worked 'in service.' Two bus rides away from where we lived. I was the only black kid in the entire school and jeeringly called "electricity" because of the many thin plaits I wore at my mother's insistence that they would result in long, beautiful, straightened hair. Then a younger black kid enrolled. There were then two targets. I felt I had to protect her. Luckily, dad was in town. He took me to the zoo, my favorite place and with a few questions realized what was going on. He didn't say anything. He brought his boxer friend Archie to the house and Archie taught me how to throw a solid punch. After that nobody's eeneymeeny got past ... miney moe ... before what they caught was a fist in their mouth. There were limits to that deterrent. When you're released for lunch and the hallway is crowded with a hundred kids, who do you punch when you don't know which one of them yelled "nigger".

I had different school attendance days than the public-school kids in my neighborhood, which meant I was also an outsider at home. I was lonely. I needed books, and now I was too ashamed to go back to the library. It turned out to be a blessing.

I discovered second-hand bookstores. No more children's section. A new freedom which led to my discovering at twelve, a 12th century writer whose book mapped my road to masturbation. I discovered naughty tales in *The Decameron*. The gardener whose robe fell open exposing him while he slept. The Mother Superior unable to stop herself adopting a superior position atop him. At home, alone as usual, I found my substitute for the gardener. First by rubbing myself against the edge of the mattress and then folding it back and mounting it.

While straddling my mattress with the book in hand I explored two delights at once. And I rode my mattress just as hard as Mother Superior did the gardener. The tension from folding it up pushed hard between my legs and felt so very good. When I got off and the mattress resumed its flat position, I patted it gratefully like it was a pony. With something so good I couldn't keep it to myself. So, I introduced the neighborhood girls my age to the joys of masturbation.

Riding the mattress was not my ultimate aim. I was after something bigger. I wanted a pony. My dream was of being another Little Beaver, the young sidekick of my favorite comic book hero Red Ryder. My pony and a hungered-for air rifle dream died when my mom and step-dad separated. They had been just about to buy a house which had a small corral and stable. My dream died, and I lost another dad.

For consolation my grandmother agreed to horse riding lessons. We went to the riding stable in Balboa Park. It felt so right: a horse made eye contact with me; horse poo smelled great. Someone my age was riding a horse in the ring. That could be me one day. But "we don't teach coloreds" had no response we knew.

We can form a moment's hallucination, suddenly, illogically

and implacably. Worthy or worthless, hidden inside us, becomes the trim tab of our life's journey.

My pediatrician recognized the signs of stress. I had a skin rash all over my body and my fingertips were bloody from constantly biting my nails. The bacon and egg sandwiches were amplified by the cookies I had started stealing from the grocery store each day after school. My shop-lifting had begun along with gaining weight. The doctor told my mom to get me out of St Agnes immediately. She did, I transferred to the local public school and at last I had the same holidays and vacations as the kids on my block.

7

IN TIME, MUM FINALLY found the man who could 'set her down' the avowed goal that she held and that surrounded every success story she related from the private lives of her friends and clients. She heard a lot. The stories, related over the shampoo bowl, in a steamy mixture of privacy and intimacy. Like the bartender of the day, as dad was, the hairdresser was recipient of stories.

She had found a construction worker who was paid good money. She wouldn't have to work. Now though he needed financial help to redeem his house in Compton. The deal was made, they married, and we left San Diego.

Compton was a neat three-bedroom house on a corner lot with a sweeping front lawn and a sheltered back yard. Mom was home every day. I got on okay at school. A nice girl lived across the street and we started developing a friendship. Around the corner was Jimmy and I fell in love with him immediately. I wasn't alone in liking Jimmy, there was competition. As I watched her dance at a school assembly, I decided for the first time consciously, that my body didn't compare, was much less attractive. Mine was sorely lacking or rather too abundant, okay fat.

7

That I was still fat was a betrayal! My mother's promise that when I started my period I would magically slim down was exposed for the lie that it was. I would not trust or believe anything she said for the next forty years or more. I had no problem going over previous years and gathering evidence that she lied to me. Often. Telling me that: I was pretty, that I was smart, accompanied by the reassurance that it was only puppy fat and it would go. I vowed I would never believe anything she said. Gathering evidence over the years was easy enough and I build a strong wall against her.

In the room next door, I could hear mum and her husband making love, giving direction, and moaning in appreciation. I was glad. Finally, I got to listen to someone 'doing it. In discussion with others near my age I found listening to parent screwing wasn't unusual and a couple had even grabbed a peek using the "I just wanted to..." excuse, stalling to get a better look.

But mum wasn't the extent of his interest. Most of the time he enjoyed humbling and humiliating me at cards and games to the point of angry tears. He was the adult and held the power and I couldn't kick the game board as I would do with other kids. Another part of the time he sought to fondled my breast and look pointedly and knowingly at the place I stockpiled my stash of mummy wrapped used pads that I was too embarrassed to put in the trash. Stored until I could secretly sneak them into the refuse. I knew what he wanted and he wasn't going to get it. It was sort of a game. An occasional feel was the most he would get and only if I couldn't block it.

Mom was happy, she was home each day when I came in

from school. I had thick slices of lunch meat in my sandwiches. It was heaven and he wasn't going to spoil it.

But when I caught him feeling up my young cousin, I became a powerless little girl and I had to tell my mommy. Our Compton stay ended that evening with my stepdad's shotgun being pointed at him by mom as we packed the car. Mom's stay home dream was over. We headed north to the Westside to my aunt, Jessie Mae. Several hit songs she had written had moved her from the low-income East Side to Sugar Hill, and a house with a studio apartment next to the garage, and a one-bedroom apartment on the side of the house with its own entrance.

We moved into the apartment and mom regrouped and went to work as a shampoo girl with a famous Hollywood hairstylist, Gene Shacove. He was the role model for Hal Ashby's movie *Shampoo*. Mom was surrounded by a concentration of Rich White Ladies and gained greater admiration for them. She came home telling of their even grander RWL feats and achievements.

Shacove's was mom's kind of environment, and she picked up tips on running an up-market salon. She watched, listened and saved, and with her sister's help, she was soon ready to open her own place. Of course, Shacove loved mom and didn't want her to leave but understood the need to have her own salon. Not a shopfront on the main street like the other black beauty shops—hers was in an office building, complete with receptionist where she catered to the denizens of black society and kept up appearances.

I still felt unattractively pudgy. My "Puppy Fat" wasn't leaving. so mom sent me off to our new doctor to "give me something" that would help me lose weight. After the diet pills prescription from Dr. Foster, I started playing tennis, every day during summer vacation. On the tennis court I had a sizzling forehand and would have been a better player if two-handed backhands weren't so frowned upon back then. The Skatium, a roller rink, opened nearby, and mom bought me skates. I was at every session possible. I didn't stop moving. Gliding alone or with a partner to "Shaboom" by The Cords—not the watered-down version by The Crew Cuts—backwards or forward, it was a dream. I loved the feeling of merging with my partner, lying in his arms as we raced backwards at speed, on the edge of ruin. All the good skaters smoked so I started sneaking my mom's cigarettes. The best skaters wanted me for their skating partner, and I was invited to hang with the cool kids and skate with them at the white skating rink in Hollywood.

My activity resulted in a 24-inch waist separating a 39-inch bust and 36-inch hips. I'd also finally made it past 5'4 ¾" to 5'8". I was fifteen, and I looked pretty good. I'd finally done something right. Mom was pleased with my weight loss.

Now I was getting attention from boys. Before my teens I had discovered bumping bushes, and porn cartoon flip books "Tijuana bibles" that my aunt kept hidden, but not well enough. I liked the ones with Popeye eating more than spinach. With attention I was getting, I was even more sexually curious but mom's only advice to me was keep your dress down and your panties up.

I got a boyfriend. My aunt's stepson. He respected my youth and didn't push for sex. One night his best friend said there was something important and private I should know about. He had my boyfriend's customised car that he loved. We got in the car and it moved itself to a dark secluded spot all the kids in my high school were familiar with. As we started to talk, he said he'd be much more comfortable sitting in the back. Sure. What he was saying was so interesting that I didn't want him to stop and moved to the back with him. He had a bottle of booze and I took a few sips, feeling quite sophisticated. I hadn't had alcohol very often. He looked down at me and with a smile asked "What will you do if I try to rape you?" I reversed the bottle holding it by the neck and said "I'll hit you with this!" He twisted my arm. I dropped the bottle. My aunt told me not to tell my mother what he'd done to me, and that proved that I'd been the one that had done something wrong, not him.

Since I was told not to tell my mother what had happened to me, in frustration, I focused more anger towards her, more resentment. We did not get along. We barely spoke to each other. The Hair War continued, but it was a guerrilla war on my part since I didn't dare openly rebel. I was lucky she was a hairdresser: she kept my hair looking good despite the mandatory swim class at L A high school, kinking it up. Black girls hated swimming because we couldn't keep our hair straight. We looked like Marge Simpson or an alien with scarves, chamois skin, and several swim caps, swelling the size of our head, attempting to protect our hair from kinks.

Mom was pleased when I started dating a doctor's son. I was actually dangling multiple boyfriends, enjoying their jealousy, and when they fought over me, went steady with the winner. I collected boys. Cute ones to complement me and make other girls jealous, and athletic ones so I could wear their lettermen jackets to football games and track meets. Basketball players were too tall. I tried one star player. His belt buckle made my chest sore when we were doing the slow drag, dancing so slow your feet barely moved. But your pelvis got a good workout grinding to the music of Johnny Ace's "Pledging my Love." And it felt better than my mattress. If you'd been popular on the dance floor, you'd go home sore from the erections. It was accepted that it was a girl's fault if a boy got hard. She'd caused it. Eve in the garden. I maintained control over their wandering hands but was undeniably aroused later when my 'going steady' boyfriend's curious fingers breeched my panties. When I told my masturbation friends, they were scandalized. That was a no-no. But it felt so good. Good girls didn't do it—and especially didn't talk about it—if we did, we who found pleasure in sex wore a label. My friend Odie Hawkins told me once that I was a slut when being a slut meant something. Who taught that it was wrong? You could get married in California at twelve and younger with your parents' permission—even if you don't want to, in other states you can't have an abortion even if you do.

* * *

Mom was filled with the striving of the wannabe class and doing things the proper way. It was assumed at eighteen I'd make my debut and go to an all-black university. Her connections ensured my debut would be with the most socially prominent black women's club in Los Angeles, The Links' Cotillion. John F. Kennedy had been a guest the year before. I picked a good-looking green-eyed boy for my escort. But I was as uncooperative as I dared. I was surly, and complained about the number of fittings for my ball gown. The dress took many, many hours. It was a most exquisite dress that I had no appreciation of. Mom's friend Anna Lee, who had made my christening dress, hand-sewed individual pearls, smocking the voluminous skirt of the silk tulle ball gown. It was made with love, and I carelessly destroyed it, scrambling into the back seat of a two-door convertible after the cotillion, escaping what I told mom was a pretentious occasion that I had participated in only because she'd insisted. As another blow in our continuing hair war, I had her rival do my hair for the big event. Huge mistake. Mom was a much better stylist.

The Cotillion was held at the white-owned Los Angeles Hilton, perceived a better location than the black Elks Club on Central Avenue where the other debutant ball was still being held—the downhill slide of the East Side and the businesses that had supported the black community was starting.

The perception that white was somehow better than black would ruin Central Avenue and a few of mom's society friends whose income came from those black businesses. Black dollars began to flow into white businesses but not the reverse. And as the black businesses began to visibly suffer from the decline, the outflow increased.

After the Cotillion I finally met, and was going steady with, the boy of my dreams. Then I broke up with him because he decided that he was going to be a Baptist minister, and I was Catholic; I thought different religions shouldn't marry. I wonder who taught me to think that? It didn't matter. Within the year, before I turned nineteen, my ex had a new girlfriend. I'd been caught smoking and shoplifting. I was graduating at the bottom of my class and destined for a hick college, in a hick town. Except I wasn't because I was pregnant.

Avoiding pregnancy was a girl's responsibility I'd been taught by everything I heard or saw. Who started that? It wasn't a woman. I must have been a spectacle trying to find a home remedy that would interrupt a pregnancy. I took hot scalding baths, jumped from various heights, water skied, and stayed pregnant. The only real chance that I knew of: the sympathetic chiropractor who inserted a catheter tube into your uterus to cause a miscarriage. I wasn't compelling enough in communicating my need and stability, and he turned me down.

When Mom found out, she invited the boy over for a cup of coffee and a talk. She did the talking. His cup in the saucer sounding like castanets in the background, as he repeated, "yes, ma'am," to everything she said. Mom was instructing us how we would go to Las Vegas that weekend and get married! I refused. He would have to leave university. No reason to wreck two peoples' lives. It was my fault. I shouldn't have been home alone trying on my new swimsuit when he'd dropped by. I didn't want him to do it. He insisted. It was my fault that he couldn't help himself. I looked too seductive. Just like the rape, I didn't fight or flee; I froze and condemned myself for what was happening. Overthinking, out of body. It was happening. I was letting him do it. That made it my fault. I was to blame. I was sure I had to be. I wonder what made me think that?

I was an embarrassment in perky maternity clothes, with a ringless finger, and resentful attitude, pushing back the pressure the family put on me to get married or go to a Catholic unwed mother's home and agree to an adoption. About two months before I gave birth, I was rescued by Jai, an older man, a Marine who had pursued me while I was in high school. It was okay; he would marry me. Mom got the news when Jai dropped me at home after the marriage chapel and a minor car accident. I made sure I scored another point against her.

Mom: Where have you been?

Me: Out.

Mom: What did you do?

Me: (closing my bedroom door) Got Married. Goodnight. (door slam)

1. *My mother Olivia, with a special friend while working on Catalina Island.*
2. *Dad at work behind the bar, 'Big Red' charmed me as well as all the women.*
3. *The White Family. Gram Percilla is delighted and planning to spoil her granddaughter. "Big Red" is proud of his beautiful wife and child and Mom is perfectly satisfied.*
4. *Damn Shirley Temple curls and Dad who is truly fading out of my life.*
5. *With the best skater at The Skatium. My regular backwards rexing partner.*
6. *I make my debut to please my mother, then wreck the dress climbing into the back seat of a convertible after the ball.*
7. *Paula and Kandis, my beautiful babies and me*
8. *Maulana Karenga, first black LACC Student Body President shares a new point of view. Cultural nationalism stirs.*
9. *Mohammed Speaks newspaper article about the Malcolm X debate Karenga and I organized.*
10. *Dr. Martin Luther King, Jr with the Western Christian Leadership Conference members. I'm in the deep end at the far end with Dr. Wyatt Tee Walker Photo: The Tom and Ethel Bradley Center, CSUN*

8

Just after I turned twenty-one, another baby arrived, and I felt trapped, my world limited. I didn't fit the "mom" job description too well. Jai and I got an apartment, and with the second child, we got live-in help with the kids, and I got a job wrapping purchases at an expensive department store that paid me just enough to pay her—and presented an excellent opportunity for shoplifting. The home help didn't speak English, but she was a friend of a friend, so I struggled to learn a few basic Spanish phrases to communicate better. I mostly failed.

I let mom turn me into a blonde; the ads all said they had more fun. My husband, Jai, and I bought our first new car, a Buick convertible, and my straight blond hair could blow in the wind. We paid the price listed on the car window because that was the price. Buying a car was a new experience. My dad, the used car/furniture/wine salesman, choked when we'd told him. We didn't know why he didn't tell us about negotiating before we bought it.

Jai was a wonderful father and a good husband. I was immature and just loved falling in love. I fell in love with several men, none of whom was my husband. It must have been rough for him. I treated him badly, but what did he expect? He had bought damaged goods. What reason did I have to think highly of him if he thought so little of himself? It was the "I wouldn't be a member of a club that would have me for a member" game that I would play repeatedly. I thought it was called "life," and it was; I just wasn't getting the lesson.

One of the things about guilt and denial and disrespect for self is how easily they affect balance. They bond and forge self-replicating, catch 22 links that are wedded in a portable, take any wherever chain of self-disgust and loathing, occasionally disrupted when you experience a rare moment of self-approval.

After one brief affair the next transgression was easier and even less satisfying. The next, just as unsatisfying and more frustrating. I had enough of my life. I wrote a note, confessing my wrongdoings, placed it prominently, and sat down on the kitchen floor. I turned on the oven without lighting it and stuck my head in. At some stage the floor became too hard, and I had a headache from the gas. I staggered off to bed, forgetting the confession note which Jai found when he got home from work that morning.

We talked and tried to put things back together. It didn't work. Getting away with so little cost only opened the door wider for me. Freedom was just outside.

Having help with the kids gave me a chance to study. Jai, who wanted to be a radio DJ, and I both enrolled at Los Angeles City College in broadcasting. A little unsure, I stayed close to him for support. I also took journalism. I think I was always pulled toward writing but didn't trust that I had the ability — that I would be, could be, any good at it, much less the demand of "be the best." I was frightened and intimidated by writing but attracted to it—still loving words, still the bookworm.

I couldn't deny as fact that I was terrible at being a DJ. When I opened the mic to talk, I couldn't say a word. I froze. Mic fright. The teacher, William Wintersole, was an actor—new to teaching and open to trying anything. He discovered making the studio too dark to see the mic, I could talk when the mic was open. I took my exam in the dark passing the class. DJ-ing was not going to be a career option. I focused on the radio administrative skills.

★ ★ ★

I dived into college life, pledged a sorority and examined the student body president candidates. One, with prominent, black-framed glasses perched imperiously on a weathervane nose, held my attention. He was slight with a slim mustache, close-cropped hair and illustrative hands. His hands frequently caressed his insights, his striking fingers making a point. And you knew he was right! I was aroused by his wit, his incisiveness, his cogent arguments, his validity. He was so bright! The words just flowed, and he glowed. His words stirred me, and I knew I was going to vote for him, and there would be something more. The totality of him stirred an uncommon and certain knowledge that we had a bond, that we would be good together.

He was to be Maulana Karenga[14] LACC's first black student

---

14 Dr Maulana Karenga, https://www.officialkwanzaawebsite.org and https://www.encyclopedia.com/history/encyclopedias-almanacs-transcripts-and-maps/kawaida#

body president. Though light of melanin, Karenga was the proudest blackest man I had ever met. Especially in a time of "if you're white you're alright; if you're brown, you can hang around, but if you're black get back". He was first person I sensed who wasn't somehow ashamed of our African heritage but proud of it. I managed to "bump into him" on a frequent enough basis that we were soon having lunch together. I listened by his side as he "taught" Richard Wright, Malcolm X, shared the opening of *Souls of the Black Folk* and opened our eyes to the 320 sections of the library. I told him about my husband and my daughters, Paula and Kandi. Soon he would come by and tell them folk tales about Anansi the Spider at bedtime.

My shackles start to fall. I had gotten used to being called colored, negro, and Negro, now black was what I was choosing to call myself. Even my three-year-old daughter Paula identified, and was pleased, when her fair-skinned pediatrician agreed with her that, yes, he was a black doctor. Karenga scolded, "You're out working hard, making money to buy presents for your kids on Christmas, then you tell them some fat white man in a red suit brought them." The girls and I embraced being "beautiful black women created from the soil of Africa," and Karenga became my then lover and forever friend. Karenga was later able to find his soul mate, regretfully I haven't yet.

My mom went berserk when I got rid of the blond hair and went natural. To her my nappy hair was a disgrace. I was banned from her salon; the receptionist would tell her I was there, and she'd come downstairs out in back of the building to talk. I was bad for a business that now served Mrs. Louis Armstrong, Mrs. Nat King Cole and Mrs. Martin Luther King,

Jr when in town. The Golden Rule was the person that has the gold makes the rules. I needed mom's contributions. So, I agreed, whenever I was likely to be spotted by one of her crowd, I would make sure I was wearing a wig or my hair would be straightened.

* * *

I was excited when Karenga invited me to go with him to hear Malcolm X speak. We knew that Malcolm didn't allow white people to attend meetings at the Temple and it was a thrill to go somewhere white people couldn't. After the talk we went to Shabazz, the only Muslim restaurant. Hesitantly, we approached Malcolm as he ate, introducing ourselves as students and Karenga, the Student Body President of LACC. Malcolm invited us to join him. He told us of an opportunity we represented: "Well you know I've been having difficulty getting on campuses in California. If I speak at your campus then that ought to open things up." He'd met with students off campus but never before on campus sanctioned by the administration.

We arranged a "debate" with Malcolm and Edward Warren, the local NAACP president to satisfy the administration. Ed was happy to participate; it widened his platform. He was fighting the film industry's racial portrayals and employment discrimination.

Karenga and I organized and publicized the first official campus visit in California of Minister Malcolm X, which resulted in an overflow crowd in the largest hall on campus. We filled the hall again a couple days later to listen to a rebroadcast. The debate was well covered by the January 1962 issue of *Muhammad Speaks*. The three of us had pulled it off. Malcolm gave Karenga a Fruit Of Islam pin and offered me a Muslim Girls Training pin.

Karenga and I continued going to the temple to hear Malcom speak. I was deferential to Karenga. He had so much more than me to say, and I wanted to show him respect and support. I supported the belief that our men had suffered inordinately from the abuses of Mista Charlie, and we black women had to do what we could to help them heal and not create new problems for them. Men were on the front line. To show them respect, we had to be behind them, supporting, not in front leading. I wonder who'd taught me to think that?

I liked that I lived furthest and Malcolm dropped me off last. This gave us time for sitting and talking. When it was just the two us the conversation ranged more widely. Our conversations reflected the day's events, how things were going with local political campaigns, whatever we were reading or watching, our children and their future. We were both determined to have a son. I loved when I could make him laugh or use a word he didn't know. One night, sitting in his car, we talked so long we forgot the radio was on and the battery went flat. Brother Malcolm needed a push to get the car going. I sneaked past a sleeping Jai, I was good at that, and got the keys to his car so I could give Malcolm the push he needed.

I wasn't taken by his leader, Elijah Mohammad, despite Malcolm's belief and support of him. The Black Muslims' way was not for me. The men became the FOI[15], the Fruit of Islam,

---

15 https://en.wikipedia.org/wiki/Fruit_of_Islam;

and the women had, to me, no equivalent value. They could only aspire to the MGT, Muslim Girls Training[16]. I preferred jeans to long gowns and head wrap, and I was not taking a seemingly obedient role to any man—or giving up my smothered pork chops. I remember responding once, "You know, Brother Minister, there's no way I'm giving up Karenga or my bacon!"

I never had a sense of Malcolm being anything other than moral, loyal, and ethical. I never ever lost respect for him even for a minute. I felt respected by him. Although I do admit sometimes while talking with him, my eyes would focus on the lips the words were coming from. But no disrespectful thought ever took place. Well, mostly. Looking back we had bonded over our love of words. I was a nerdy kid always reading, whistling or riding my bike. My favorite of all things was getting the new *Reader's Digest* and taking the test in the "It Pays to Increase Your Word Power" section.

Malcolm had a thirst for knowledge and a love of words. Whenever I used an unfamiliar word, he would stop me: "Sister Ande, now what does that mean?" And pretty soon he'd be including the word in an appropriate sentence. I loved that. I was delighted whenever I used a word Malcolm didn't know. He had no hesitation in asking and incorporated whatever was useful. I admit I did show off sometimes. I enjoyed using words that were precisely shaded and descriptive, like "trenchant" and "cogent" rather than "sharp" and "clear" in discussing some point. We both liked to play with words.

Most importantly, after the 'legal' murder and the shooting of seven members of the FOI by Police Chief Parker's police,

---

16   https://en.wikipedia.org/wiki/Muslim_Girls_Training

Malcolm spoke at the service. He went to the root and asked the most significant question I'd heard: "Who taught you to hate yourself?"[17] That question has echoed through the rest of my life, only changing the object or verb.

The first time Malcolm and I had a meal away from Shabazz was for lunch. We met at Curry's Ice Cream Parlor, a favorite lunch spot of the local black business people. It was down Western Avenue, past the landmark Golden State Mutual Life Insurance building designed by Paul Williams, the noted black architect of The Beverly Hills Hotel, the LA Airport Theme building and around 3,000 projects that are still treasured. Golden State was the largest black business in the West. Its move to Western and Adams signaled the end of Central Avenue and the Eastside as the heart of black business. The migration was north and west. When I walked into Curry's, Malcolm's friend Sam Cook was on the jukebox with "Bring It on Home," the echoing "yeah" behind his voice belonging to a then unknown Lou Rawls whom Sam and JW Alexander had discovered.

It was my first time being in public with a recognizable person. A controversial person. I checked out the people checking us out. Once we started talking, I didn't notice anything but his voice and his lips forming them. I have fragments still, but it was as though he opened his mouth, I went into trance, absorbing every word through my pores, not my ears. I can remember his patience, his soft smile, and the gentle cadence of his voice, but the words he said went deep

---

17   https://www.youtube.com/watch?v=kboP3AWCTkA

inside me, stirring deep racial memories... I had always known. I had just forgotten for a while.

After I came down to earth and we were leaving the restaurant Malcolm stopped and looked at me. He inclined his head slightly. I plotted the trajectory, my eyes tracing the angle through the plate glass window and continuing a path across crowded Western Avenue to see two faceless men in an anonymous, gray Plymouth four-door. "You know, when you're with me, you'll get your picture taken."

His "Smile, Sister Ande," took on another meaning. I'd already noticed the plain, unremarkable sedan that was totally out of place. If the FBI had employed black agents, they would have had cooler cars. But J Edgar Hoover's COINTELPRO was active, and the black men they recruited weren't agents. Black men were only used for undercover spying, planting evidence, and creating dissent wherever they could between black activist groups like the Black Panthers and US Organization, co-founded by Karenga. The testimonies gained helped imprison Maulana Karenga and smears were spread after.

* * *

Special among the people in the movement at that time was a phenomenal woman who worked behind the scenes. Gwen Green supported the men who were leading the movement. A. Phillip Randolph, Bayard Rustin, Whitney Young, Jr and Martin. On the West Coast, Gwen was civil rights leader Martin Luther King's right hand, his go-to for an efficient response to any organizational support problems: what was going on, where he needed to go, who he needed to see, where the allies and the roadblocks were, and how they aligned. Gwen knew it all, and she could strategically map the appropriate response.

She was with Tom Bradley, for both campaigns to be the first Black mayor of Los Angeles as well as getting him elected to the city council before that. Gwen was running things for Robert Farrell, a more courageous-than-me freedom rider, who was elected as an LA city councilman. Back when I was in high school 'Bobby' had come out on a cold rainy night to bring me a rose when I was sick and I've never forgotten. And he was cute too, still is.

Despite the dangers, at Martin's request, Gwen joined Hosea Williams on the Southern Voters Registration Strategy. Gwen helped make The March on Washington happen. In her 90s she was still active organizing a women home care workers union.

Gwen and I were both friends of the very fabulous Florence Antoine who'd introduced us. Florence was a character who knew everyone else who was fabulous! She was politically astute and had connections to every black politician in her San Francisco hometown. Florence was a close friend of SF Mayor Willie Brown, and in Los Angeles had continued collecting local personalities, including KGFJ DJ, The Magnificent Montague, whose shout "Burn Baby Burn" took on a new meaning in Watts.

When we met, I was twenty-one, and Gwen about 14 years older. She was with the Western Christian Leadership Conference (WCLC), a fundraising affiliate of the Southern Christian Leadership Conference, Martin Luther King's organization. I became a volunteer. Her workload there had increased, and she laughingly said she needed someone who could do the running around and who would work for trading stamps[18].

Gwen was exacting, so I must have done OK because she assigned me to chasing after Dr. King to arrange and confirm his itinerary on the West Coast. That was exciting! And when Gwen told me I would be Dr. King's personal assistant for the time he was in Los Angeles, mom was excited too. To mom Dr. King was king. At that time people hung on to his every word, sought his advice, and stuttered in his presence. Gramma Booker thought he was good but was a fan of Malcolm, whose more militant stance frightened mom.

Dr King was based in Georgia and travelled frequently, I had to chase him down to talk. After being passed through several southern telephone operators trying to connect my "person to person" call to him, I thought I had begun to sound like the operators.

"Martin," I drawled, "How do you like my southern accent?"

"Ande," he responded, "you sound just like a cracker!" He made me laugh! I was delighted to find that he was a real person with a sense of humor! Gwen always referred to him as Martin, and so I did too.

---

18 They were issued by stores with purchases and were exchangeable for goods — like loyalty points today, except they were stamps that went in books.

9

THE SOUTHERN CHRISTIAN LEADERSHIP Conference members were flying into LA for a connecting flight to the starting place of the tour. In between flights we held a press conference. I was so nervous. I had chosen a look to impress but didn't notice if it affected Martin. The person walking behind him had grabbed my attention and made me catch my breath. Wyatt Tee Walker. And something happened as an instant glance passed between us.

We were drawn out of the room together as soon as the press conference ended. Wandering around the check-in counter holding hands, we shared our worlds. When we returned to the group, a change was visible. Martin examined us and exclaimed, "Ande and Wyatt are in love!" The attraction was unambiguous and obvious.

Dr. Wyatt Tee Walker was married with children. A minister, the high-profile director of SCLC and MLK's chief strategist. I was a sexy, immature twenty-one-year-old, filled with insecurities and self-doubts, who fantasized about love at first sight. Which could be a problem.

That night mom was vibrating, her hand shaking as she handed me the phone. "Andrée, it's Dr. King." When I answered, Martin greeted me with a couple of comments before turning the phone over to Wyatt. Wyatt and Martin were close friends and had known each other since seminary days. Between deep, heartfelt sighs, Wyatt and I made plans. My hours would be long. They could, probably would, include overnight. I had a lot to process. These feelings were new. It was hard to wait for them to come back to LA.

Wyatt had a brilliant strategic mind, a soft Virginia accent, and a sexy smile. The anti-civil rights goliaths in the south would discover this to their shame when he turned their tactics against them. See his profile in Malcolm Gladwell's book, *David and Goliath*.

When Wyatt smiled at me and said my name, I didn't fight my feelings. But under my casual, free-sex attitude, what I wanted was an always-was, always-will-be, ends-of-the-earth-together, heart connection. Maybe this was it? I would have to make the most of his short stay. I also had a job to do. I ran errands for Martin—taking a broken watch to be repaired, arranging transport to appearances, at the hotel mixing drinks for guests after working hours. Whatever the task, I was there to serve!

Malcolm, accompanied by the Fruit of Islam, was in the crowd outside a church at 52nd and McKinley on the East Side where Martin was speaking. My Aunt Jessie Mae had lived across the street so I was in a familiar neighborhood. It seemed shabby, smaller. The migration to the West Side could be felt as well as seen. I'm sure my perception of the area was affected by the company I was in. We were in a limo provided by the mayor, escorted by an official from his office and accompanied by one of the ministers' wives. I had already noticed women liked to be around Martin. When I exited the limo, I saw Malcolm and excitedly went to greet him, hands open. "*A 'salaam a'laikum.*" A shriek caused me to look back to see the minister's wife, emerging from the limo, staring at us with a look of horror on her face. My mother wasn't the only good Christian woman Minister Malcolm's militancy frightened. That evening Martin was curious. He said several of the women in his organization had been talking about Malcolm. Perhaps one of them might have been Ella Baker, who radically believed that, in a participatory democracy, "strong people don't need strong leaders." It wasn't a belief shared by the men of SCLC.

Martin wanted to know my connection to Malcolm. He was interested to know what I thought about Malcolm, how we met, and how long I'd known him. Martin was a good listener; he asked good questions. I was comfortable. And I could only say what I felt, and so I said, "He's like you. He's a man to emulate. He has integrity and courage; he speaks the truth, and he cares for people." Finally, I had to admit that Malcolm probably was more representative of my beliefs and values. I felt Martin's non-violence was laudable, but I wasn't turning the other cheek. I would not be placated—I wanted to punch, hit back. I think I've always been angry.

Basically, I felt Malcolm and Martin were very much alike and significantly different. They both had the same objective, same passion, same intensity, but different paths they would be willing to go down. Martin would give his life for the beliefs and values that we call freedom, Malcolm would kill for them. I told Martin about Malcolm's love of words, his sense of humor. His admiration and respect for women, belief in community economic support and especially, the way he could get his message across to inspire others, just like Martin. I told him that I thought they'd like each other. He seemed appreciative. And we laughed.

Ultimately, I swung away from revenge, reprisal, retaliation, and the rest of the R's and accepted Martin's belief that love is the most beneficial, the most sustaining and sustainable lifegiving way. Martin did cause a shift in my thinking then about spanking my kids. It had been done to me; everyone I knew did it or had had it done when they were young. We would share stories about our toughness, trying to top each other with our story of a spectacular beating. Martin didn't spank his kids When I asked Martin what was wrong with correcting your kids, he said correcting was good but spanking was something different. Physical discipline wasn't African tradition. It came from slave days, From the need to subjugate and make the slaves docile. From when we were routinely whipped, called nigger, and dehumanized. In family it was often explained away as being for the child's own good, as necessary to toughen, them to handle the treatments they will get growing up black.

Each time I broke a rule, failed to do a chore, or said or did something I shouldn't—in other words, was a human—there was a demerit placed by my name. Posted on a chart in the kitchen where everyone could see them. If the punishment level was reached, a "spanking" was scheduled. to be executed on Sunday at 2 p.m. While my friends went to the movies on Sunday, I searched our yard to select the switch my mother would use. Too thick hurt, but too thin stung and hurt more. Trying to get away with something that wouldn't hurt would get me sent back out to get something she'd accept. If I didn't cry soon enough or hard enough, the blows increased until I did. My resentment increased as well.

I found it hard to unlearn the reflexive . Just by being aware caused me to try to change. Even a small change made a difference..

I was learning—not just from Martin but also by being around him. I was seeing behind the public view. Being Martin's PA, I stayed by his side all day and after the day's speaking, meetings and interviews, I'd relax with Martin and Wyatt at their hotel. It was where I'd made my debut. Local identities and compatriots would stop by for a chat and a drink. I learned religious figures, civic leaders, and their girlfriends liked to party too and how I could ruin perfectly good Scotch whisky by mixing it with the requested milk.

With such a limited amount of time, Wyatt and I would hang out until late. Not wanting to say goodbye but not daring to spend the entire night.

I saw a free and easy Martin relaxing late one night with only the intimate circle around. I was sitting on the floor at his feet leaning back against Wyatt's legs, glass of Jack and Coke beside me laughing. We laughed a lot. I guess being on the edge, facing danger as they did, laughter can keep you centered. But Martin told a joke that had me blushing as well as laughing. The joke was funny, but the subject, oral sex, colored my cheeks as my head sank lower and lower until my face was in the carpet. Martin called attention to my red face, saying incredulously "Ande is blushing." Attitudes were changing, but even the suspicion of practicing oral sex raised eyebrows. One bartender I knew would break a certain suspect's used glass instead of washing it. Martin ended the joke saying women could reciprocate by joining a 'special' Ladies Auxiliary. I had already joined. With my husband's teaching, I had found that if I put a piece of Sees peanut brittle in my mouth, I could suck that as well as him.

⋆ ⋆ ⋆

Wyatt was only going to be there days, not even weeks. I was love-stricken and pushed that thought aside. I wanted him to give me something, a memento of our mad passion. There was a jewellery store at the Hilton where I'd taken Martin's watch. I had spied something sparkly that I liked there. I hinted to Wyatt I'd like a token of our relationship. When we went past one night, I "discovered it," pointed it out to him. He didn't pick up the hint and I didn't mention it again. Gramma Booker had a story about a man and a woman and a gift, and the punch line was, "Woman, listen. When I'm hard I'm soft, and when I'm soft I'm hard." I told myself that just being with him was enough, and I'd wanted him as much as he'd wanted me. I wasn't expecting and didn't require gifts. It would've been nice, though.

Their tour ended; it was time for them to go back to Georgia. We said goodbye at the hotel. Then Wyatt called: "Come to the airport; the plane's going to be late. I've got to see you again." And like the first time, we were again walking around the check-in areas. Sharing heart-to-heart. He joked that they were always transiting Chicago, and if I lived there—he trailed off as he remembered to call home. He rang to advise his wife of the later arrival. I listened to the call, "Hey, big stockings."

The affection, the warmth and love flowing through the phone, and I felt hope drain away. I didn't have a chance. There was no way it would turn out well. On the way home, I stopped at the local cocktail lounge, ordered a straight sour mash whiskey from the glass smashing bartender, and dropped a coin in the jukebox. Ray Charles sang it: "Born to Lose." I felt it!

I didn't want to live without Wyatt. Phone calls between us were infrequent, often coming from dangerous places in the deep south. I was frightened he'd be killed. I was frustrated. If only I lived in Chicago. My dad was living there and so was a high school friend.

My depression deepened and led to my first serious suicide attempt. I was on a date with a childhood hero at a club where Lou Rawls, an ex, sang onstage. That made things worse. Before Wyatt I'd had a brief moment with Lou Rawls. He told me Jai had threatened to stop playing his records on air if he continued. It could have been true. But I was in deep depression, reliving my lost relationship with Lou and my inability to be with Wyatt. Pills and booze swallowed together while Lou sang on stage. I was such a drama queen! I passed out from the pills and alcohol after making it up the stairs to the front door. My childhood forever beyond my reach dream date used my key to dump me inside my front door. I wasn't the only one intimidated by mom. He closed the door and ran away without a word. I think he changed his phone number too.

Some part of me fought back against the drugs. Even though I'd passed out and didn't remember, I had phoned the fabulous Florence Antoine and babbled my farewell. She mounted an effective rescue. I woke up, flat on a gurney, in restraints and was soon water-boarded by a nurse, forcing a container of tepid LA tap water into my mouth and up my nose. Mom was worried but maintained her cool. Her psychiatric social worker friend interviewed me and they decided on a course of action. I was sent off, without the kids, to spend some time with my dad in Chicago. Paula was mom's favorite, so Kandi was separated from her sister and sent to her grandmother in Texas. Mom preferred light skin. Kandi was dark and looked like her.

10

Chicago in 1962 was dreary and foreign and unwelcoming. As Wyatt had suggested, it was also a place he and Martin transited often. I arrived in time to catch up with him at a fundraiser. Backstage Aretha Franklin asked me to help with the long zipper in her gown. I was so nervous about seeing Wyatt again, I barely processed it was The Queen of Soul. Zipping, while absently wondering how someone could get so much makeup on a dress. It wouldn't show, but how would it be cleaned, and how long…? I was overthinking, again. The critic in my head always available.

I didn't know what to say to Wyatt, so I clumsily told him about the suicide attempt to show him how much I cared. He recognized my instability. I was bad news, and I didn't see him again for ten years. I was staying with a married school friend I hadn't seen for years. That wasn't working out either.

I had arrived in Chicago full of hope, and after I crashed, the reality was that I was living with a friend who was working at the post office. She lived upstairs from her despised and despising in-laws. I had practically no money and no job. I hated it when I had to choose between walking to interviews or eating. Mostly the bus won.

One cold and miserable day, I'd been to agencies looking for work, taken a typing test and interviewed. Promise but no work yet. On the way home there was a cheap steak house with the skimpy T-bones on a grill in the window. The smell blowing from the exhaust stirred me. I stood there, sucking it all in. Food is love. In my pocket was train and bus fare back to my friend's grim manor where I'd skipped eating today, aware of looks tracking me whenever I went into the kitchen, especially near the fridge. In my pocket was enough for the steak, but I'd have to walk home. Or, I could take the train and only face the long walk home down the avenue where a man had put a knife to my friend's throat and told her to "keep on walking just like we're lovers" and then raped and robbed her in an alley. No, I had to do without. That hurt. I was my mother's only and favorite child. I had to have my sadness soothed. Food still provided that.

I moved in with Dad and his girlfriend. Their fridge was available and soon it wasn't as important. I hooked up with some Johnson Publication folk through a friend from home. They lived in a nice high-rise building in Prairie Shores and were a group I was desperate to belong to. Through them I got hooked up with Oscar Brown Jr.. The Johnson Publications friends were cool. I wasn't. I postured and pretended I was, but in reality, I was in a low-paying job in a warehouse, filling orders for a mail order company. Encouraged by Agnes, Dad's girlfriend, I went out with a friend of hers. He was a ponderous old, smelly cigar-smoking man who lived in a dingy bachelor flat.

Christmas was coming. I was so broke and so far away from my kids, the least I could do was get them gifts, and the only way I could see was to have the old man buy them for me. He gave me money for their presents. I slept with him. I felt like a whore— one that didn't charge enough. I knew I was selling myself. It was the lowest part of my life. I sawed at my wrists and made sure everyone saw the bandages.

Then everything changed: new job, new place to live, new man in my life, all because of friends of the fabulous Florence Antoine. The job was working at the black radio station WYNR. Her friend was my boss—and married. My new lodging was a south-side, three-bedroom apartment with another friend of Florence's. Onita was a very sophisticated NOLA (New Orleans Louisiana), black-educated, and very bright, a good Catholic girl who shared the apartment with Mary Alice and Tina. Mary Alice was a soft-spoken, petite school teacher and amateur theater member who would later win an Obie, Tony, and an Emmy. Tina who liked bus drivers and any man in uniform. Mary Alice and Tina were my friends, I made Onita my role model/mentor. There was no spare bedroom. But it was summer and I was welcome to sleep in the living room or on the covered balcony. Tina sometimes shared her bed and had sex with me. I hadn't bumped bushes since I was twelve, and I enjoyed it.

At the radio station, I was hanging out in the newsroom with Thom Beck, the news reporter[19], when the newswire announced Medgar Evers had been murdered in his driveway at home in Mississippi. I was devastated at the loss of that sweet, gentle man. I'd liked him, even though I'd only spent a day showing him around Los Angeles. Smugly, I'd suggested LA

---

19   https://youtube.com/watch?v=OJhj2qr5cyk&si=EnSIkaIECMiOmarE

might be a safer, better place to live. Immediately, Medgar let me know that was true in some ways, but it wasn't his home. He'd made his choice. He had no hesitation and died for it. I was angry and frustrated. I knew they'd get away with it and no one would be arrested.

I buried myself in having fun, not letting it get to me. Having single roommates my age was new and so was meeting women who were bold and breaking new ground. like Yvonne Daniels. At WYNR I was working with the only female DJ in town, one of too few in the whole country. She blazed that trail and made me her social companion. She was high visibility because she was also the daughter of Billy Daniels, a very well known, popular singer. Yvonne was having a secret affair with one of the DJs from a rival station. I provided cover for their relationship.

Chicago was a non-stop party. There was a lot for black people to do. I was free of child responsibility other than sending money home, and was making up for the good times I thought I had lost being a mom. One of the roomies would wake me Saturday morning before noon, wrapping my hand around an icy martini, and the day would begin. I even missed the March on Washington in exchange for a Motown party. I met Dionne Warwick. Onita went to the march. My roommate got to be a part of the change that we hoped was coming. I wish I had been there.

I went to New York to see Major Lance who I'd dated in Chicago. He was at the Apollo and Redd Foxx was also there. We had become friends in Chicago. He showed me around Harlem, and I fell in love with the Big Apple. A few weeks later Onita and I moved there. She went to work on becoming Dr. Onita Marie Estes-Hicks PhD and I found a job at a black radio station: WLIB, voice of liberty—Radio Harlem as their Traffic Manager, scheduling ads.

Onita was already my instructor and role model for navigating a new world which now threatened to include interracial dating. "Onita, Mr. Woo called," I said. "You're dating Peter, who's white, and George, who's black. Now a Chinese guy?"

"Coochie," she responded, *"black, white, purple, or pink, mens is mens."* Her response made me curious.

Working at WLIB in Harlem was only a few blocks from the temple Malcolm X headed. There was a restaurant there. The food was good and healthy. The bean pie was joy singing in my mouth. Meeting up with Malcolm there was always a delight. I was filled with new experiences from living in the Big Apple. Malcolm was a good listener and heard things that hadn't been said aloud. When he asked me if I went out with white men. I was caught. I didn't know what to say. I stammered and then told the truth. "Brother Minister Malcolm, I met this nice guy. I like him—bright, enjoy being around him, but he's white, and you teach that all white men are the devil."

"Well, sister Ande," Minister Malcom responded, "with your intelligence and awareness, I'm sure you can make that decision. It's only with a child you say snake, baby; all snakes are bad. When you do that, it's out of caring about the safety of the child, to protect them. Too many black people in America think that because they were born in America that America has their interest at heart. That most white people accept that they have equal rights. But, Sister Ande, a chicken born in an oven ain't a biscuit." I started dating any man that appealed. Onita was right: mens were mens.

I saw Opera for the first time at the Met. I'd listened with my Gram Percilla on radio. But there I was peering around the pillars of the cheap seats at *Faust*. Saw Diana Sands and *Blues for Mister Charlie*. Blacks were more visible in theatre and film, making inroads and influencing. You couldn't un-ring the bell: Diahann Carroll winning a Tony for *No Strings,* and Sidney Poitier an Oscar for *Lilies of the Field*.

★ ★ ★

It was while I was working in Harlem and living in The Village, I became consciously aware of my "code switching". My world was expanding and with it, the faces I presented. Working in Harlem. Living in the village. Seeing opera, live theatre, movies in foreign languages with subtitles. The Apollo! Dating white and black. Sex with men and a woman. Bringing Harlemites to the Village, introducing them to the relevant, the cool stuff, like Chumley's, a legendary speakeasy that had no identifying sign. You had to know where it was. Uptown and downtown, I was able to fit in. I think every black person learns to code switch in kindergarten. It's a survival technique.

It also concerned me. Was I selling out? Was I acting white? Malcolm's words: "If you don't stand for something you'll fall for anything." Strong. Centered. That was what I was striving to achieve, but what I believed was shifting. I was uncertain. The depression didn't go away, though now and again, I felt great. The suicide thoughts were also still there, but the execution was halfhearted. Enough for a bandage on my wrist, but cut across and not deeply enough. Lithium was still the treatment for bi-polar. So glad I wasn't diagnosed then.

Lithium must be monitored closely, I was too capricious, too inconsistent for that.

★ ★ ★

Dr King's public dreams became more detailed, seeing not only civil rights and equality but economic access, equal opportunities, and his bombshell—his call for an end to the war. He was facing attack from within, younger people who thought he was too slow. I was also guilty.

Martin held a just-out-of-jail press conference that I used my radio station ID to get into. When Martin noticed me in the crowd of reporters, he smiled, recognizing a friendly face. Except I wasn't. I was angry. I was frustrated. Martin seemed pleased to see me until I attacked, and then I think he was sad. "Why didn't you stay in jail? Why did you leave?" I hurled my questions at him as though they were bricks. With him in jail, the struggle was reported in the valuable real estate above the fold on the *New York Times*. His getting out let them off the hook and the struggle slipped off the front page entirely. It felt like a betrayal. With him not in jail, the movement was losing traction.

I didn't know—we didn't know—that Hoover's FBI was blackmailing him, making and sending tapes of his encounters with women to his wife. But Hoover was also rumored to be watching President Kennedy who was having an affair with actor [20] William Campbell's ex-wife Judith[21]. I wonder if the watchers ever compared their sexual prowess? Based on the

---

20 Star Trek actor (TOS & DS9) and Gene Coon's close friend.
21 https://allthatsinteresting.com/judith-exner

passionate sounds I heard one night from the room next to Wyatt's, Martin was excellent! But the orgasmic cries of "Oh Doctor, Oh Doctor!" made me sad. It sounded like she was in bed with the public figure not the man. Our need for contact, comfort, warmth and belonging is hard-wired in us. What Martin did was human. Faced with the loneliness of the road and the threat that death could come at any moment, he stuck to his vision of equality.

A few days after the press conference, mom was on the phone. "Andreea, Gwen called me."

"Yes, Mom."

"She said Dr. King saw you in New York."

"Yes, Mom."

"And he said you were wearing your hair nappy!"

Busted! Thanks, Martin.

When Malcolm showed up with Cassius Clay for an interview at the radio station, I could see how comfortable they were together. I saw a teacher pupil connection, one with love and respect going both ways. I used their presence to get revenge on one of the white guys who worked with me. Out loud, in front of them, I called him out on his paternalistic attitude and absolutely dissed him. And there was nothing he dared say or do. Malcolm X and the Champ were my team; they had my back.

I think he got his revenge when I was fired from my job at WLIB. I had acted without authority, followed my radio training and pulled all the commercials following the assassination of President Kennedy. Even though other stations followed that policy, and I'd worked like a dog to reschedule the ads when it was appropriate, management didn't like my taking unilateral action. I was a good traffic manager and quickly got a new job at WMCA where I hated the music. The radio station was promoting some British group called The Beatles who were about to make their first trip to the States.

I wasn't the only one who got in trouble over Kennedy. Malcolm did too. Malcolm was suspended by his leader at The Nation of Islam after he said, about the assassination, the "Chickens had come home to roost"[22].

A 700-year-old saying shared in modern speech that meant even a president with Kennedy's popularity and Camelot armor couldn't be protected; that children have been bombed in church, people protesting for civil rights beaten, dogs turned loose on them, that America had become such a violent society that an American president was able to be assassinated. Martin had said roughly the same thing, calling it, "the climate of hate." When Malcolm called to tell me about it, I was concerned. His influence now rivalled his leader. He was a threat. He was becoming more influential and not limited to the United States. Africa was stirring. Seventeen countries had gained independence in 1960, and Kenya was about to win theirs.

It was no longer only civil rights. When Malcolm moved away from Elijah Muhammad and The Nation of Islam, he became an orthodox Muslim and made the hajj[23]. El Haji Malik Al Shabazz raised the stakes, calling for human rights. The explosion of independent black nations at the United Nations gave him a chance to be heard and he made new alliances with

---

22 A saying that the past comes back to bite you. Originally "curses are like chicken; they always come home to roost."

23 A pilgrimage required of all Muslims once in a lifetime.

African and Islamic countries in order to bring charges against America in the United Nations for denial of our human rights. That marked him for death.

Black leaders were pushing back against the established order, demanding more and expanding the issues and alliances. Even Martin had broadened, had become anti-war, and more anti-racist as he now demanded economic justice for all. Martin challenged both the economic system and the war machine. He planned a poor people's march on Washington bringing back old alliances, unions, and other like-minded people, and new alliances with people of every color and every race; and like Malcolm, that marked him for death.

I was tired of the battles, I was tired of the fighting, I was tired. I went back to California, met hippies and joined up to be responsible to no one but myself. I left Malcolm and Martin to the battle, they got assassinated and I got stoned.

11

I was back in LA cruising down Crenshaw Boulevard listening to soul radio KGFJ on Sunday February 21st 1965. The Magnificent Montague had the Temptations singing about sunshine on a cloudy day. Into that squawked the breaking news. Heartbreaking news! In NYC Malcolm X assassinated. Tears flooded my vision; sobs shook me so hard, I was ripped apart, screaming out loud in pain. Steering so erratically the grief forced me to pull the car over, and stop. Pounding the steering wheel doesn't help, nothing helps, but to wait till I am voiceless, again. Malcolm is gone. Shot. He's dead. What I had feared had come true that Sunday morning.

On Malcolm's previous L A visit we'd caught up. It had been a while. There were many changes in both of our lives. The most important for him was that he was more certain than ever of what he was doing. He was sure he could bring the US government in front of the UN to face charges of failure to protect its black citizen from racist terrorism. The US made and upheld laws that were systematically entrenching the powerlessness of black people, and empowering whites. To overturn many of the laws would go against the lawmakers' own best economic interests. They wouldn't do that on their own. It would require an outside force, and a greater one.

Change was happening at the UN. Russian Jews were there successfully challenging their mistreatment. Countries were declaring and becoming independent. Some of those countries didn't even comprise as many people as we had Black people in the US.

I didn't understand completely why Malcolm's focus was international. Back then I was still focused on racism as a personal thing, a one-on-one. So, I had listened more carefully when he shared a personal identifiable threat. While he was in LA, a car that had been following him pulled up beside his on the 110 freeway, and one of the black men in the car mimed pointing and shooting a gun at him. They drove off laughing. He told me not to be surprised when I hear he's been murdered. But I was.

Things didn't improve. My life was mostly dreary and disillusioned. I was living with my mother again. I was in a separate apartment. Without a permanent job, I was Kelly Girl-ing it. Working for the temp agency, doing clerical work. But that wasn't working too well. I'd refused some tasks because they involved doing business with South Africa, where anti-apartheid revolutionary Nelson Mandela was in jail. Apartheid was wrong and I was doing nothing at all to support them. A put-out employer said "If you don't want to do the job you shouldn't be here" and assignments dried up.

The bright spot was when, after collecting my unemployment payment I could hit Route 1 with the top down on my 2-seater sports car. I would meander up the coast, sucking in the sights, marveling. Always there was the stop at Nepenthe in Big Sur for good food and to listen to the surf. Finally, into San Francisco, to Haight-Ashbury, to a friend's place where I'd be lifted by some cannabis and good company.

I had been tripping on Owsley acid in Golden Gate Park at a love-in when I heard Watts had exploded. Damn! The revolution had started without me. I had to get there quick. I had a desire to participate in bringing about real change, and if that meant burning down the old, I am OK with that.

When I hit LA I don't even go home. I head straight for Watts to the part where I know things will be happening! 103rd street. I park a way down the main drag, and walk past Jordan High. It was named for Stanford University's founding professor, a eugenics supporter who wanted to limit racial mixing and the reproduction of those he thought unfit. Like black people. My mother and her sisters were schooled there. The less melanized Jordan in Long Beach still carries the name, David Starr Jordan High School and ironically their mascot is the black panther.

103rd is still where It's happening. All around me. I poke my nose in everywhere. In one place it's getting warmer, the smoke thicker. Time to coolly but quickly exit the store.

A woman moving in the same direction smiles at me, a smile of some satisfaction, her arms overflowing with clothing, holding on so tightly, a couple things slip away. "Go ahead, I'll get them". I let her go by and pick up small dresses and pants. Outside putting them back in her arms, she beams, so happy she has smiles for days. She says, "I got all new clothes for my kids, they going to start school **this** year with new clothes!"

The Nat Diamond's Empire Furniture where my dad had sold overpriced, overstuffed, long credit term, high-interest rate, cheaply made furniture, has smoke coming out of it as well as heavily loaded people. People ant-like, doing a stop-and-share with each other every few feet. Everywhere. Working together. Helping. What was happening? I see strange things everywhere I look.

I see strange things everywhere I look. Cooperation, that's what it is. People are helping each other carry sofas and fridges. And it is the same when I go into the next building, it too is burning. A variety store and it has stuff, cheap junk really. I start grabbing, there's nothing I want or need, it's the Carnival mood that has captured me. I feel unrestricted.

The National Guard arrives. The bullets start flying, and I can't find anything big enough to hide behind. The police stop us leaving the curfew area. We had felt free and united, now we are suspect and about to be judged. I am stopped at a police roadblock and searched. Oh shucks! The woman with the clothes. To help her, I had stuffed whatever I'd been holding into my pocket. It still had a price tag on it, and the police took it.

They saw nothing worth detaining me for, didn't notice or didn't care about the small carton of evaporated milk I'd picked up somewhere and tossed in the back seat. I was snotty later when mom asked for a can of the milk for her coffee. All markets in our peaceful middle-class community were closed. We were located about a mile outside the white demarcation line. Close enough to be suspect. "Stop calling it a riot", I frostily told her and handed over a can from the carton, because people gotta have milk in their coffee. "It's a revolution."

It was both and more. It was over-policed poor people rising up in protest. Police Chief Parker was publicly racist. After he took over no black police officers partnered with white, and a more militaristic policing became the standard.

The black population had increased in the 25 years to 1965 from roughly 60,000 to 350,000. Restrictive covenants covered 95% of the city. Some properties black people were able to buy were only because they had been taken from Japanese people who were put in WWII camps. Black people picketed because they couldn't live in Carson, the suburb next door to Watts, and were refusing to accept the combination that suppressed their access, income and accommodation.

We fought back. It was a revolt.

We destroyed property and looted. It was a riot.

The police and the garbage collectors were together when things calmed enough for a trash pickup. Where there was an old appliance or piece of furniture to be taken away the police were there asking for receipts for the replacements. Police confiscated anything new and undocumented. Over 30 people died, more than 1000 injured. It was the end of asking please and being appropriate. And the beginning of more neglect.

After Watts, I fared well. I had been registered with the Urban League, a black organization that specialized in finding jobs for black people to integrate workplaces. Desilu Studios was looking for a clerical person, and because I'd worked in radio, the Urban League figured television's practically the same, so they sent me to the interview.

PART II
I TRAVEL UP THE STREET TO A FOREIGN LAND.

12

"**Put on the wig** when you go to the interview. Don't you show up with your hair all nappy," mom warned me. Naturals had yet to be broadly embraced. I understood the underlying concern that I wouldn't present well. Appearance was everything to Mom. We couldn't be real, messy, humans. We subscribed to 'respectability politics. We had to be better citizens to prove that we deserved a place. So, I attended the interview, my afro crushed beneath the straight hair style wig that matched the suit I wore. And gloves. My tiny rebellion was they were leather driving gloves.

Desilu Studios was just north of where I lived. That was lucky because there was no way I was taking any job over in the Valley where there were sunset suburbs that blacks weren't welcome in after dark. Mulholland Drive marked the border I refused to cross. The Hollywood Bowl luckily was just inside. Universal Studios was just past it, and Warner Bros was in Burbank, definitely no-go territory.

My interview was at 780 North Gower in Hollywood. It was a few blocks south of Columbia Pictures and around the corner from Paramount Studios.

The main entrance had a severe guardian behind an

enclosed desk who controlled the button which remotely unlocked the door. They kept the door locked? I was a little intimidated.

Ernie Scanlon, the Desilu Human Resources guy who interviewed me, was old Hollywood. His dad had worked at studios before him and probably his dad before him. Nepotism was how you got employed in Hollywood. That's how you got into the unions, even the creative ones. That's how black people were restricted to service jobs, except for security guard. Blacks were the Desilu shoeshine guy, janitors, cooks, and the actors that played janitors and cooks and maids.

During the interview I pulled out my radio experience, evidence I knew something of the entertainment industry, and stressed that temping as a Kelly Girl showed I was adaptable and used to working in a variety of situations. I assured Ernie my typing speed was fantastic, and it actually was.

Then I whipped past my lack of shorthand by saying I had fast longhand, a bit of shorthand and never a problem. In reality I had always had problems with languages. Shorthand was another language I didn't get. At best in my night school class, I'd learnt some of the brief forms. Like Dear Sir, which was written with the symbols for d and, I think, for r joined together. It had a great look. I liked writing that.

Ernie didn't challenge me, or even ask what my shorthand speed was, a perfectly normal interview question at that time. I think he knew he wouldn't be impressed with the number. Ernie had been warm and welcoming, even a bit funny. I had seen and heard no threat from him. I read him as not racist, and when he commented on my driving gloves my honest feeling came through. I laughed and admitted to being an active fan. Turned out he was also a Grand Prix racing fan. I'd recently come back from watching a race and we spent the remainder of the interview talking about Grand Prix racing. The track at Watkins Glen, and who would be at the Riverside and "What about that Bruce McLaren, can he ever drive!" I was definitely in with a chance.

I worried. I'd been the first black hired a couple of times and not very successfully. Both jobs had rules that were procedural and rigid. Gas company service rep, municipal center switchboard operator. Radio stations had been different. I'd enjoyed them! I was pretty sure the movie business was going to be a fit.

I got the job! Like any zoo or attempt to include a new species, Ernie brought in two of us. We had nothing to say to each other. The university-educated, serious accounting male and the 'out there from the hood' female. Our subspecies didn't match. But we were proud to see each other there and we did give a warm nod whenever we crossed paths.

★ ★ ★

Desilu was an anomaly at that time: a studio and production company with a woman at the top. Of course, the man was the head. Desi was President and Lucy Vice President. Still, Lucille Ball was a first! Not only was it the first independent production company, it was a smart, profitable way to keep her handsome Cuban musician husband Desi Arnaz at home, off the road and away from groupies. Her home btw designed by Paul Williams, black architect of many iconic Beverly Hills commercial and residential buildings.

In person Lucy was addressed by all as Miss Ball, with a deferential bob of the head. I reacted that way automatically years later while walking past her shopping on Rodeo Drive.

Lucy deserved the respect. She backed up her beliefs with action. She challenged television network executives by casting her husband on her show when they were concerned the public wouldn't accept the all-American redhead being married to a Cuban bandleader on TV despite their being married in real life.

That Lucy did it by forming her own production company, producing the pilot herself, and selling it to CBS instead of to a sponsor, as was the custom, is a myth. They didn't produce the pilot. And Desi saying in his memoir *I Love Lucy* was the first show to use three cameras doesn't make that true either. New York was where all the TV shows were produced with a kinescope copy airing in the west three hours later. And that's where Lucy and Desi did something special. Kinescopes were not as good quality and degraded further with each viewing. Lucy's company actually was one of the first in Hollywood to give up the kinescopes and film the show. It was more expensive but it gave better quality.

Lucy's company covered the film expenses and also (and more importantly) retained the rights to them. Reruns and residuals were born! The whole country benefited. And it gave her the ability to keep her family stable in California instead of moving to New York.

Desi had the company buy the equipment used to film *I love Lucy* with money from CBS and structured a deal so Desilu owned the equipment and rented it back to the production company for each episode. These then became standard practices in the industry.

The story I like best is how Lucy saved *Star Trek*. When everyone was saying 'dump the loser' Lucy held firm and kept the show going. Every actor and Trek person needs to remember to light a candle for St Lucy, patron saint of the residuals, the possible Guardian Angel of Star Trek.

Desilu prospered and the studio included two additional lots; on Cahuenga Boulevard in Hollywood and in Culver City near MGM. When Desi and Lucy divorced, she bought his share, and became President.

13

1965-1967 WORKING THE THREE Desilu lots:[24] Desilu Culver City: Where the Star Trek revised pilot was shot. Desilu Cahuenga: Where a young Bill Cosby was making history starring in *I Spy*, in what I think was the first interracial equal co-star series. Desilu Gower: The home of Bing Crosby Productions, and Hogan's Heroes, Mission: Impossible and Star Trek. And all the Lucy shows: *I Love Lucy, The Lucy Show* and *Here's Lucy*, as well as specials.

Desilu Gower was pretty good size. Paramount was next door and I found there was a path to their commissary winding through the western sets where *Bonanza* was shooting and past a huge water tank that always stirred my imagination. It was a reservoir where at-sea shots were done using miniatures. They could create storms there that looked real. I was starting to discover how the magic was made.

I was the Desilu floater clerical support. I don't know if the job existed before I started there. I was an assistant that was available to work in any area that needed clerical support on a temporary basis. I got to explore and learn. I worked all

---

24 https://youtu.be/yaQeMzlQ_Zg or With Lucy and Desi https://youtu.be/8RQgmfEmHw0 https://youtu.be/YfIBIh9ghvU

over the Gower lot, and the other two lots as well. Telephones answered, things sorted and filed. Being the floater suited me perfectly. Star Trek was one of my casual assignments.

My favorite assignment was working in the Art Department. I was able to watch designs come to life. I could see the sketches for sets or wardrobe, a planet or some space-age equipment come off the page, assume shape, become reality and then I'd see it on my TV.

In payroll I got very friendly with actors waiting for much needed checks. In casting I met hopefuls desperately wanting a role, a big break, or even just a few lines.

A couple of times I worked with an executive, covering for his regular secretary. Fear of exposure of my shorthand deficiency made me nervous working there. I did get sprung. After taking dictation, I was attempting not to freak out as I tried to read the forms that were meaningless squiggles on the page. Finally, the guy asked "Okay, how was that?" I responded "Yeah, it's fine," and then, as casually as I could, "What was it you said after Dear Sir?" The way he tip-toed around my inadequacy told me he was a social liberal, and I realized the schwartza (me, the black person) had been given a break for a change.

I was the regular lunchtime relief on the Gower Street entrance. There I controlled the door release button. You couldn't walk onto the lot if I didn't press the buzzer. Oh, the power. Which I of course abused. I may tell you about it later.

I enjoyed going to other lots. While Star Trek was reshooting the pilot, I worked for them at Culver City.

The man who ran my favorite learning place, the Production Department, had an old school southern vibe. Jim Paisley was very pale, a former ginger whose hair had gone snowy white, with faded blue, almost icy eyes. I sensed that if we had to wait for him to hire a black person we'd be waiting forever. He was courteous, but he slipped up. One day, as he turned from speaking with me and started to leave, he reached out and patted my head. I wasn't his dog or his bitch and I quickly fired at him, "Need some luck?" Blood flooded his face, rising from his neatly knotted tie to his white hair roots. It was an old slave era tradition 'rubbing a black person's head for luck' and I'd nailed him. He kept his hands to himself after that.

Whenever and wherever — I responded to needs on the three lots: Payroll, Art Department, Casting, Reception, Mission: Impossible, Star Trek... I started to like casting and I became a tyrant at reception.

Although working in payroll was boring, I had fun whenever I could. Frequent calls from Greg Morris made me laugh. He had finished shooting the Mission: Impossible pilot and was needing that check. We became friendly. I could relate to his situation and offered to call him immediately when the check was ready. I mentioned to him I was looking for a place to live. He lived in a nice spot not far away from mom. He said there was a For Rent sign on a duplex around the corner from him. Greg eased my mind about applying for the apartment. The owners were old black ladies, four sisters who decided to live in one building and rent the other. A very nice neighborhood. North of Pico and off San Vicente which was a sort of Mason-Dixon line. Black below, white above.

Paula 7, and Kandi 5, my two kids and I moved in. Two bedrooms and two baths upstairs, downstairs a living room with a wide window, a formal dining room and a big kitchen.

13

My husband Jai was a DJ at an FM jazz radio station. One of his advertisers sold the kind of high-priced cheap furniture that had burned in Watts. They gave Jai enough credit that he furnished the whole place for me. We were still married, and I wanted him sometimes and sometimes I didn't. It was go away, come back. That wouldn't turn out well either.

14

I was tired of wearing a wig or getting my hair straightened. I could imagine how singer Abbey Lincoln had felt. She was one of the few that had a natural at that time, but had worn a wig when she co-starred in the 1964 film *Nothing but a Man*. The film was earth-shattering, not just ground breaking. A black couple in the politicized South struggle to keep their courtship and marriage together within a social and economic system that destroys relationships. It was a kick ass-film and the lead actor was too.

The lead actor, Ivan Dixon, was nothing like he was on TV. In this movie he was muscles for days, a wet your undies thinking of the possibilities, chocolate delight. And better than that, the lead role he played, Duff Anderson, grew as a character into the imaginable, then the possible. He was relatable, all too human, blaming "the man", or considering the easy path. Then Duff steps up, revealing an increasing manliness and maturity. Taking responsibility for raising his abandoned four-year-old son and finding an economic solution.

I loved the scene when he brings the boy home to live with him and his wife. He won my heart when he put his arms around me... and held me so tight I could feel ripples from his biceps sending a secret message. (Abby Lincoln, on screen, was just standing in for me) Those muscular arms saying they will protect me, will keep me safe, they'll stop anyone hurting me ever again. His warm, dark, chocolatey words coming to me from the screen, giving hope to my needs and satisfying my cravings: "Ain't gonna be easy," he tells me. "Gonna be alright." Watching the movie, I cry away old hurt, fears, the monsters in the closet, vampires and zombie werewolves, and the demand that I not tell my mom about the rape. I let go of my dream of letting go and actually feel safe, whole and enough. If I could manage to meet someone like Duff.

Nothing But a Man was also the first time I remember seeing a drama for general release that starred black people. Ordinary looking black people — even Yaphet Koto, who wasn't considered good looking by a lot of those who appreciated thinner noses and paler skin. I'm surprised looking at photos now how handsome he was. I didn't feel that way back then. Who taught me that our noses and lips were unattractive?

Anyway, Duff was my hero back then. Duff was Ivan Dixon, and Ivan Dixon was in a TV comedy series called Hogan's Heroes. And Hogan's Heroes was shooting on the Desilu Gower lot. He was where I was. Of course, I was in awe of Ivan. After a few nods at a distance, he smiled one day as I was about to go past. He motioned for me to approach. Getting the courage, I introduced myself by saying, "Underneath this wig, I have a natural." I'd expected him to be a little impressed. He said, "Take off the wig." I wasn't expecting that. At work? Mom would kill me. "Oh no. I can't do that". His scorn was obvious. That wasn't what I wanted.

I reminded myself I was a first. I had to behave in a way that represented a positive image of black women. It wasn't yet time at work. Ivan would have to wait until I felt it was.

I had watched and liked Hogan's Heroes, but a comedy series wasn't how I saw him. I didn't understand why a talented dramatic actor like Ivan would even be in a comedy series. It was the usual reasons. He was an actor, it was a part for an actor, he needed money, and besides he didn't think that the show would last past the pilot. Unexpectedly, Hogan's Heroes ran from 1965 to 1971. Ivan bailed out after the fifth season. The only one to leave. He was replaced by Kenneth Washington, later the only black actor on Petticoat Junction. Comedy was no stranger to black actors. For early black actors there were no lead roles. Willie Best made more than 100 films. He was treated with dignity on the set but as a fool on screen, except by Will Rogers who was a good friend of his.

★ ★ ★

Now that I lived around the corner, Greg and Leona Morris had become friends. I loved his humor and kindness, and she was a dynamic and together lady. Seeing his car go past in the morning meant he was working, and I'd better get going myself. He was doing well on Mission and working frequently.

Later, on the wave of his Mission: Impossible success Greg released an album of love songs[25]. Not sung, not a note, just dramatic readings of the lyrics. I don't think it was an artistic success. The real success for Greg was that his wife was turned

---

25 Greg Morris: "For You"

on by his mellow readings. He told me that one day while listening to the album. "her love come down on her," he said with a cheeky grin and a bit of a brag. He was so good looking. And so very much in love with Leona.

When I'd visit him on the Mission: Impossible set, if they weren't busy and I didn't leave the sound stage soon enough, the series leads, Martin Landau and Peter Graves would corner me for a hug. One in front and one in back, while Martin's wife Barbara Bain seemed to tolerantly watch the boys at play making me part of their sandwich. The fat kid from Jr High School was in a new world I never imagined and I enjoying being the center of attention of two good looking famous actors.

Working in The Casting Department I was seeing actors close up. Reading the script and imagining it, I could compare who came in for an interview and who got the job. Of course, I wanted to see more black actors. And may have mentioned that a few ... hundred ... times. Casting several shows at once, lots of new faces. Mostly men. What unique potential.

The casting director Joe D'Agosta, shared the story of how a previous secretary had found her husband in the casting book, The Academy Players Directory, where all the actors are listed with 'head shots'.

I pored over the directory, selecting and discarding until I came to the man whose face answered every question and told me everything I wanted to know. Raymond St Jacques. Yes, he could! I met him at the main gate and escorted him to the office while trying hard to make an impression, subtly signaling I could be available. I used every bit of charm and did my best to ensure we would meet again. He was enchanting. I was hopeful. Maybe?

I walked him back to the entrance, said good-bye and used his "Tell Ivan hello for me when you see him," as a reason to stop by the Hogan's Heroes set. I told Ivan about my effort. I thought I'd done pretty well. Ivan laughed. "He's got a lot of balls for a gay guy." I was stunned. He didn't conform to my expectation of gay. But he didn't walk ... his wrist... Everybody knew from the way they acted. Where did I learn that?

15

AT THE STUDIO, THE most fun was working on the different TV series. Mission: Impossible, Mannix, Star Trek. I was learning about how the pieces fit together.

The back-to-back nature of tv episodes required expeditionary planning in order to make each episode distinct, watchable and most importantly, on budget. Call sheets, and production reports are just what they sound like. The call sheet had the time each cast and crew member were due in hairdressing, wardrobe, makeup and on set if actors needed to be fed or any special requirement. It showed the scene numbers for the day's shoot; as well as production notes about the location, special equipment or other requirements, transportation and if necessary, directions to get there.

The production report reflected the completion of the day's shoot: what had been done, where it had been done and who did it. The most important thing: where was the production in the shoot? Hopefully on schedule and on budget.

The production office was Star Trek's hub. Creator Gene Roddenberry's secretary Dorothy Fontana, was my chief go-to person. She was well organized and professional. An aspiring professional writer, who had trained as an executive secretary in order to feed herself. I could only aspire to be as good as she was at both. Dorothy was reserved. She spoke no unnecessary words. I thought she was older than me. Turned out I was a few weeks older than her. She seemed self-contained but behind that mask, she definitely was interested in rodeos, cowboys, and writing for television. Dorothy never missed the National Finals Rodeo. It was an almost sacred event.

Bob Justman was Star Trek creator's Gene Roddenberry's right hand and his go to guy. When I arrived, he was the associate producer and also the assistant director of the first two episodes.

Bob's PA, Silvia Smith, often gave me well intentioned, but not always welcomed, advice. Silvia was Jewish and married to a black man. She took me under her wing. It was more like she appointed herself authority of how I should be and the judge of my behaviors. I was never totally comfortable around her.

Silvia and I ridiculously had an issue over steak. I preferred a well-done T-bone; she liked a filet, rare. She swore well done just wasn't done but I couldn't stand the sight of blood on my plate. I hated it running into the baked potato, which hopefully was already erupting butter, sour cream, chives and bacon sprinkles.

I enjoyed Bob's sense of humor. He often lifted the mood in the office and he was first to send funny interoffice correspondence. His office was the home of many of the series' props and weird creatures. It was, of course, Bob who nicknamed Gene Roddenberry The Great Bird of the Galaxy.

Roddenberry was big. Very big with an imposing beak . He kept his head cocked at an angle, eyes on me. Understandable because I was younger, goodlooking, with big boobs, great legs, and was just a little flirty. There was something of my dad in him that I responded to. Another horny old dude bs artist kinda guy. He and I got on very well.

With Gene Roddenberry there were more pluses than minuses. One was that he showed me opals for the first time. I fell in love with them. He and Majel cut and polished the stones and made jewelry. They gave me a pendant that I loved. And, most importantly, he was always patient and kind with my daughters, as children and as adults.

Gene Roddenberry moved to Executive Producer. A new producer was hired. To Bob Justman's frustration it wasn't him. It was a guy called Gene Coon. Another Gene! I wasn't about to call him coon. Which made me use Bob's "Great Bird" nickname to distinguish them. Coon wasn't a popular name in my community. The word 'coon' was an insult. It was considered disparaging and offensive, and contemptuous (and also formerly the name of an Australian cheese that's recently been rebranded). When I met the new Gene he seemed just a little tense, coiled, but holding back any sudden moves. Gene could have been cast as the tough no nonsense gunnery sergeant, or the cynical wisecracking principled editor. I had to distinguish them by adding Coon or Roddenberry.

On the lot I was feeling comfortable enough that I started wearing my dresses a bit shorter. OK, they were miniskirts and that was a shocker for many people. I got a couple of anonymous interoffice mail memos. "Miniskirts are not appropriate for work" read one bluntly typed in all caps. I didn't care! My legs were great and I loved showing them off. Although I still didn't dare take off the wig yet.

I was learning 'the biz' and had become aware that I was

pretty good at my job. I had been asked to show the ropes to a young college graduate. He would shadow me for a few days and I would share with him what I'd learned. His last name was a giveaway. Both parents were powers in the television industry. No Way! I flatly refused. Shocked them! "Why?" they asked. I told them I wasn't training anyone to be my boss. It shut them up. No more was said. I knew he'd get whatever job he wanted. In Hollywood it was who you knew. I was jealous.

I started getting more frequent assignments to work with Gene Coon. After I'd worked with him a few times I stopped noticing that I'd thought him a middle-aged grim, grumpy-looking guy. He was that, and also a guy with a great sense of humor plus he was very bright. I especially like bright. We got along well. I didn't have to be reminded or told twice to do things, and most importantly, Gene got my jokes and I got his. Gene had a mid-western ethic, and I had that of my East Texas Freedom Colony ancestors. We travelled well together. Gene said he liked my legs and short skirts; asked me to work for him full time?

Now I had a choice of no more floating. Working for one person. I liked the people; I liked what Star Trek was about. I'd had a look at the whole studio and it was the right place for me. The job also paid a bit more.

I questioned myself briefly, "Oh God, I'm a young black woman. Do I want to work for a middle-aged white guy called Coon?" Yes! What if someone calls me Coon's Coon? Someone did!

Although I'd still have to relieve the reception desk at lunch for a while longer, I was now officially working on Star Trek. Nichelle Nichols, George Takei and I were going where no one

15

of our kind had gone before. A black officer on the bridge, an Asian who wasn't playing 'a yellow peril', and the first black executive secretary with the best legs on the lot.

1. *My desk was first stop for scripts. They came from the writer to me for distribution. I kept the originals in my files.*
2. *Ricardo Montalban and me. The only actor I wanted a photo with.*
3. *Me and Desilu parking lot guy next to my sports car. He always looked after me.*
4. *Stanley Robertson LA Sentinel column with a mention of me.*
5. *Godfrey Cambridge. Godfrey introduced me to the movie world.*
6. *Me and Gene Coon. In background NBC's Stan (Stanley) Robertson.*
7. *The two studios. Mission: Impossible, stages 6 & 7. Star Trek 8 & 9*
8. *The most excellent researcher, Joan Pearce from deforest Research.*

16

Gene Coon's smile was warm, genuine and ... rare. He drove an old car in a city where your car represented who, what and how well off you were. It was an ancient Toyota Land Cruiser, a four-wheel-drive, good for ferrying his dogs to the vet and on trips. It was a car that was odd on a lot where only stars, producers and execs had drive-on parking privileges, and what they drove was expensive and impressive. I parked in the employee's lot across from the studio entrance that I guarded at lunchtime and the brother who managed the lot always made sure I had a prime space.

Gene didn't dress well, or cool. I wasn't impressed with his looks either. Two strikes from the ghetto girl. He seemed to know his way around though. He was a writer and he'd worked on other series. Even better, he was a fast writer

Gene and I lost our first battle when I asked for a new desk. The one in my office was old and ugly. It didn't have a pull-out shelf or a drop-down typewriter table. I liked modern, efficient, gadgety stuff. The desk was so old it was only missing an ink well.

The request for a new desk became a learning experience. Producers don't have as much authority over facilities as they do over their show. Gene did his best. He manufactured a desperate need on my part to seduce him that failed "because her desk was so ugly, he turned his eyes away, and couldn't see her smoldering looks". The "my secretary needs a new desk to seduce me" interoffice mail spread to the Exec level. Gene Roddenberry and Herb Solow weighed in with guesses as to my need to have assistance in seducing. Yup it had to be about sex.

To turn things sexual at the woman's expense was nothing new. It was normal. Perceptual filters of the day were firmly in place. The back-and-forth memos are included in Whitfield's "The Making of Star Trek."[26] Actually, the exchanges, aside from being sexist, show the lightness and laughter, the take-offs and having-fun- nature of the crew. It was a great place to work. This sort of thing was accepted. No one made a fuss. I think your brain searches out examples to back it up, to make it palatable so that you can swallow it until you wake up to what's going on.

As Gene and I got through the early info sharing, probing and checking each other out, the basic information I got about him was he was a small-town boy, who grew up locally. He was born in Beatrice, Nebraska, population less than 20,000. Spent his earliest years there with his dad Jack, his mother Erma and two brothers. Another brother had died young, as was frequent in those days.

Gene was close to his family and looked after his mother. He took good care of his wife Joy and a number of dogs. Joy, an artist, also wore Joy perfume, although her work showed none. Her paintings were grim. I don't know if anyone ever bought them. One hung in Gene's office on the wall behind

---

26 *The Making of Star Trek* (1968) by Stephen Whitfield and Gene Roddenberry.

his desk. Which was probably why he usually walked looking down. That way he didn't see it when he went into his office. Gene was a good and loyal friend who had good and loyal friends. Not a lot of them. He wasn't a party guy. He and Joy didn't entertain a lot and I found an evening at his place unmemorable. Ok, boring.

Gene had been a Marine and I'd been immersed in that culture when I'd married Jai who was also in the Corps. A jarhead, Jai called himself. Gene had served closely with Lewis B 'Chesty' Puller who was the most honored, decorated Marine ever. From that I understood something about Gene's humor and attitudes.

Here's a Chesty Puller quote from the Korean War. At the Chosin Reservoir, in the midst of a fierce winter, when masses of newly involved Chinese soldiers had surrounded soldiers and Marines he said: "All right. They're on our left, they're on our right, they're in front of us, they're behind us ... they can't get away this time. Now we can shoot at those bastards from every direction." For decades Marine Drill Instructors would have their recruits recite. "Good night General Puller, wherever you are".

As I said before, Gene had a reputation as the fastest writer in Hollywood. All that speed had a cost. Gene needed an afternoon nap, several forms of caffeine, and an available supply of uppers to sustain the motion that was providing the scripts the show needed on schedule. I learned to guard his nap, score his pills, and make matcha. He also liked hot chocolate around 3pm and sometimes, when he was finished for the day, a shot of Slivovitz, a hundred proof European plum brandy. He liked the Czechoslovakian import at room temperature. As I got to know him, I appreciated and shared some of Gene's values and his ideas. He was antiwar, cold or hot. Anti-escalation, as was happening at the time during the Vietnam War. He practiced fair treatment for all people and supported equal access. For his time, he was accepting of difference, and believed in mediation. Gene's values are illustrated in The Prime Directive of non-interference, The Federation of Planets of which Starfleet is the exploration and defense arm, and the prevention and ending of wars and resolution of disputes whenever possible.

His attitudes about women? With my historical, looking back, perceptual filters firmly in place, my response is: Same old, same old, attitudes about women. "The gal at" usually indicated a woman at someplace important as in "the gal at the network". Even though she was acknowledged as giving intelligent feedback and performed her job well, it was still the "the girl at research".

17

EVEN WITH THE GENDER-BLIND spot, Gene and Star Trek were talking to us about what was happening at the time cloaked as science fiction. The Prime Directive was supposed to protect indigenous pre-eminence and values. I think it was supposed to mean No more Captain Cooks and Columbuses. Certainly, no more Congo Conference which divided up Africa between the European powers, all of which ignored the indigenous peoples[27], and screw Gomes Eanes de Zurara[28] And just like in our real world, Kirk or crew, or a guest star, in their world sometimes violated it.

The Genes, both of whom had served in the military, showed us the cost of conflict, and they both pointed toward peaceful solutions whenever possible. In the 60's the US government took a position that any expansion of communism anywhere was a world threat. When the Soviets aided the North Vietnamese communists, President Johnson backed

---

27 Congo Conference (1884-85), also called the Berlin Conference, regulated European colonization and trade in Africa, without consulting African leaders. It led to the atrocities perpetrated by King Leopold's Belgians in the Congo and resonates still.

28 Lived 1410-1474, an early writer of lies about Africans in his book about Portugal's 'discovery' of Guinea that made enslaving Africans justifiable.

South Vietnam. Like the US, their Catholic president was shot to death in November 1963, just twenty days before Kennedy.

President Johnson's Civil Rights Act, that would be his legacy, wasn't going as well as he'd hoped, so he used what he knew was a fake threat and played the Vietnam war card. The one thing that he hoped would unify all of its citizens and promote race and gender egalitarianism. It didn't work as it had with Korea and the World Wars.

Gene created the Klingons to point out the effects and dangers of a cold war that could become hot. He brought them to life and they have continued to populate the world.

The Klingons were handy for action-filled, 'finger on the trigger', 'Cold War' stories. The Cuban missile standoff, a few

years before with the Soviets still resonated. It had scared the heck out of my generation. We had grown up with 'drop and cover drills' like today's school shooter drills for kids.

As he gave us an opponent, Gene also gave us the options to go to war. But the emphases were always on peaceful solutions, creating The United Federation of Planets, The Prime Directive, The Organian Peace Treaty, Star Fleet Command, and using mediation to resolve conflicts. He also valued community and cooperation, and The Federation was a mechanism for creating more ways of working together. In his scripts Gene sought respect for all including non-carbonbased life forms.

One of differences in the two styles of Gene and The Great Bird, besides humor or lack thereof, is demonstrated by outcomes of these two Season One episodes: Devil in The Dark on Gene Coon's watch, and The Man Trap on Roddenberry's.

The Devil in The Dark: "Our" guys discover why an alien is

killing people. The creature, a guardian the last of its kind, is killing invaders to protect and allow her children to survive. Though not a carbon-based life-form, it is recognized as sentient and protected until they find a way to communicate. The creature is not killed and a peaceful, beneficial solution is found.

The Man Trap: An alien, in the form of a human woman once loved by Dr McCoy, is killing people in order to survive. Even though the life form is known to be the Truganini[29] of that planet, the very last of her kind, they kill her.

Gene gave The Great Bird of the Galaxy total respect for the universe he had created, and contributed his touch to fine tuning it. Because of Gene's sense of humor, the exchanges between McCoy, Spock and Kirk were bound to happen. If you read Gene's war novels, *Meanwhile Back at The Front* or *The Short End*, you will recognize the same style of humor that he added to Trek. It was just who Gene was.

Star Trek offered a voice of possibilities that paralleled what was happening in the wider world outside the studio. Martin Luther King's opposition to economic injustice, oppression and the Vietnam war was also clear. Gene was a lot like MLK; they had a similar sense of humor. They each teased me, and both were intensely influenced by the same philosopher, Reinhold Niebuhr, an American theologian. He was an evangelical, critic of capitalism and ecumenical influencer who taught at Union Theological Seminary in New York. A prayer he used is widely known as The Serenity Prayer, "God, grant me the

---

29 Truganini, 1812–1876, is often described as the last full-blooded Aboriginal Tasmanian, although Tasmania's Aboriginal population remains strong and resurgent to this day.

serenity to accept the things I cannot change, courage to change the things I can and wisdom to know the difference".

Gene and Martin were visionaries who wanted wrongs righted, and they proposed solutions. They spoke of strong moral lessons, in human terms concerning personal redemption and opposing war. No wonder I felt at home with Gene. My kind of people.

Since I was working with him, I was allowed to watch the editors cut the film, and saw the illusions our talented cinematographer Gerry Finnerman created with his camera. I was sucking it all in! The more I learned, the more I saw the magic and influence that the results held. Being a TV producer gave you the opportunity to point out injustice and oppression, to howl in a way that informed as it entertained.

Gene was a good listener. He liked hearing my take on the events of the day, and sometimes was surprised by his new awareness since our realities were not the same. After a while I was just myself, didn't need to code switch or pull my punches, at least not very often. Sometimes though, I just didn't have the words. We were just two howling at the world, doing the best job we could, because that's who we were. We were immersed. It wasn't 9 to 5 even if the hours were supposed to be.

18

Nichelle Nichols who played Uhura amazed me. I was in awe of her. A black woman who actively demonstrated and inspired. For me, she was a supplier of awakenings. She made me aware of how much about life I didn't know and modelled being brave enough to experiment. She was encouragement and support for a lot of us.

Nichelle and I took time exploring our connectedness. A few hi's, and nods, with lots of 'so glad to see you here' smiles. We checked each other out. On the physical side we were both good looking and looking good. We were both wearing wigs so hair wasn't counted. After a few general questions and we found that we lived in the same general 'hood. She was further south and a bit farther west. We knew a few local people in common. There was a spark. We went to the same dry cleaners, Jenny's. A small business owner who sponsored my husband Jai's jazz show.

Nichelle had worked with the very talented singer, songwriter Oscar Brown Jr, whom I'd had a crush on in Chicago. He had introduced me to Gandhi, 'and Satyagraha' the non- violence practice that connected me to MLK. Nichelle had worked with Duke Ellington and become friends with his son Mercer, the warm gentle soul I'd worked with at WLIB in New York. I was again being connected to people who had touched me. Though she was an actor, her love was music and our connections were musicians. With Nichelle I relaxed and didn't worry about who I needed to be and I got in the habit of just dropping by the set and sometimes dropping by her house. I liked spending time with her.

It was nice having someone close to me who was experienced in my work world. I felt comfortable enough to tell her about Ivan Dixon. His suggestions now included my taking off my panties (I was still wearing them and a bra back then). He was married but that didn't stop him having affairs. I knew that, but he carried himself like a king and I felt like a subject being asked to kneel. Well, yes, I guess he wanted that too. The thought of saying no, scared me a bit. Who was I to refuse? Sex wasn't a big deal… "free love" was ok, said Margaret Mead a cultural anthropologist and fabled RWL[30] who some young women in Tahiti had fun telling her free sex was a cultural practice. Guys were quick to bring up that 'research.' Besides I enjoyed good sex. There wasn't nearly as much as you'd think out there but because of the past I still had difficulty saying a strong no. I talked to Nichelle Nichols about my concerns. She 'schooled' me. I was an attractive prime black woman with great legs, and I would be counted as a notch, a one-night stand, a score. Guys would talk. There was lots of contact between the small group of aspiring Hollywood black actors. They frequently knew every other person on an interview. They hung out on Sunset at The Old World Cafe.

---

30 Rich White Lady a mythic superhero

Or played tennis in West Hollywood, and they liked to brag. What picture, what women, how much, how often.

I think it would have been painful at a casting call to look at the other black men in the room and know, no matter their 'type' they were seen as same. Even worse to be waiting to be interviewed by someone who may think they know more about being black than you do, because they wrote the script or are directing it.

Nichelle worked hard because it wasn't easy for her. It was the 'black people have to be twice as good' thing. In Hollywood there is a caste system. Separation starts with the shooting budget. Above the line people are the stars of the production. Below the line are the worker bees, production and postproduction costs and things like insurance.

The division of the actors is based on the part they play on the show. That would include the lead, guest stars, and regular cast members. They are Contract Players, represented by agents who negotiate their salaries. Day Players are performers with speaking roles hired on a semi-regular basis without long term contracts. Their agents having less negotiation muscle and clients can be paid a set fee not much above the union rate. And in Hollywood everyone is interested in who gets paid what.

Unlike the men on the show, Nichelle had no assurance of inclusion in the scripts or how many lines beyond, "hailing frequencies are open, sir". The writers wrote for a men's world. Women were mostly sex objects or love interests or a burden to be carried. The women settlers seldom even held the horse reins on *Wagon Train* and Star Trek, the 'Wagon Train to the Stars', wasn't much better. Overall there just weren't a lot of lines in the scripts for women. The writers except for a few like Margaret Armen, and especially Dorothy Fontana, were men who mostly saw women traditionally. Star Trek, amongst its contemporaries, shone with about 20% of the scripts written by women. For a brief period Nichelle had a contract, but Bob Justman suggested it be dropped. He thought they'd made a mistake in making her a series deal. "They could have *bought* her for less," he said in a memo. He suggested she'd be better value on an "as needed basis." Because of their failure to provide more inclusion in the scripts, she had often been paid four days salary for one- or two-days' work. It was suggested the new offer be made on a "take it or leave it" basis and would pay considerably less. Grace Lee Whitney, who played Yeoman Janice Rand, also had the same treatment.

That made Nichelle no different than any temporary worker. I had been one and could relate — needing to be available whenever they called, not esteemed, salary based on the union rate boosted by an agent. No wonder she got tired and wanted to quit. Nichelle never let it show. She was always 'Ms Thing' serenely above the ordinary! Working hard to make everything look effortless! Nichelle never got to show all her of abilities; but being black and female she couldn't be ignored either. There were very few black actors who had it any different.

Although Nichelle got on well with the actors and production team, the crew didn't all have the same opinions. Let me go back some years. California had been a favorite mustering out for the military and a lot of good ol boys didn't go back down South. Mostly they took law enforcement jobs and skilled labor jobs. We had some crew members just not used to working with black folks.

The makeup at the studio resembled 'The Malibu divide'. The folks who lived on the beaches were the social liberals, while the folks in the hills were a red state of social conservatives.

I wasn't aware of Nichelle's issues. Sadly, as she says in her autobiography, she didn't even know she had fan mail. They deliberately forgot to tell her. The unions were becoming more aware of change. Yes, 'we' were invading 'their' territory. The threat was already apparent. The Directors Guild had taken on minority apprentices, and the Writers Guild started their inclusion program, called "Open Door" in 1969. Guilds and craft unions would be 'invaded' next.

Nichelle was a gracious lady and a lot of people from work were invited to her annual 'chittlin' party. Her mother's huge cast iron pot spanned two burners on the stove and was filled with chitterlings. The effort to clean and cook that many pounds of pig guts, plus their terrible smell, all made it a rare occasions dish, and depending on your upbringing, a delicacy or a comfort food. I would try to distract or chase away newbies who wanted to try it. I didn't want to share, and tried to stop their visits to the cast iron pot. "It's not your culture" I would rage, dramatically, while checking my internal gauge to see if I could stuff in a few more bites.

I needed Nichelle the day Ivan spat out what I had dreaded from anyone, and never expected from my hero. "You know, you are nothing but Coon's Coon" Ivan snarled as I searched for another reason to tell him why I was still not wearing my hair natural. It was something too blatantly racist for a white person to say it. They wouldn't have had the guts, even if they had the ironic delivery to carry it off. I thought it would come from a black person, overly impressed with their sharp wit, prefacing it with a wink, snorty laughter following.

No! Coon's Coon spewed from Ivan's mouth with a venomous scorn that soaked me in shame and made me vulnerable to doing anything to regain his approval. When I told Nichelle, she was pissed off and reminded me what I was there for. It wasn't about pleasing Ivan, or to find love. It was to demonstrate to the people that provide my paycheck that I could, would and did do the job ... excellently. Besides, on Star Trek, we were going where no one had gone before. I'd felt that way with Malcolm. I'd felt that way with Martin and with Gene Coon, no matter his name. We were making a difference.

More than anything else that Nichelle showed me, she demonstrated the dignity and awareness that the women in my family were said to possess. That I didn't feel. My mother and I were still not close and Nichelle provided the hip cool big sister, social aunt, nurturing granny presence without being any of the three. In so many ways she led. Her presence, her carriage, her integrity. The way she looked and the words she spoke. I started wearing makeup and she accomplished what my mother had failed to do. She got me to wash my face and to make sure no matter how I felt that I at least looked good.

I always tried to be casual when Nichelle was around the office, but also to show off to her that I knew my job and was taking care of business. I showed off one day when she was there and I playfully answered the phone with my very best 'keep it low, keep it slow and milk your 'vo ewells' broadcasting voice. "Coon's Coon". This was my way of saying to her that I was OK, that I had it together. She was there when Ivan had hurt me, she had consoled me. I let her know those words couldn't ever hurt me again.

* * *

When my aunt Jessie Mae died suddenly, I was shattered by the unexpected level of grief over the first close family member that I had known to die. My aunt and Nichelle were very much alike and I hadn't had a chance to say good-bye. The two of them had shared a 'cool butter wouldn't melt in their mouth' way of carrying themselves, perfectly at ease with who they were. Wherever they were.

After the funeral I headed for Nichelle's to talk and be consoled. Nichelle wasn't alone when I dropped in, unannounced as usual. A new boyfriend was there. I was so full of grief I barely noticed him. It wasn't long before she took me aside to say privately that I should go home. I was confused. What had I done or said? I apologized for interrupting. No, it wasn't me. It was him. Her boyfriend was looking at me much too much.

Now I have to admit I may not have noticed, but I'm sure I was looking good. I remember that dress. One of my all-time favorites, a classic, very elegant knit that would look good forever. Extremely short, it was the only thing I had in mournful black. My mother-in-law's gift to me when I visited her in Dallas. She had taken me shopping at the very up-market Neiman Marcus. It was still a time when blacks were not allowed in their dressing rooms or their cafe. This was my only experience of 'not allowed' signs and segregated treatment. Nichelle's treatment was disturbing and I was a little cool toward her for a while. But in time, I realized it wasn't personal. I appreciated her honesty and directness. I recognized that was all part of her ability to be who she was. She wasn't afraid to say, gently, firmly, with love, the nicest "no you won't".

Nichelle and I had discovered we were related. Not the family tree kind of related. We were what she called ex-wives-in-law. Nichelle's first husband Foster Johnson, Kyle's father, had been married to Jean King and had two daughters with her. Jean married my ex-husband, Jai. So, we had an 'enemy' in common.

I knew about the new wife thing from the relationship my mom had with dad's wife. They could be toxic. Star Trek ideals had already started to influence me and I went for connection not combat. So did Jean! What a fantastic woman! She was a member of The Blossoms, a group I'd admired since high school, who were back-up singers with The Righteous Brothers. Their hit *You've Lost That Loving Feeling* was a favorite of mine. Jai had married another fabulous woman! She and I became friends. She was going to be in my daughters' lives and I was thrilled we got along. Sure enough, Paula and Kandi were 'Mama Jeannie-ing' almost immediately and thrilled to have Kyle and two more sisters!

19

When I learned about Jeannie, Jai and I were still married, but we hadn't lived together for years. Jai taught me to appreciate good sex and financially supported me. I had needed and liked but not loved him. My mom had drilled into me that a woman needed 'a man who would set her down'. Someone who would bring in enough money so that she didn't have to work. That wasn't enough for me. My heart wasn't in our relationship. Since the early days of our marriage, I'd been on my way out. Maybe it was losing my dad as a four-year-old, or my much-loved stepdad as I entered my teens. I expected to be left and so I left first, then lured them back. Again, and again. Go away, come back. I knew I didn't want Jai, and I didn't want to lose him either.

I was alone at Jai's place waiting for him to come back. I started snooping. The photo next to his bed was mine, but I found Jeannie's photo in the drawer. The words inscribed on her photo shrieked that I was replaced.

I was really angry with my ex-husband. This I demonstrated by trying to wipe his face. Yes, as in wipe it off the face of the earth. Then I discovered he didn't mind hitting me back. As we tussled and he hit me, I broke things. A punch from him, and a picture came off the wall. My foot through it. Then he blackened my eye and the shock of the pain told me that he must die. I spotted a carving knife in the sink. Even though he shoved me, I grabbed for it and slammed it into his chest in one economical, efficient stroke. When I looked down, I found that he had slowed my momentum just enough that I had missed the knife.

I had plunged a spoon deep enough into his chest to break the skin. He was scraped and bruised rather than stabbed and dead. The Universe looked after me! I am grateful. It would have been hard to explain to my children how I'd killed their father. It was a sobering moment for both of us. I picked up my things and left without a word. Not from either of us. I got in my car and drove, weeping to the nearest police station where the police dismissed my tears and complaint and ignored me. I didn't mention I'd hit him first and they could see my swollen eye and the bruising around my neck. They could not have cared less. Like the comic who asked "What do you say to a woman with two black eyes? Nothing, you already told her twice."

Since they weren't going to do anything, I went back to his place. There was construction going on down the street. I gathered lots of ammunition, bricks mostly — which I loaded into my front seat. Ready for a quick getaway, I rolled down my driver's window next to his car and did target practice. I threw some bricks at his roommate's car as well. He never did like me and I was certain he had contributed somehow. I didn't win and the resentment plus the guilt from my actions just made me take longer to be friends with Jai again. I'm glad we got there.

I was at work very early the next morning, walking onto

the lot with my head down, wearing dark glasses. I went into the makeup room. The makeup artist, Fred Phillips, usually finished with Leonard Nimoy by 7:30. I was in luck, Fred was there alone. I sat down in the makeup chair, pulled off the glasses and said "Freddie, fix the eye. No comments, please." He couldn't resist one. He gave me a smile, his hands gently holding my face, his eyes looking intently into mine and promised "I'd never treat you like that".

He fixed the black eye and also designed a makeup plan for me. He gave me the works and I got up looking fantastic. He also made a list for me of exactly what he had used to sculpt my face, and I went shopping and started using every trick he had taught me. After that, when I got made up to go out, there was a drastic change in my appearance. When I carried my make up bag into the bathroom one night, getting ready to go out, my cousin Gil teased that a different person would emerge. Freddie had taught me to do magic. I was pretty enough; his advice made me stunning. There were now two of me. One of me got a little insecure.

20

What did I do at work? It was mostly dealing with the script and everything concerning it. When the scripts arrived at my desk, I stamped, signed and entered them into my registry. Then I sent them out to be duplicated and when they returned, I distributed them as required.

I read everything that came from the writers in their earliest form and herded them through the changes as they came in. I commented on them when I was asked, circulated all the script changes and kept everyone up to date with whatever they needed. I was the central repository for things to do with the script, the research notes from research, the responses to the scripts from the Network's departments and the producer's and crew's responses. I shuffled and distributed a lot of paper and I loved every moment of it. More than anything I had Gene's back, making sure he got the information he needed. I transmitted the words he wanted to the places he wanted and smoothed the road for him when I could. And I did a few things for him that were personal. Like scoring the pills that he used.

My interest in scripts and watching the development, from story treatment to shooting script, was accompanied by an interest in the writers. My science fiction experience started with a Ray Bradbury short story 'The Lake'. Karenga introduced it to me. He started to explain the story over the phone. Stopped, started reading instead of explaining. I relaxed, tucked the phone under my chin, stretched out on my bed and closed my eyes, as his words intrigued. I had found my milieu. Now, in addition to reading Ray Bradbury, I was reading Isaac Asimov, Theodore Sturgeon, Norman Spinrad and of course Robert Heinlein, the "dean of science fiction writers".

Since I was so connected to the script it was understandable that I would get to know and like some of the writers. Harlan Ellison and Theodore Sturgeon became friends. Both writers were well known and well regarded in Sci-Fi. Both had bunches of awards, they were brilliant writers. Ted became a nudist and Harlan became very good at suing people.

For the first couple of weeks after I took the job with Gene, I still had to be lunchtime relief. Life on the reception desk at the Desilu main entrance was fairly boring except for Harlan Ellison. He no longer bothered to stop and check in at the front desk. We both knew he had an appointment in the Star Trek office.

Our game was to see how close he got to the door handle before I would push the loud buzzing door release. Our form of chicken; just a bit flirty. Bursting through the front door from Gower Street, Harlan would be looking at me, while racing towards the locked studio access. My hand would automatically reach for the release, knowing he was late again and in a BIG hurry. I would hold off pressing it until his hand was almost grazing the handle. Would it be locked when he wrenched it toward himself or...? It always opened in time and sometime I felt that I'd unlocked it way too soon. That I was chicken.

When Harlan temporarily moved into one of the offices a few doors from me, it was a chance to get to know him better. Harlan was a talented, tumultuous terror and cute. In his lifetime Harlan sued a lot of people, including James Cameron over *The Terminator* and 20th Century Fox. He had a lot of battles, most of which he won in some way. He became my buddy and l was on his side.

Harlan was working on what should have been a shooting script of what became the award-winning Trek episode City on the Edge of Forever. He had been given a desk in the assistant director's room, a small room near the end of the hallway down from my office. I don't remember any other writer having that treatment. They especially wanted and needed that script as soon as possible. Harlan had been chosen because he was an inventive, creative award-winning writer and the idea he sold them was brilliant... just a few problems with the script ... and the show format. He did have a bit of a reputation and they must have thought bringing him physically closer meant they could watch or confine him.

But Harlan was Harlan. No one could control him. Instead of writing he was on the set whenever he could. He justified spending time there by saying he was studying the actors, picking up things that belonged to the characters. And at least once he escaped by climbing out a window on the Gower St. side.

Harlan started hanging around my office. I was good looking and single; he was having marriage trouble. I was comfortable with him. It was common in my community to see Jews as allies. I had briefly worked as a temp at the University of Judaism. Curious and interested in the people, I read Max I Dimont's *Jews, God, and History*. The book gave me 4000 years of Jewish history and was a great read. I liked the title, the order in which the three words appeared.

Harlan had gone to Selma, Alabama and marched with Martin Luther King, Wyatt Tee Walker, Fred Shuttlesworth and the rest of SCLC in 1965. I hadn't gone. James Meredith was going there to support voters in a March Against Fear. I was not going. The first peaceful non-violent attempt to march from Selma had been swarmed by club wielding cops, smashed into by State Troopers, and not a few private citizens helping to uphold the law that restricted protest. I had seen the photos of the bloodied demonstrators, in suits with blood-spattered shirts and bruised faces, and those were the ones that weren't in the hospital.

Harlan and I argued. "No, heck no, I wasn't going anywhere South." He insisted I had to go; it was My People's Protest. Mom settled it. She had seen the photos too. She said she wasn't going to look after my kids while I put myself in danger.

Because I stayed home, Harlan put a curse on me, making me an honorary Jew subject to 4000 years retroactive persecution. My kind of guy. Not afraid to call it. I loved his wit, his intelligence, his beliefs, his valuing people, all people. He just didn't like assholes. We shared strong beliefs. Harlan and I were such a good fit, he felt like part of my family.

Down the street, half a block away from the front door of the studio, The Bird and Majel had rented a 'nooner' getaway apartment, where they could spend time together. I checked out their love nest. In the same building there was a sign offering a two-bedroom apartment to rent. I was still looking for a place, and it ticked all the boxes. A two-minute walk to work, home for lunch and the kids could go to the local school. There were very rich people living a few blocks away so the schools had to be good.

I got 'the oh no, you're black' look as soon as I showed up. I wasn't even shown the apartment. I was told that my children were the wrong age as well, they were too young. Then, he changed it to no children were allowed there at all. Then he remembered he had already taken a deposit. A lease agreement was going to be signed that afternoon. I knew it was all BS. The rental equivalent of red-lining. I'd heard so many lame excuses, so often for so long, that when I called about vacancies, I started telling them I was black so they didn't waste my time.

I told Harlan about it the next day and he was furious. He gathered the details I could recall from the conversation with the apartment manager who had 'interviewed' me. He took the info and left. When he came back, he was gloating. We could nail them for discrimination in housing, which was illegal at that moment. He had the proof we could use to sue.

He had represented himself as a male 'me', a clerical at Desilu with two kids the same age. He was not only accepted; he was offered the available apartment and could move in as soon as possible. We now had material and I could force them to rent to me or sue them. By the time we finished the paperwork he'd brought back the apartment was rented to someone else. Maybe they'd rent to the next black person. We had to think that we'd won some sort of victory. They knew that they might not get away with it again.

From Harlan I felt kinship and support. A Trekker feeling? Then Gene made my day!

Having failed to get an apartment, a private school near studio had been the best I could do for my girls. With private school fees for two kids, things were tight and they were tired of eating beans, without meat. "Hey at least there's an onion in them", I had to point out more than once.

Gene had a problem with a new dog and asked me to keep it over the weekend. When I was unpacking the dog bag, I found a package of steak. Assuming it was an accident, I phoned Gene and sarcastically asked "How does the dog like the steak cooked?" Gene responded "just braise it lightly".

I hung up the phone. "Kids, run to the grocery store, get a can of dog food. We're having steak for dinner tonight."

21

I MET GOD (GODFREY Cambridge) — and the lights got brighter and the city bigger.

I often wandered over to see who was in Bill Cosby's bungalow. There were always a bunch of guys there. Cos was entertaining and he stood up for them.

For example, there were no black stuntmen in the union. Cos got Calvin Brown a job as his stunt double. He had refused the tradition of accepting a white stuntman whose skin had been 'painted down'. Calvin had worked in the background as an extra, till he'd been asked to fall out of a tree and discovered how much it paid. He became a founder of the Black Stuntmen's Association.

There were connections to be made in the bungalow. I was looking for one. That day the guy I focused on wasn't the finest or even fine, but he was the funniest. His name was Godfrey and he invited me to a film premiere.

Kleig lights, limos and a red carpet. Just like I'd watched on TV. I was wearing a black diamond mink coat I'd borrowed from Jail's dry cleaning client Jenny, in a limo looking out at people straining to see in. When we stopped on the red carpet to be photographed, I put my feet the way mom had showed me from the Powers Modelling School. She had taken lessons to be able to gracefully float down stairs.

The glitterati in those days were documented in fan magazines, and my photo was in one. Me on the other side of the spotlight, on the red carpet, on Godfrey's arm. I was looking so good that he did too. The caption 'My Man Godfrey'. Showing the article for friends was fun, flashing it at anyone I didn't like was even better. At that time no one I knew had ever been in a mainstream magazine. Mom bought several copies of the magazine for her hair salon. I had let her straighten my hair. I was sick of the wig but still not ready to be natural at work.

Godfrey invited me out again. The next date was dinner in Beverly Hills. It was at Henry Mancini's home, an Oscar-winning film composer.

It was a small A-list dinner party and one of the guests was motion pictures' Million Dollar Mermaid, the 1940's-star Esther Williams. There were a couple of other guests who made the films that I'd watched in the 40s and 50s and were distant gods. I felt hopelessly out of my depth. This wasn't something I'd encountered before and I wanted to fit in. Honesty and authenticity would have been the only thing that worked. I didn't have much of that. I'd been raised to project a me that would suit the occasion. And I usually did it well. This was different. It was 'Old Hollywood' and I'd already almost come undone at the door. When the maid reached for my coat, I was a bit protective. Yes, I'd borrowed another one of the dry cleaner lady's mink coats.

We were seated at a table with Esther Williams and her actor husband Fernando Lamas. I had envied her ease in the films I'd grown up watching. I was a poor swimmer, lacking confidence in or on water. Turns out mom had, in her opinion, almost drowned and had passed the fear on genetically or through her breast milk or something. Esther Williams was a professional swimmer who smoothly duplicated on land her ease in the water. Always gaining whatever prize she was after; the way white ladies did in the movies.

At the dinner table I didn't see much of the confident women she played on screen. She was a deferential Mrs. Lamas--he was the star. I had code switched instinctively and thought I was doing ok. I was still stressed from attempting to defend the mink coat and I could use a drink. There was no booze on the table. Then a waiter appeared next to me with a single glass of wine on a tray and said that magic word "wine?". I spun in my chair grabbing for the glass. The waiter deftly avoided me and put it on table where I quickly grabbed it and sucked in a bit of life –ah, red. Esther Williams spied my gulps of wine and inquired of Lamas, "Where's your wine dear?" He didn't hesitate, his finger pointing directly at me, voice accusingly raised, "She's drinking it". Martin had cured me of blushing in public, and so, with what I thought was style I snapped my fingers and said "Waiter more wine." But inside I was dying from shame.

Later with the Mancini kids I was more comfortable. I guess because I was the youngest guest, female and black, Mancini's kids shyly approached and began asking race-based questions. Not dinner conversation in polite company in those days. Racial things weren't spoken of. Mancini was embarrassed and apologized. Just a dad worried that his kids are maybe being inappropriate to his guest, which made him real to me, ordinary not mythic.

Seeing through this new filter made the difference. Even looking at the miniature mountain of what I recognized from photos as caviar I had thought it looked like the stuff mom threw away when she gutted and cleaned fish on Friday nights. But when I finally tried it, it wasn't as bad as I expected. The caviar was just some fishy egg bubbly things that popped in your mouth and was pretty OK, if you put them on the little pancake and added enough sour cream and onion. When we left, the maid returned the mink. I could breathe again and I made sure to drop it off at the dry cleaner lady before I went to work the next morning.

I knew Godfrey Cambridge was a comedian but with a little research, I found out he was also a serious actor, an uncommon combination back then. As a comic he rated with Cosby, Mort Sahl, Dick Gregory and Richard Pryor. *Time* magazine said in 1965 that he was "one of the country's foremost celebrated Negro comedians".

Godfrey was born in New York to parents from British Guiana (Guyana) which I had never heard of, and was schooled in Nova Scotia. He had quirky looks with a well-grounded sense of who he was and his value. He was an integrationist, his onstage humor was wry and ironic, subtly poking fun at white people without anger almost as though "it's just so ridiculous." He had famously sparred with the conservative David Frost on his TV program and was friends with George Plimpton, the famous New York high society journalist and a founding editor of esteemed literary magazine *The Paris Review*.

Godfrey's theatre background was of works I knew nothing about. He'd performed Jean Genet's 'The Blacks' and received a

Tony nomination for *Purlie Victorious*, written by and starring Ossie Davis. Godfrey had a clownish physical profile but with an incisive intellect and cultured identity. He was the perfect guide to a world I had never seen up close, and very exotic to my upbringing. This was a guy I'd like to get serious with. Somebody to "set me down". I thought there might be a chance.

God took me to my first awards show. It was the 1967 Emmys. Star Trek was up for Outstanding Dramatic Series and Leonard Nimoy had a supporting actor nomination. What made it particularly exciting was Ivan Dixon had been nominated too, and I was hoping to see him collect a statue.

I didn't have to borrow another mink. I caught a sale at Joseph Magnin and found a hot pink classic empire gown with a matching floor-length coat. And white kid gloves. Real kidskin with silk lining, the traditional 16-button evening gloves that extended past the elbows nearly to the shoulder. All on sale! I was Audrey Hepburn at a price I could afford! My outfit was a standout in the halls of the local Elementary School.

I'd forgotten when I accepted God's invitation that it was Parent Teacher night and because of the East Coast TV schedule, the time I needed to visit the school was just before the Emmys began. I had no choice. I had to go to the school already dressed for the big night. God had been understanding of the importance of showing up to speak with my kids' teachers no matter what. The limo waiting outside the school was noticeable in the all-black working-class neighborhood. It made a good story.

Because of the school visit we arrived at the Emmy theatre just as the show was about to start but before the TV cameras rolled. Godfrey had stopped to sign a couple of autographs and so did I. I didn't hesitate. I signed Mary Wilson, the member of The Supremes I slightly resembled. And then we were on the escalator descending to the Emmy banquet just as the telecast started. I was the first image seen. A thrill for my family and friends and a perfect serve to my officially ex-husband. There I was, in living, glorious, beautiful hot pink, as the camera held and tracked with us down the escalator.

My first Academy Awards was also with God.

Tom Bradley who became the first black mayor of Los Angeles was running for City Council at that time. Gwen Green was running his Mayoral campaign office and had gotten me to volunteer. I had a large 'Vote for Bradley' badge pinned inside the flap of my envelope clutch. Tom saw me across the room, and gave me the nod. I open my purse and flashed my Vote for Bradley button back at him. He flashed back an award-winning grin. Black people were becoming more visible in Hollywood. Tom didn't win that race. Sam Yorty his opponent played the race card. Made people believe that the moderate ex-police lieutenant was a black militant thug.

I had God's attention, I wanted more. I worked to be sexy, fun and funny. I borrowed one of Gramma Booker's Bibles to search for quotes. I found biblical quotes that could be interpreted as sexual or funny. Godfrey travelled often and I would leave the Bible citation with the hotel desk to give him when he checked in. He told me he was getting funny looks from the hotel staff when the first thing he asked for when he got to his room was a Bible.

When God invited me to accompany him out of town, I had hope we were getting closer. The first trip was to San Francisco. He was performing at the luxury landmark Fairmont Hotel.

He flew out from New York and rented a Lincoln Continental in LA. We drove up, romantically taking my favorite Highway 1 along the coast.

We stopped at The Esalen Institute in Big Sur. Godfrey as usual spoke their language and we became guest for the night. Fritz Perls, the German-born psychiatrist who developed Gestalt therapy, and whose work I would become familiar with, lived there. I didn't meet Perls but again Godfrey had broadened my outlook and showed me something very new.

I was absolutely up for our next trip. God was headlining in Las Vegas in the 500-seat Bagdad Theatre at the Aladdin Hotel, one of the most luxurious new resorts on the Strip. It was a big, big deal.

I had just the outfit. Another Joseph Magnin bargain. Silver and black metallic stripes, the shortest mini I'd ever worn provided a good look at my 39-inch D-cup boobs. With it, some huge Lucite earrings with double thick eye lashes, and full Fred Phillips make up. To try out the outfit; I wore it to dinner at a ritzy Beverly Hills restaurant. I took in the environment, and adjusted my internal setting to match the cool, classic image that I wanted to project. I felt I was gliding as I followed the maître d to our table. As I passed the trio playing background music the three of them stopped playing mid-note, and their eyes had me for dessert. It was a perfect Vegas outfit.

In Las Vegas, since God was the star at the Aladdin, we had a 'villa', one of two adjoining suites that shared a private pool. I was in the pool rejuvenating, just floating, one hand within reach of the edge, when I was shaken by a young girl screaming for her mother. A woman came out of the neighboring suite and scooped her up. I was relieved, about to say something friendly when the child pointed at me, and in tones of shock, anger, and fear, screamed "the maid's in our pool". They learn early if we're not careful.

God went off to Italy to shoot a film and when he came back, he'd brought me a handbag. I was disappointed. It was just a plain black leather bag, nothing sparkly, a plain buckle was all. It was nice leather, obvious quality. The bags had these two 'G's. I didn't know what or who Gucci was, pronouncing it "gucki". I just knew the purse came in a soft cotton bag inside a green felt shopping bag. I'd never had a bag that had its own bag, or a shopping bag made of felt.

One night, while waiting in God's backstage dressing room for him to shower and dress, I recognized a match to the buckle from my handbag. It matched the ones on another visitor's shoes, George Plimpton. I was a Paris Review reader, especially the interviews, and had also seen him on television. I was very impressed by his reputation and accomplishments. George Plimpton was from another world, another person I never dreamed I'd be alone in the same room with.

Desperate for something to say to express my admiration, be recognized as worthy, to make some connection, what I came up with was ... "The buckle on your shoes is the same as the one on my purse" said complete with the gestures that would have been perfectly appreciated and understood on Crenshaw Boulevard. The look I got instead of a 'gotcha, we are so cool, connect', was the distaste of noticing you've stepped in something disgusting. It wasn't that I'd done something revolting, it was that I was revolting.

He and I actually did have something in common. We both

appreciated the amazing Archie Moore, the longest-reigning World Light Heavyweight Champion of all time. Plimpton had sparred for three rounds with Archie and published his experience for Sports Illustrated. Archie was my dad's friend who had showed me how to throw a punch when I was 10.

Maybe I couldn't risk visiting a memory of a school hall full of white faces and the frustration of not being able to identify and punch the mouth nigger had been shouted from. In any event I had screwed up. I had code switched the wrong way. More than anything, I hadn't had the ease to be myself.

I kept Godfrey's attention for quite a while, leaving the double entendre Bible reference messages to be picked up at his hotel. I knew I'd blown it when I ran out of Bible quotes and left a quote from the musical Man of La Mancha song, The Impossible Dream.

God lost interest, we stayed friends, and I resumed my hunt. I knew more people now and had access to more places. My world had expanded! There were new possibilities.

22

Ros Taylor. The first Rosilyn in my life. We met in my office. She'd been dropped off by her agent and was waiting to meet Gene. I wanted to know where she was from. That wasn't Californian she was speaking. She talked southern. Rosilyn was petite and beautiful, a dark chocolate Playboy bunny from a small town in Florida who'd won a contest to go to Hollywood and become a star. Her sponsor had insisted she use a stage name, Cindy Lou. He thought Rosilyn was too sophisticated a name for a little black girl.

I was still wanting to get a better place to live. Somewhere with a good school so I could be relieved of the private school fees I was paying. Rosilyn needed a place too. Her agent had a suggestion. Why didn't we share? He knew just the spot in the Hollywood Hills. The house next to him was available and he'd make the arrangements. It was in Nichols Canyon, an obscure canyon off Hollywood Boulevard next to the better-known Laurel Canyon.

The house on Zarada Drive was modern, cantilevered off the side of a fairly steep hill. It disappeared down a driveway, and was hidden from the street. The hills across from it were still wooded they hadn't yet built the Mt Olympus development. Deer used to come and visit and I bought a salt lick to attract them.

Nichols Canyon Road didn't lead directly anywhere else. It took time folks didn't have, as it wound round and meanderingly to Mulholland Drive, which did the same thing along the Hollywood Hills. It was a place for taking your time, for appreciating little things. Ricky Nelson, the actor/singer lived around the bend, and gave great candy every Halloween.

When I was a kid in San Diego, we lived on the edge of an untamed canyon. Our club house was a small cave we were comfortable sharing with a few snakes. I had felt connected there as I also did in this canyon. Didn't often see neighbors because of the foliage that hid many houses. There were no folks wondering how I got there or if I might be able to clean for them.

As a new person in town and without a brilliant resume with loads of credits, Rosilyn didn't have a lot to do. Lucky for me she was at home and didn't mind doing the cooking. Her cooking was as country as her stage name and could make you weep with joy. She cooked string beans that were so in love with the company of ham hocks, you felt the need to eat them together in one bite. There was creamed corn volunteering to be pulped straight from the cob and cornbread light enough to fly. Rosilyn was a perfect roommate.

The parties that Ros and I threw were well attended by the brothers and sistas grateful to find some 'homies' in the hills. A few black folks were moving into the more welcoming West Hollywood area. I remember a black woman, at one of our parties, covertly asking me "Whose house is this? Who lives here?" and her surprised pleasure when I told her, "Me".

Diahann Carroll's, *Julia*, the first TV series starring a

22

black woman was still being called unrealistic. I was living it. Black and white Hollywood flooded through the house, smoked reefer on the balcony, dropped speed in the kitchen and watched as I occasionally did something stupid like taking acid and walking on the roof. Especially when I was depressed, feeling worthless. My Bi Polar was still undiagnosed. I had noticed that it was hard to feel depressed while taking speed or smoking weed.

As I mentioned earlier, Gene had a need for speed. I had a connection, a very hip doctor who was part of the entertainment industry and served their needs. *'Dr Hip'* gave me things that quieted my head and put me to sleep. I wasn't trying to kill myself. Sometimes I needed to quiet the chatter. I believe that if you are old enough to make a serious decision like voting for President, you can make a choice about the pharmaceuticals that support your drug-taking decisions. I believe that was *'Dr Hip's'* belief as well. It didn't hurt that it made him best friends with a lot of very interesting well-known folk.

His practice included Playboy bunnies, actors and other personalities. A doctor to the B list.

I saw the Jacksons kids there. I wonder what *Dr Hip* would say to a parent's request to suppress puberty, to prolong his kid's high-pitched voice and keep it from cracking.

I wasn't hesitant to let the doc know I needed assistance. The kind of pills that made you get extra energy, an extra level of go. One thing for sure though, *Dr Hip* was a 'whatever you need and supply' pill person. He didn't just write a prescription for the drugs, he had pharmacy-sized bottles of the pills that he handed out. Around 3 or 4 in the afternoon it was time for the white one, and that would get me home, dinner cooked, kids to bed, dressed up, and made up for Clubbing at The Candy Store, the forerunner of the Studio 54 type private clubs for 'the beautiful people'.

For a time, this was the coolest spot in Hollywood. I'd sometimes see D'Urville Martin, Fred Williamson and a few other black actors there as well as at The Factory. I'd get home from there about 2am, take an orange and turquoise Tuinal and put a glass of water and a Black Beauty next to my bed. When my alarm went off about 5 hours later, I'd pop the Beauty and close my eyes again. Soon my eyes would pop open and I'd be moving, 'show time'. Because of the pills I was quick, and competent, and THIN!

Cocaine was getting more popular. That things were speeding up was no joke. Amphetamines were not made illegal to buy without a prescription until 1965, and available easily and without stigma until the War on Drugs in the 70s. That war is not on drugs, it's on people and has now been going on for over 50 years, with no less drug use and ever-increasing private prisons, broken families, and broken black lives, since we bear the brunt of the enforcement. The penalties for crack cocaine are not the same as for powder. In 1986 the penalty for crack was 100 to 1 times that of powder. The 2010 Fair Sentencing Act made it less but there is still a disparity. I think it's now only 18 to 1. Portugal showed what a reasonably sane drug policy can do[31]. The war on drugs is a failure, but somebody's making too much money to allow change. The opioid-Sackler example is a clear one.

---

31 https://transformdrugs.org/blog/drug-decriminalisation-in-portugal-setting-the-record-straight

23

I WAS CONTINUING TO learn. I paid close attention to everything, especially the scripts. Gene had started to discuss them with me. What worked, what didn't. I was understanding the elements that made a good Trek episode. The episode must have a framework of action. Something had to be going on from the teaser opening. It had to grab. And, much as a soap opera does, it had to build the story around people, their struggles, their needs, fears and desires. Science and imaginative technology are nice, but the stories that impact are about people and their jeopardy or about someone they care about. The act endings had to make us stay around, endure the ads to find out what going to happen to someone we care about and what happened to them had to apply to a universal theme or need.

I started to think about things that were important to me and how they could be expressed using science fiction rather than pleading or lecturing. I understood what Gene would expect from the writers. I was delighted when a new script landed on my desk because I was the first to read it and for a little while it was exclusive just to me. I often let Gene know he was going to have to do a lot of work on a script or that he would be pleased that the writer had actually nailed it. He seemed to take my impressions seriously and I felt my opinion was valued.

OK, a glimmer of possibility. Maybe. Maybe, I wanted to be. Could I possibly be? A television producer? Maybe. It was a pretty big deal to even entertain the idea that it was something I could do. I didn't know any black producers either male or female. As ridiculous as it was, I could feel myself wanting to let myself think about it. Being the one who was able to select or write the story. It could be a story that had meaning as well as action. You could reach a large number of people. It's definitely a place from where I would love to howl.

My smooth sailing was interrupted, my confidence had a wakeup call. Shorthand shafted me. Gene usually just wrote a draft and I cleaned it up and sent it. Now, he suddenly wanted to comment on something he'd received. When Gene realized I couldn't take shorthand and was hopeless at any language other than English, he didn't spare me and for a while he referred to me as *Miss* Dumb Bastard. It wouldn't have been polite to just call me a dumb bastard. He knew how to rub it in. I ignored something so obviously a joke. OK it did hurt a bit … OK, a lot. I'd gotten away without shorthand and had hoped to continue. Besides, if he told the writer in person that would have been better than a long memo. I tried to sell him the idea that he should do more telling writers rather than writing writers.

Gene didn't fall for it. I'd bragged about how fast I could type and he had seen evidence of that so he decided he'd get a Dictaphone. A dictating machine would allow him to record and me to transcribe it. At that time very advanced. With my super typing speed, I would be able to transcribe without a problem. Gene got the Dictaphone. I admired, unpacked, and set it up. I always love new toys! As with all things tech I was looking forward to using it.

I made Gene a cup of tea, gave him a copy of the material he was ready to dictate, and I left him to it. Gene dictated and dictated and dictated. He ended up dictating a memo that was massively long. Because it was a lot of extra work transcribing something that long, I had to come in on a Saturday to do it. My office was on the inside studio side of the building and with my windows open I socialized with passers-by and made Saturday more fun than a week day. I had a great time. Miss Dumb Bastard ... not really. I was earning double time while having fun. But I felt humiliated by the name. Not quite as bad as Ivan Dixon with Coon's Coon. But not good either.

When Gene realized he had written a very long memo, he was embarrassed. He drastically edited the memo before it went out. But it was still 18 pages long. Nothing changed, except the extra pay helped.

★ ★ ★

What's worse than feeling incompetent is when something happens to your kid. One of the best things about living in the canyon was the kids no longer had to wait at the studio for me to finish work. They went to the same school as Michael and the other Jacksons. A bus picked them up and dropped them off at the bottom of our hill. Ros was usually at home. The kids had liked hanging out at the studio. They had wandered freely and knew how to behave but there was one time that I was totally freaked. Paula, my 7-year-old daughter, came into my office in tears, sobbing so hard, I dropped everything. I didn't know what had happened and I had to find out what was wrong. My heart was racing, fear stirring up some inherited trauma and I was desperately trying to get information so I could 'Do Something'! My anxiety was transmitted to her and she cried harder. Finally, she managed to get out, "Bill, Bill, mommy!

Oh my God! What has he done to my child?

She could feel my growing anger, and forced out. "I ... I ... went into Bill's dressing room."

Oh shit. He will die ...

I didn't need to breathe. I was ice, my mother's daughter.

"And what happened? What happened?" Deliberate, precise, cold

"He, he, he...."

"What!" I'm my great aunt, shotgun loaded.

"H ... his ... ha ... ha ... hair!"

I took a moment. It was OK. I understood. I was breathing again. Paula had gone into Bill Shatner's dressing room without knocking and seen him without his hairpiece. Traumatized the kid! And Bill. Imagine what would have happened if someone had seen a seven-year-old burst out of his dressing room in tears. Tabloid time!

Appearance, especially hair, was another area where I realized I had lazy attitudes. I had never questioned, just taken the attitudes on board. Who made losing hair such a snide joke? When I told the story of my hair war with my mother at TED, I ended with, "Doesn't matter what kind of hair you have. It's just nice to have some."[32]

---

[32] Now with thin hair after 40 years of dreadlocks, I'm so glad there are weaves.

My kids were settled, I loved where we lived but my rent was higher and I needed more money. When I asked Gene about a raise, he said that would be above his pay grade because there was a standard rate for everything. So, I looked around for another job. As much as I liked working on Trek, I needed more money. Women at work were not paid like men at work. Still aren't!

By then I'd gotten to know the guys from the script service as well as the people in research. They all had contacts on other lots and I heard The *Monkees* TV show was looking for a good production office person. I applied and was offered the job. Unfortunately, the pay wasn't any better. I told Gene and it didn't seem to be any big deal to him, so I was surprised when he later said from then on, I'd be working overtime each week. I was about to protest when he clarified. It was guaranteed overtime and I didn't have to work for it. He'd found a way to up my salary, I realized I must be doing a good job, in spite of being Miss Dumb Bastard. One place I don't feel proud of was how I handled power.

24

I was on the receptionist desk as lunch relief when Charles Bronson came in. He was the 'die hard guy' before there was a Die Hard. He was a few years from his breakout film Death Wish, but I recognized his face immediately. Jill Ireland, who was not yet married to him, was on the Star Trek set filming "This Side of Paradise". I knew all of that. I'd distributed the call sheet. Maybe he was a movie tough guy, but here I was the one who could push the door release to let him in.

I had the power. I decided to show him who was boss. I asked for his name. Then, I made a show of finding the guest list and looking carefully, line by line. I said, "Oh I don't see your name on my list." A beat, then "I have to call". I called the set and went through the formal procedure of checking with the 2nd AD, who of course couldn't understand why I was calling, because the man was so well known. I slid the sign in sheet to him, I said, "OK Just sign the sheet," passed over a pen and coolly waited while he signed. Checked he spelled his name right and then gave him the blessing. "You can go in now."

I made a big deal of pushing the buzzer and disengaging the door. He was such a mild sweet guy. He stayed totally cool, just said, "Thank you very much" and laughed — I'm sure it was at

24

me and my attempt to show power. Maybe it was the way he looked. Had I interpreted what he portrayed and responded to that instead of to him. At the time I thought I was cool. I'd stood up to the man. I felt good the rest of the day, I'd shown the man and walked tall. Definitely wish I hadn't done that. It was not my proudest moment. Years later I had bragged about it to Marjorie Fowler, one of the few women film editors in old Hollywood, and she was horrified. Bronson was one of the nicest men in Hollywood. I was lucky he wasn't one of the ego people. They would have gotten my ass fired.

25

Remember, this was TV not a space launch and Trek producers had the attitude we don't have to be scientifically accurate; we just have to sound like we are. That wasn't good enough for the researchers at our research company Kellam de Forest Research. De Forest Research were going to let you know what was accurate and then you could make the choice.

One day my de Forest researcher friend Peter Sloman was struggling so hard with the grammar of one of the Trek alien languages that I felt his agony. I tried to get him to lighten up by saying "Peter, no one will know." The look he shot back shut me up. I know the feeling. You do your very best, whatever you gotta do, because you know, even if no one else knows. Peter's specialties included sciences and languages, plus the military. He was the Vulcan language specialist. Even if you didn't understand Vulcan, Peter still made sure the syntax was correct.

Joan Pearce was The Chief Detector at de Forest. Her expertise was everything and she specialized in British anything. Joan was one of my favorite people to work with, as well as hang out. Crisp, direct and no nonsense at work and play. She was a joy to be with. Her level of professionalism, her knowledge, sense of humor and warmth made me lucky to be her friend away from the lot.

Research was located in the upstairs of a dusty old building near stage 10. It was over-crowded with books. Telephone directories from all major cities were a vital asset.

Desks were crammed in where they could fit and be within the easiest way to communicate, shouting distance. Phones ringing, bringing weird or esoteric questions. If it couldn't be answered right away, before getting up for a reference the question might be shouted out: "Hey somebody, in 1885, jeans: buttons or zipper? Joan's was usually the first response. Joan might call back "zipper invented 1891 — Levi's, buttons, no zipper until 1947".

There was an uprising in the 80s and Joan and the gang left Kellam and started a new company, Joan Pearce Research. So much for Joan always being referred to as Kellam's assistant.

26

Of the cast I was closest to Nichelle. I thought Leonard was warm and friendly, though reserved. Dee Kelly and Caroline, his wife were both very nice, friendly and comfortable to be with. Jimmy, was ok, sometimes I thought he was up himself. And Walter I don't remember. I regret we didn't connect.

But, Oh, my! I officially met the very cool George Takei on the set. I remembered him from LA High School. We were fellow "Romans". George served one semester on the Boys Senior Board and was the president the next, the semester he graduated. He wasn't thinking acting then. Instead of the drama groups at school, George was an Ephebian, a civic-minded group that was interested in city government. No wonder he ran for City Council. After nearly winning, he then went onto the board of directors of the So Cal Rapid Transit District and served for over ten years. We also both went to Mt Vernon Junior High. All without meeting.

At LA High George and I were both friends of Johnnie Cochran, the OJ Simpson "If the glove doesn't fit you must acquit." lawyer. They served on the Senior Board together and Johnnie and his girlfriend Sandra regularly double dated with my boyfriend Paul Martin and me. Paul was one of Johnnie's lifelong friends. Paul was special, he was my first love.

George introduced me to the idea of eating raw fish, instead of deep fried. I love food, eating, talking about it and trying new dishes. I was making a lunch dash to Olvera Street, 'the birthplace of Los Angeles' to get the best taquitos in town, when George jokingly asked if I could pick up some sushi in Little Tokyo which is near Olvera Street. I had no idea what he was talking about. George explained sushi and started telling me who made the best. I was curious. I was willing and wanted to try this soou-she. The only place that sushi was available was in Little Tokyo. I wasn't going there by myself. George volunteered without much hinting. He was the perfect choice to show me. He was the Helmsman after all.

In little Tokyo, I was all eyes. I'd never paid much attention to the area. I was totally in a strange land. George guided me to his favorite place, and we climbed up on tall stools at a bar. I was comfortably used to bar stools but instead of a mixed drink, I saw a hand ballet. We watched the sushi being prepared. I was fascinated. I'd had prime rib served at the table at Lowry's on Restaurant Row, but aside from hamburgers and hot dogs never watched my food prepared.

While we watched and started eating, we drank Sake. I'd never had that before either. I thought the little jugs with the clear liquid and small cups were cute. George failed to tell me about the alcohol content. I was a sour mash bourbon drinker and thought that serious whisky was brown.

The sake I threw back that night warmed and relaxed me. And was stronger than I expected. I fell in love with sushi and tried to kiss George. He was gentle with me in his rejection of my advances. I took a while to recognize how wrong my thinking and expectations were. Anyway, we were better as friends. I cheered him on. He was one of the first Asian actors to be a non-stereotypical grinning fanatical evil Asian character and was on his way to being a cultural icon. Unlike the few Asian characters on TV, he didn't have an accent, wasn't a martial artist, plus he held rank, he was an officer.

George and I stayed in contact until the 80s when I complained to him about LA's public transportation. He was on the Transport board and I think took it personally. Another one of those trivial differences becoming estrangement. It was hard to explain to him that after living with excellent public, Los Angeles transport seemed primitive. It's improved.

Another person who broke the ceiling was Dorothy Fontana.

She found that changing her name to DC Fontana got her work seen by more people. But Star Trek was the show she wanted. And she got there! One of the few, the proud, the female. When Bird promoted her to Story Editor, it was a much better use and acknowledgement of her talent. She did him proud with *Journey to Babel* and another six or seven scripts. But despite her efforts, there was still the pressure to keep the women as smiling eye candy.

27

PENNY UNGER WAS THE woman who slid into Dorothy's secretary's chair. She was more like me, felt more my age. A big smile and a bigger laugh. Penny was a Hollywood kid. Her dad Maurice 'Babe' Unger was a producer and director. He produced several series during the 60s, *Ripcord*, *The Lawbreakers* and *King of Diamonds*, working for the Ziv production company. Growing up in the industry, Penny was very efficient but relaxed. Nothing stressed her, and she made things look fun and easy, almost like there was a party going on.

The Star Trek Writer's Guide alluded to smoking cannabis. It may have happened. I do know that Penny could take a pack of filter cigarettes and carefully empty the tobacco out without tearing the paper. Next, she would take some nicely ground cannabis and tamp it down inside, meticulously smoothing until they looked perfectly normal. I don't know who they were for but she was The Great Bird's secretary.

★ ★ ★

I had hopes for a black male actor on the show. Don Marshall came aboard. He was my homeboy, also born and raised in San Diego. His sister had been my babysitter. His dad Scooter and my dad were best friends. Two extremely good-looking men who knew it, spent a lot of time together and with the ladies despite their marital status. So even though Don was handsome and fun to be with, we were 'kinda family', anything more than a hug would have felt a bit incestuous. His character, Lt Boma, Starfleet officer, was an astrophysicist and a popular Trek character.

Don had already been signed for a television series that gave him a lead role so he appeared in only one Trek episode. He made his mark and his character appeared in two Star Trek novels, *Dreadnaught* and *Battle Station*s. He was my homeboy, also born and raised in San Diego. His sister had been my babysitter. His dad Scooter and my father were best friends. Two extremely good-looking men who knew it, spent a lot of time together and with the ladies despite their marital status. So even though Don was handsome and fun to be with, we were 'kinda family', anything more than a hug would have felt a bit incestuous.

After working in casting and often suggesting a black actor for a part, I can say casting people just didn't think of it themselves. Like the fish in the ocean that pays no attention to water. If the part didn't specify 'Negro' it was automatically white.

28

HE WAS BLACK, HE was formidable, he was determined. He wasn't part of our crew but he deserves to be recognized: Stan Robertson, our NBC Program Manager.

I'd heard about Stanley before we met. He was a distant relative of Gwen Green who had introduced me to MLK. She bragged about him. After 14 major eye operations, attending a school for the blind and majoring in journalism at LA City College, he became a reporter at the largest-circulation black newspaper in the west, the Los Angeles Sentinel. It wasn't long before Stanley was their Managing Editor. He became Associate Editor at a national black publication, Ebony magazine before he took a gamble and gave up print success to pursue a communications degree at USC. With his poor eyesight he had chosen a challenge as well as a passion.

Stanley started at the bottom as a page at the local NBC affiliate in Burbank. It was a long bus ride. His limited vision meant he was unable to drive, but getting to Burbank by public transportation allowed time and subject matter for creating a weekly LA Sentinel column, LA Confidential.

In his column as well as praising actions he agreed with, he called out "the we ain't ready club members", those black people he saw who didn't fit his dress or behavior criteria. Maybe it was something he was wanting to protect himself and others from. I cringed sometimes when he told of some incident he'd witnessed. The fear was of embarrassing a whole race. In any event Stanley was the self-appointed arbiter. His weekly column gave him credibility and influence of which NBC was certainly aware.

Stanley Robertson worked his way up from page to become Stan Robertson, NBC film program operations and was offered to The Great Bird of the Galaxy as a Program Manager for Star Trek.

The Stan Robertson the Great Bird described to me sounded like a progressive hip, black man that would recognize and implement this new age space trip together with him. I didn't want to disturb his fantasy. I thought Stanley Robertson was a man willing to be called Stan who belonged to the corporation, the people who signed his check. For me he was too old school, too conservative, and I thought his story sense sucked. I liked Stanley and admired his intelligence and drive. He was a brother, I wished him well and publicly supported him. But he was a Corporate man.

The Great Bird didn't realize what he was getting. With the frequently applied liberal blindness of seeing what you want to see, he would have looked at Stan and seen an intelligent, cool, aware ally, a likely follower of Martin Luther King and perfect for the job. To say that Stan was ready for the job is modest. "I was around before they knew what tokenism was," he is said to have told a TV critic in 1970.

The Great Bird had agreed to appointing someone who he assumed would be on his side. I watched the reality set in. Stan was the network executive and he was black, a combination rare at that time. The Bird was hogtied. It was a situation where he could be called racist if he was simply calling out uncreativeness. To my knowledge he never stopped regretting Stan's appointment.

With all the shit Stan would have had to endure; he kept his eyes on the prize. Stan Robertson was named a VP for motion pictures at NBC in 1971, becoming the first ever non-white in that position. After leaving NBC he held the same position, at Columbia Pictures, also a first where he established the first creative access program at a major studio to develop minority writers and directors.

Stanley did the hard yards. I'm pleased that at 75 he produced a biographical drama *Men of Honor*[33], about another African American first who achieved against incredible odds. I like to think he felt that it was his story on the screen and an acknowledgement of what he had achieved.

---

33   Drama released 2000 https://m.imdb.com/title/tt0203019/

29

It was time-out time and Mexico City was the place. June wasn't coping at all with loss of her mother. I needed to make her better. June and I grew up like twins that lived in different cities. She was an only child like me, but she and her mother Jessie Mae had been close friends. Only in her 40s, Jessie Mae's death was sudden, bewildering, and we were never able to find out what caused it. Her husband refused an autopsy and her doctor, noting that she had a lung condition, signed the death certificate with no hesitation.

Jessie Mae hadn't trusted her lawyer to be the executor and the will was never signed so June's stepdad inherited and took control of all the money and property. It was the one management mistake she made.

Jessie Mae's husband did let June stay in the house her mother bought for her. But June was trying to start a design studio and was stressing out over a new boyfriend. I had to do something to help and Mexico City seemed like a good idea.

I met Lorin, a brother from Delaware who was studying at a university there. He was definitely much younger. I ignored June's digs about younger men and indulged in long walks with him through Chapultepec Park and late nights in his tiny flat on top of a building with an outdoor shower.

When I got back from Mexico I couldn't wait to stop in Penny's office and toss her the package of cigarettes I'd brought back. Of course, it was cannabis and I'd used her method. Emptying the tobacco out and refilling it with cannabis. She was impressed with how well I'd done it, plus the fact that I had the daring to bring them through customs.

I was so proudly showing her how well I learned her methods, that it took a while to notice that Penny couldn't help bringing up a mention of the new Assistant Director.

I'd been back from holiday for five minutes and she had mentioned we had a new Second AD about 600 times. It finally got through to me without her saying it directly, that we'd finally got the black one. The one black person in the Directors Guild Trainee program.

★ ★ ★

Charles Washburn, the new Assistant Director trainee, was a good guy, as straight as the part in his hair. Charlie was a southern boy from Memphis, Tennessee, with a good education, good manners, and a belief that if he worked hard enough and took the right steps, he could achieve his dream of being a director. Charlie was the first African-American to apply to and graduate from the DGA's eight-month AD trainee program.

Charlie was an outstanding Second AD. Meticulous in preparation, his production reports and call sheets could be depended on. It only took him one day to win the trust of the senior AD, Tiger Shapiro. Charlie soon took on many of Tiger's tasks with his approval and graciously accepted his nicknames. Tiger called him 'Washrag' or 'Washtub'. Charlie even took 'Washbottom' with a smile.

He started being called Charlie Star Trek from the way he manned the phone. Anytime you called the set, you could be sure he'd be the person who answered. No matter where he was, when it rang, he got to the phone first, answering "Charlie Star Trek". Charlie was incredibly good natured, his smile, which rarely dipped into concern, always returned. You could rely on him. He got the job done. He was one of the reasons Trek had a great crew. His willingness and good humor rubbed off. It was a crew that worked well together. And their caring, about the cast and the show created an onset atmosphere that was good for actors and guest directors.

Charlie wanted to be a director. He did all the right things, was competent, capable, likable, polite, hardworking and rule following. But he was black and the door wasn't yet opened. Charlie worked harder and became a very successful First AD and Unit Production Manager working on lots of TV shows and feature films. He even got a couple acting spots from favorite directors. He married and moved from Carson, the suburb next to Watts that had finally integrated, to the San Fernando valley and added a bit of color there.

Hollywood was tough on people and dreams and a directing slot was never to be his. He deserved better. Nonwhites had a long way to go still. The unions were verrry slooowly giving ground.

30

When the episode "*Arena***"** was finished the Gorn, the reptilian creatures who had battled Kirk, the female with a mini skirt, were moved into Bob's office. Wah Chang and his partner Gene Warren who created the Gorn, also created masks, props and creatures used for the show, including The Keeper and the Salt Vampire and the Tribbles. He also designed and built the tricorder and the flip-open communicator which influenced mobile phone designers.

Wah was one of those people you could hear coming. That was a result of the heavy clanging metal braces that caused him to swing his legs from the hip, one after the other, arcing out and plunking down. And clanking. His braces had to be unlocked for sitting and locked for walking. At 21 Wah, a promising sculptor, contracted polio, which was still around, not yet eliminated by the vaccine that arrived in the 1950s.

He was the man responsible for many identifiable Trek aliens and he wasn't a member of the prop union or likely to be. The prop union wasn't interested in being inclusive and the Desilu studio prop makers were supported by their union. They warned the studio that non-union made props could not be used on Star Trek.

He would happen to drop by to visit with Bob Justman, the Associate Producer, to have a friendly conversation. At some later date he would drop by for another visit and just happen to have a prop that would be perfect for inclusion in the episode Bob may have mentioned and Bob would buy it. Wah didn't design for Trek, he 'just happened' to make things they wanted and needed and purchased. The union was safe from invasion of those that were different and Trek had another diverse input.

I was always pleased to hear him coming because I knew something interesting was happening. Many things that the show imagined and predicted are in development or in use today: tablet computers, tractor beams, tricorders, flip communicators and wearable badge communicators. There are hypo-sprays, replicators, cloaking devices and Siri. There are other talking computer voice interfaces and AI. There's Uhura's Bluetooth headset, portable memory devices, automatic doors, teleconferencing and GPS. OK, we are still waiting for warp drives and transporters.

31

Lorin from Mexico City came to visit me on his way back home to the East Coast. His timing couldn't have been worse. Before I'd gone to Mexico City, I'd been dating an actor from Trek. Percy Rodriguez was handsome and very smooth, bright and fun but he wasn't a possible 'set me down' guy. He had a wife back home and intended to stay married. He was a 'Canigger', he jokingly told me, a black man born in Canada with a Portuguese heritage. Like my Coon's Coon, if he said it, it was OK, it was his joke.

Percy played Commodore Stone in the Trek episode *Court Martial*. He was the first black actor to play a flag officer on Star Trek. That was a BIG deal! There wasn't a lot of work for actors, especially meaningful roles during the 1960s and 70s. By portraying characters of authority like Commodore Stone with his gravitas and that deep authoritative voice, he succeeded in breaking the stereotype barriers. It wasn't the only time.

He was like TV's Jackie Robinson only he wasn't alone. There were more. A very few actors who were in a relatively quiet way getting these nondomestic-servant roles that television was very reluctant to give to black actors. Percy was picked for the regular role of Dr. Harry Miles on Peyton Place, which had been a steamy best-selling novel, a blockbuster film and then a prime-time soap opera. A headline in the Los Angeles Times read "A Doctor's Role for Negro Actor". The inclusion of an African-American family in the top-rated drama was a pivotal step forward for blacks on television. Critics grudgingly accepted a black doctor. There were complaints that if the medium wanted to show a more realistic, multicultural view of American life, a minority character who was also a surgeon was perhaps somewhat unrealistic. They obviously didn't know that a black surgeon, Dr Daniel Hale Williams, performed the first successful heart surgery in 1893.

Percy had been shooting *The Heart Is a Lonely Hunter*, in Selma, Alabama and when production was unexpectedly shut down for a couple of weeks, he came back to LA and I had to make a decision. I was too old to play around. Lorin was staying with us in Nichols Canyon and we were getting along very comfortably. I delivered the 'it's over' notice to Percy, who took it well, and invited me over to his place for a glass of wine to tell me what had happened on the film. What was Selma like to a black man now, so long after MLK. Besides, it was the least I could do. He was cool about my dropping him.

He said I looked good except my natural needed a bit of a trim on one side. It would just take a moment. He had scissors. I left with a bandaged ear! Maybe he was more pissed off than I thought. I learned how easily a smooth manner can unexpectedly inflict an injury. Like a shark attack. Perfectly, he became the narrator for the Jaws movie ads.

I went to dinner one night with Gene and his agents Reece and Dorris Halsey who had become friends of mine. At home that night Lorin struck a blow that left no outward damage.

Lorin gently told me he thought I was an Uncle Tom. I tried to explain that I was just exuberant, glad to be with some good friends who happened to be white. Lorin just didn't understand my fitting-in strategy. When I looked back, he may have been right because sometimes I had been a one-woman minstrel show. I was hurt by what he said. I didn't think I was a Tom, maybe I was. Where did I learn it?

1. *Johnny Cochran and George Takei, Los Angeles High School Student Association.*
2. *Ted Sturgeon Book*
3. *Harlan Ellison book*
4. *Me and Lorin in Mexico City*
5. *Me and June in Mexico City*
6. *Gene Roddenberry book*
7. *Party in Justman's Office*
8. *Call sheet for Percy Rodriguez* Court Martial *episode*
9. *Dancing with Ebony bachelor*
10. *Me and Ivan Dixon* Hogan's Heros *wrap party*
11. *Charlie with Leonard & Bill, photo from Larry Nemecek (Dr Trek)*

32

GENE WAS DOING HIS bit for integration and was part of the 'Open Door Program' of the Writer's Guild of America, West. It was WGAW's contribution to open up the writing aspect of the industry by mentoring and teaching people who normally wouldn't have that opportunity. Gene mentored the first (only?) Native-American writer on Trek, who also won Star Trek a first Emmy[34]. And Gene gave a free-lance writer a break even though his story had a similarity problem. Gene's boys were Russell Bates and David Gerrold.

Gene liked mentoring. Perhaps because he didn't have children. He was a nurturing man and his pack of dogs wasn't satisfying that part of him.

I knew we were still learning the very personal stuff about each other. We were friends now and I felt free to ask why he did it. My "why" questions discovered Gene shared deep feelings about the unfair treatment of the First People where he was born.

The county Gene came from was the land of Chief Standing Bear, who participated in a trial that changed the status of

---

[34] *How Sharper Than a Serpent's Tooth*, co-written by Russell Bates, won an Emmy for Outstanding Entertainment which was given to the show's producer not to Russell.

the Native American. There was no recognition of Native Americans' rights until the court determined if Standing Bear had a legal right to a writ of habeas corpus. Was Standing Bear a person? To deny his legal right to the writ, the court would have to conclude that he was not a person, not a human being. Chief Standing Bear gave eloquent testimony and for the first time in the US, in their native land, Indians were declared to be people. Humans.

When Russell Bates entered his life Gene was glad to be able to help promote and support a young native American. Rare grins occupied Gene's face every time Russell came into the office. They spent hours together. Russell was making progress; he was a talented writer and Gene enthusiastically read and commented on his work. He would have an episode to submit soon. Then suddenly Russell was gone. I tried to find him. The phone was disconnected but there was a message from him. Russell had received a sign, a particular animal, was seen in a place, in a way that said Russell must return home immediately. It was tribal business and even a chance at Hollywood couldn't stop that. No time for goodbye, no plans for the future. Gene was gutted!

David Gerrold was the most immediately successful of his 'boys' and a from-the-heart Trekker. David had an idea and Gene liked it, encouraged it. When the research report on the story treatment came back from Joan, I laughed. Big phony, I sneered. The report showed the idea had already been published. By Robert Heinlein. Well, if you're gonna steal... Gene understood and knew better. You are all the things you experience and read and live and imagine. It comes out unconsciously. It had happened to him with his first Trek script *Arena*.

32

Double-checking with Kellam de Forest to make sure. It had to be Kellam, the man. Not Joan Pearce, the 'gal'. And once Kellam had verified that it was too close to a Heinlein story, Gene got on the phone. He telephoned the master to personally plea. To Robert Heinlein, he sold the story of a young sf writer just starting out, talented, his first sale and accidentally, unconsciously some similarities and ... He stuck up and sucked up to help David. I was jealous of Gene going to bat for him like that. Then I saw Gene's changes. When I saw them, it was too much. Now, Gene didn't do anything to David's script that he didn't do with all the scripts. It's about where you put your attention. It was me. I was taking this personally. It was as though David was taking something from me. I had envied Russell but I was jealous of David. I could see his talent and passion. And, he was a young white boy and all doors were open to him. Ultimately it was good for me because for the first time I told Gene about my dreams, that I wanted to produce and to maybe, write.

Gene said he thought I had writing talent. That was something I could develop and that would be an asset. He suggested Strunk & White. I was excited and went straight to a bookstore seeking the magic that would make me a writer. A book that would share with me the must do, should do, could do, always do and how you do.

It was a damn book about grammar and punctuation! Whadafk! Then I thought maybe he didn't think I was worth it. Maybe it was a putdown. I never had a problem thinking less of myself and so I did, big time, and David's success was a dagger in my heart.

I consoled myself with the idea one day I would be a producer and hire all the writers I wanted. It wasn't putting a person on the moon. You just needed the ability to judge the potential of the story, choose the right pieces and put them together. It wasn't much different than selecting an outfit for an occasion. Knowing the outcome that you were trying for, and what you wanted to project. It was just a matter to me of the choices, of taste, what you put in the pot. And I began to focus on that goal. That I would be a TV producer. And I'd howl!

So glad I outgrew that crap. I'm pleased I was there. I'm glad for David and Russell's success and I'm embarrassed that I was envious. We never know what's around the corner and what seemed so bad, when looked back upon was a necessity, a tempering, a growth opportunity. Again, it's where we put our attention and what we tell ourselves about it that makes the difference.

A couple of years ago I got this on my Facebook page from David Gerrold: "Well, look who I found! Hugs and smooches from one of your biggest fans!". And in response to my reply, David wrote, "You are and always have been one of my heroes. I remember worrying that my script had to be good enough, not just for Gene, for you as well. You were the one who always looked like she knew what she was doing. I'm so thrilled to hear you're doing so well. I'll let Dorothy know I've touched base with you."

33

HARLAN, IN THE MIDST of a feud with the show and especially with Gene Roddenberry, asked for my help. After his script had been rewritten a bunch of times, by practically everyone, Harlan was pissed off enough that he had put his alternate identity Cordwainer Bird author name on it. This indicated to Hollywood insiders that it had been written by Harlan Ellison, screwed up by the production company and was now a piece of crap. Bird went berserk. I heard him swear: "He's not putting his @*## name on my show."

Harlan called me, or sent word through our friend Ted Sturgeon, I don't remember. He asked me to get him a copy of his original final draft script of City on the Edge of Forever. I think it was his second revised final draft script and Harlan needed it to submit for the Writer's Guild Awards. Think about the time. Typewriters, not computers or word processors. Carbon paper. No photocopy or scanners at home. Harlan had typed the script using carbon paper and he'd turned in his last readable copy.

I remember I liked his version best. I think I felt they had softened his stance, especially where I felt he was calling out white folks on how savage they could be, calling out a deadly 'replacement theory thinking' then that we hear now. The actual shooting script had been rewritten. The story editor, Steven Carabatsos's rewrite particularly pissed him off. I was glad no one knew about my one-night stand with Steven. D.C. Fontana, Gene Coon and finally Gene Roddenberry had all had a go at it.

Harlan needed his original submitted script. I was the keeper of the writer's originals. Harlan asked. I owed. We were family. And while the office was at lunch, fairly empty, I surreptitiously photocopied the script he wanted. It was also a day of liberation for me. The little cubby hole where the new photocopier was located was stuffy and hot and I was wearing my wig that day. I went into the ladies, took it off, stuck my head under the cold water and restored my natural. I was ready. Harlan and I were not going to take any shit from anyone. I waited to see if anyone reacted to my hair. No one said a word. There were a few looks and mom was pissed off when I told her. I'd finally pleased Ivan. But it didn't matter any longer. I'd wear my hair any way I damn well pleased!

'City' is a great episode and a favorite. The lead, who the captain falls in love with, will, if she lives, start a peace movement that will result in Hitler winning WWII and conquering the world. If that happens, the Enterprise and the Federation will not exist. It makes me think of some "what if they hadn't died" I would have liked to have seen. Maybe Abe Lincoln survives the assassination attempt and puts in place legislation and enforcement that results in systemic equality? Just like with 'City', what you wish would happen may not work out as well as well as you think.

Lincoln spelled out his feeling about black people during the

Fourth Debate in the 1858 election against Stephen Douglas: "I will say then that I am not, nor ever have been in favor of bringing about in any way the social and political equality of the white and black races, that I am not nor ever have been in favor of making voters or jurors of negroes, nor of qualifying them to hold office, nor to intermarry with white people."

"... while they do remain together, there must be the position of superior and inferior, and I as much as any other man, am in favor of having the superior position assigned to the white race." See? He could have made it worse.

34

Many people joined the battles to save Star Trek and make the network aware that we wanted the show on the air. I was feeling more and more connected and invested in Trek and went out of my way to personally contribute to the series. When they had the big save Star Trek drive handled by Bjo and John Trimble, I introduced Gene to my friend Thom Beck who I'd worked with at WYNR in Chicago and was now working in LA at a popular radio station KRLA. He was a member of a satirical, anti-Vietnam War group, The Credibility Gap. Len Chandler, the folk musician and songwriter was also a member. They joined the campaign to keep Trek on the air and although it was local and didn't get the coverage and impact of Bjo's wider Save Star Trek letter writing effort, they added a totally cool aspect for the fans in LA. Trek was clearly a favorite of a wide range of people. We all found something.

I reckon we all have favorites. While 'City' is one of mine, I have special affection for Devil in The Dark. From the time Gene walked in the door still laughing about something Janos had got up to, he was revved up. Janos Prohaska was our special alien guy and would pitch possible creatures. If they worked, Janos would rent them to the show and be hired.

Usually curious about everything I had stayed away from the unveiling.

Janos felt a little creepy to me. Not the guy himself. Nice man, a good actor, tall and good looking. To me he became whoever's outer skin he inhabited. Especially the apes. He moved like them, acrobatically leaping up onto tables and other things. He became an animal, a horny animal. After one encounter I kept my distance.

I don't know if Gene told me about the 'egg' Janos laid while demonstrating his new unnamed creature to Gene and the guys. The story goes that Janos came in, costumed weirdly, and lay on the floor looking like a big rock. Then, Janos started to wiggle around, humped a bit, and then scooted off, leaving a rounded stone behind as though the creature had given birth. It does sound like Janos, and Gene had certainly given birth to an idea.

The Horta was an idea that would become a story and screenplay in record time, in days. A record for Trek and most series. The usual length of time from idea to screenplay is at least six weeks. Gene Coon was one of the fastest if not the fastest writer in Hollywood and I helped by visiting Dr High, the pills man. It also meant that I could bring back Pink's chili dogs[35]. Pink's and Lucy's, El Adobe chicken tacos were our favorites.

Dr Hip was sympathetic about the need for an extra energy boost and happened to have a few bottles, and when Gene took possession of the very large pharmacy-sized bottle, he shared

---

35 Both became famous and are still around. I miss having Pinks when I visit. Occasionally I have hit the afternoon sweet spot without a long line, and scored a couple of chilli sauerkraut dogs. They're plant based now as well. Lucy's is still there but fairly posh and very political. The salad dressing still rocks.

some of those with me. Party time for me, machine gun rapid words per minute for Gene, words that again target bigotry and otherness.

This was bigger than race. It was about life forms. It starts out like the usual monster movie and is the only episode that doesn't feature one of the main cast in the opening teaser. The monster is around. Keep your eyes open. The guy is scared to death and gets killed when the monster shows up. The outcome though is radically different than the set-up expectation. It's just a guardian protecting babies. She isn't a monster. Ever forgiving, even when she's dying, the Horta communicates through Spock, telling them the location of a life-saving pump despite thousands of broken eggs which were destroyed by the miners as worthless. We understand that she's not evil. Just protective like mothers everywhere, no matter the color, the shape or what kind of life form.

The miners lynch mob arrives and attempts to attack the Horta. Kirk and Spock stop them and explain that when it killed humans, she was only protecting the future generation eggs. Dr. McCoy successfully treats the Horta's wound using a silicon-based cement.

The Horta is still different than them and the miners fear the prospect of thousands of Horta. Kirk convinces them that the Horta are peaceful and could collaborate with the miners by tunnelling for them. The miners are asked to understand that their friends have been killed because of the deaths of the eggs and the truth leads to compassion and then to the end of bloodshed and to a working relationship. Still, even when they understand the Horta is intelligent, they continue to consider it an animal.

I see *The Devil in the Dark* as a story about a colonialist and an indigenous inhabitant. An Australian First Nations friend said 'just like Cook and Koori[36]." The premise was unmistakable, maybe a cliché, but striking and inescapable. Being a different color is hard enough for some people to accept, so Gene went to a different life form. Silicone rather than carbon like us. This was bigger than the more obvious *Let This Be Your Last Battlefield* episode. Though I admit it is still one of my favorites. The white on the right side of the face black on the other person hates the black on right side other was pretty in your face obvious, but what is also there is that that battle led to the destruction of the planet. But it was SciF, that war couldn't actually happen. Today I look at the gun/race/police/virus/news/lies and insurrection that has happened in my birthplace and wonder if it foreshadows the future.

---

36 Captain Cook who "discovered" the part of the country occupied by Kooris and in that specific area, the Gadigal People.

35

THERE ARE ONLY THREE photos of me from my time at Desilu and one of them was insisted on and with Gene Coon. The second is with the powerful parking lot person. He could make a my-car-sized space appear right by the gate near the studio front door. In the third, still wearing a wig and "an I'm in heaven" look on my face, I'm cuddled up next to Ricardo Montalban, absolutely my favorite actor on the series. He is the only person I wanted a photograph with.

I knew about him before we started shooting *Space Seed*. He was 'Hollywood Royalty'[37]. An Oscar, Emmy and Golden Globe award winner and esteemed in the business. For 63 years he was married to actress and model Georgina Young, the sister of Loretta Young, an influential star of the period. Ricardo's parents were Spanish and had immigrated to Mexico where he was born. He never became a US citizen. Ricardo was made a Knight of the Order of St. Gregory the Great, the highest honor that can be conferred on a layperson in the Roman Catholic Church.

---

37 Hollywood Royalty is loosely defined as being whole families of notable Hollywood identities, such as the Houstons, the Barrymores, the Chaplins, the Carradines, the Redgraves, etc. Who makes it to Hollywood Royalty status is often debated, but it's all about family.

I noticed he limped. Not just a bit, noticeably. He had been born with the condition arteriovenous malformation (AVM) in the spine which was made worse when he came off his horse and was trampled during a film shoot.

As soon as the director said action, he moved without a trace of limp. At 'cut' he would sometimes lean if there was anything handy. Later when paralysis after spinal surgery put him permanently in a wheelchair, he used a 'jet-propelled wheelchair' in Robert Rodriguez's film, *Spy Kids*.

With Ricardo I had the same ease I'd felt with Malcom X, he elicited the same awe and curiosity. What's his favorite dish and place to eat out, I want to know? From food, we ended up talking about being a minority in the industry. He'd been the first Hispanic actor to be on the cover of Life magazine.

He had ideas of taking a few tips from black groups. I said my favorite capsule "I got the job here because of Watts" and how the Urban League had provided my connection to the studio. He knew about connection. In a time when being Spanish was more acceptable than Mexican, he made Mexican actors more visible and started *Nosotros* to reach within the community to find and encourage, support and develop, Latino creative people to enter the entertainment profession. It was an honor to have met him.

His favorite Mexican restaurant was a shock. Instead of one of the expensive Mexican valet service restaurants, his favorite was La Luz del Dia on Olvera Street, the biggest Mexican tourist attraction in Los Angeles. At the opposite end of the street to the taquitos that I'd been eating since a kid.

I ordered Ricardo's favorite Carnitas and found heaven without hot sauce, plus the best beans and rice I'd ever had other than my mom's. The queue then and for the next 50 years was out the door and down the lane. I watched grey appear in the shiny black hair of the men behind the counter operating the cash register, when it turned into a full head of silver it was replaced by another good-looking, black-haired young man.

The constant was the excellence of the food and sound coming from the women on the other side of the counter, their hands slapping balls of masa into tortilla and onto the hot grill behind them, flipping them over and onto my plate. A Dos Equis dark beer and then it was a challenge to see if I could fill the small paper container with the fresh made salsa and get outside to a table before 'the tray lady' snagged the plate and ignoring where I wanted to sit tabled the dishes, taking the tray away. The tradition was she carried, you tipped, she didn't carry you didn't tip. Rather than a woman trying to earn an income, I imagined a power struggle between us. And you often get what you look for, where you put your attention.

Last time I went there was finally a woman taking the money behind the counter but the tortilla making ladies weren't there. Their equipment was alongside a machine that turned out uniform, perfectly round tortillas that I swear just don't taste the same.

36

THE ORIGINAL SERIES GAVE me the acquaintance and friendship of wonderful people. It gave me confidence, an experience of difference as same, other as me, and a desire to use the medium to convey important information that could bring understanding and acceptance. Bring people together.

I was happy. Except for love, my life was working fine. I was spending time, even skipping lunch, learning about post production. It was easy to slip into the recording studio and watch conducting and recording music for the show.

I especially loved spending time with the editors. It was the time of the upright Moviola editing machine when film was physically cut and spliced together. Loops of film draped over and hung from the trim bin which was also where the bottle of booze was kept. I had a lot of respect for what they did. They dealt with the reality.

The producer and writer had an idea, the director interpreted it assisted by set, makeup and costume design. The actors input all the feeling and the cinematographer added light accents. What the editors had was the reality. They could do magic. The juxtaposition of clips changing the meaning of a scene, cutting changing the pace, transitions heightening and informing the story.

There was one editor whose work I liked and him as well. I found myself spending time after work in his cutting room, having a whiskey from the bottle in the trim bin and chatting, catching up on the gossip. There was one editor whose work I liked and him as well. I found myself spending time after work in his cutting room, having a whiskey from the bottle in the trim bin and chatting, catching up on the gossip. His wife was terminally ill and he was looking after her at home. He was a sweet guy and so a couple of times I went for a 'ride' with him in his big Lincoln Continental and had quickie car sex. It was a charity thing and I donated to a Worthy Cause.

The editors also contributed their talent to the making of the gag reel for the end of the season wrap party. Wrap parties occurred at the end of filming an episode when we got another one done and celebrated with food and booze. The end of season wrap party was the biggie. It had better food, more booze and included the gag reel. Outtakes from the season's shooting was logically dominated by Bill. If you have the most lines, you're on camera the majority of the time and have more opportunities of cracking up the other actors, or turning a dialog mishap into a comedy event. Nichelle's were few but funny. The biggest laugh I heard one year was when a tribble lying on the ground suddenly swings into action and smacks Leonard on the butt. That was a set-up but a hit.

37

THE BATTLE TO KEEP the show on the air at a viewer friendly time, with ever debilitating budget cuts was stressful. It could also be one of the reasons Gene left.

I think the myth that Gene left because he was going through a break up with his wife Joy and that contributed to his leaving Star Trek was another thing Bob Justman and Herb Solow [38] didn't verify and got wrong, and because of that other also got it wrong. OK, Joy didn't give him much. Sure, The Great Bird was around less often. He had a back door and often slipped in and out with no one but Penny knowing he was there. Paramount was taking over Desilu and the show budget was getting squeezed.

Before Gene left Trek, to me the most visible sign of his growing need to escape was his getting rid of his old, shabby Toyota Land Cruiser, which had ferried the many dogs he and Joy had back and forth to the vet, at a price he grumbled about. The new car was a surprise.

Gene had dumped his old four-wheel and bought an E-type Jag. That was when I knew there was something wrong. The

---

[38] *Inside Star Trek The Real Story*, Pocket Booke 1996

atmosphere was off. I liked to drive it and did whenever I had an excuse to use his car. It was such a drastic change of style for him! I recalled standing on the main street in my neighborhood talking with a friend, a psychiatrist in private practice, when one drove past. He started jabbing his finger at it, "it's a dick, it's a dick". And that's what I was reminded of by Gene's new car. What did the new car mean, why did he need a dick? He seemed to have everything together. Though perhaps he was grinding his teeth more.

It could have been the stress he was under from a memo from Stan Robertson wanting the next script to have an edge of the seat teaser, preferably any place but on board The Enterprise. Or Joan Pearce calling from Research saying a necessary plot point was scientifically impossible. It could have been a letter from the Writers Guild, an arbitration decision that would give him more pain than gain. It probably was all of them, plus the sale of Desilu to Paramount, Herb Solow's new less supportive role, the network's airtime placement, and the rarity of Great Bird sighting. Gene was a writer, he didn't really like actors and was most impressed with directors who got the script shot on schedule, and he left post production to the experts. He also did a rewrite of every script. It was necessary.

Now, it's difficult enough to come up with an idea for an entertaining script for a TV show, even when writing about something you know, but to ask the writer to come up with a script that's good, about something that's totally outside their experience, makes it pretty hard. Writers with a science fiction background had it just as hard. Experienced science fiction writers are used to creating their own future civilization, the habits, the manners, the way they dress, the slang they use, all that stuff. But Star Trek had its own, and the writers have to do everything within the Trek Universe.

Writing for TV had constraints. How long, what the acts have to be like, and what is needed in each one of them. I mean, it's a television show and there are boundaries, and it's a series not just one episode. So, how the cast acts in one episode can't be completely different than in another one, unless that's a story point, a duplicate universe. All that had to be considered.

Writers that thought 'Oh, it's science fiction; I can do anything, I can dream', well effects were very, very, very expensive and the budget couldn't sustain many of them. What Gene needed were exciting shows that you could do onboard the ship or easily replicated worlds on Stage 9. Planets had to be created, but they cost a lot. And locations took tons of money too. Despite all those restraints, you still gotta come up with a show that has something to say, because that's Star Trek.

It may have been easier with new TV writers like Norman Spinrad and freelancers like David Gerrold, but when you had Harlan Ellison and Theodore Sturgeon, imagine telling these legends what they could do, or couldn't do, what they should or shouldn't do. The wearing on Gene from having to explain to writers who wrote brilliant scripts that it was a great script it just wasn't a Star Trek script yet. And his having to fix scripts, and sometimes being required by the Guild to take credit and be resented for the un-wanted credit and for fixing the script. And on top of that, the lack of the Great Bird.

Star Trek had reflected a hopeful, inclusive future where a person like me, coming from slave ancestry, worked alongside a Klansman's son and the son of a bigot cop who rebelled against their upbringing.

It was no accident that Star Trek preached racial equality and strength through diversity. We were sure the world could change. We were showing what the future could be, innovating, exciting and value laden. The pushback in the real world hadn't started yet but it would and gains we made would be rolled back. Issues would be made simple enough to fit on a protest sign. With lies permitted as long as they fit or were profitable.

Now, I can't tell you there was a specific conversation at the end of the day where Gene told me this. One where Gene with a Slivovitz in hand, me gagging on a Tab[39], discuss the interviews we'd give on the 50th anniversary of the show. It never occurred to us that Star Trek would even be remembered in five years. We weren't doing anything special. Doing the best job, we could, because that's who we were. Don't know what else he thought then, other than that the curve of a woman's thigh was perfection.

Gene was leaving and he asked if I'd consider going with him to Universal. He offered me a spot with him on his new show when he settled there. Universal was on the other side of Mulholland, past my boundary, next to Burbank, where I'd never been. I hesitated only for a moment and agreed. The 'what else is out there' part of me needed to stretch. Working at Desilu had been a delight and working on Star Trek was special. I knew what I was doing was a job, it was also a privilege. And, it was time for me to leave. Besides, I'd slept with a story editor, a film editor, an AD and a Federation Commander. I'd just be repeating myself if I hung around.

---

39 one of the pair of diet drinks introduced in the period. One dark cola, one light sorta lemonish. The first of their kind.

38

JOHN MEREDYTH LUCAS HAD stepped into the producer's spot and I stayed to smooth things a bit. I got on very well with him. By now, I had confidence in myself and my ability. JML was the son of another old Hollywood family, screenwriter Bess Meredyth, one of the founders of the Motion Picture Academy, and writer/director Wilfred Lucas. Bess and Wilfred traveled to Australia where they made three films together. She was the first professional Hollywood screenwriter to work in Australia. John was also the adopted son of director Michael Curtiz who directed Casablanca.

JML was talented and easy to work with. I loved that he hired a black man for the role of a scientist. I had only mildly hinted to him that there were actual black scientists. He hired William Marshall, a 6'5" man that had Bill Shatner standing on an apple box[40] in close ups so he looked equal height and or filmed Bill looming over a seated Marshall. It was his set; Bill was the captain.

I have no idea why JML wasn't asked back for the next season. My interest in office events wasn't high. But I did note that Bob Justman did not move up to producer. I'm sure

---
40 A multiple use box found on every set.

he was hoping, maybe expecting, this time he'd get the spot. From his memos it was clear he wasn't satisfied and wanted more authority. When Fred Freiberger was hired, Bob got a Co-Producer credit and a raise.

Trek was in trouble. Herb was still there but we'd lost support for a decent budget, a good air-time and for the show. I'd stayed with JML and didn't think staying with Freiberger would be beneficial. I knew I'd be leaving soon and thought it fair he had someone who would stay for the whole season.

Before I left, I found a clever spot to hide a thanks and farewell bottle of booze for Bob. I was grateful for the kind efforts, even though he and Silvia weren't able to quite turn me into an acceptable Negro. No way I'd just say good-bye and walk away. Which is why it hurt when I later read this in the book, he and Herb wrote[41]:

"I soon realized Gene Coon was a romantic. He was a romantic with an obvious sense of humor, as evidenced by an accepting smile every time the secretary I hired for him Ande Richardson, the first African American woman at Desilu to become a producer's secretary, answered the phone by announcing in the heaviest, most Southern cornpone accent she could muster: "Coon's office! Coon's coon speaking." Ande was much loved by all who came in contact with her, reputedly including her onetime boyfriends Wilt Chamberlain and Godfrey Cambridge."

The only true things in this were that Gene Coon was a romantic and I dated Godfrey. The rest was imagined, a lie,

---

41 Hi, I'm Gene L's Coon. David Gerrold p 165. "The Trouble With Tribbles" footnote. JML's book "Eighty Odd Years in Hollywood also has a couple of stories on p 237-238.

a steal, or maybe filtered through Herb Solow. Nobody hired me 'for Gene'. Especially, Bob was Associate Producer and they wouldn't have hired anyone to work that closely for the showrunner. It reminds me of Bob's comment about buying her for less.

Yes, I was born in the south — Southern California. I never had or used a cornpone accent except once with Martin Luther King, it made him laugh. Maybe Bob/Herb was channeling some plantation that had a Gone with the Wind mammy. Also, I never met Wilt Chamberlain who claimed to have slept with 20,000 women, something like 20 a day, although a pimp who lived in his rental apartments tried to recruit me. Bob and Herb may have confused him with my Scrabble playing friend, Bill Russell. I guess all basketball players look alike or maybe just black basketball players.

I have to admit though, after saying in front of Nichelle, I used the Coon's Coon or a variation a few times[42]. I loved the shock value of it, something I could say and they better not.

I still don't think I ever said it in front of either Bob or Herb. I think they made up, mis-remembered and 'borrowed', a few bits. Nichelle's book came out a few years before theirs and was an easy reference. Here's what she wrote. You can guess why I like it better:

"Andi ... who I believe was the first Black executive secretary on the lot, and whose mini-skirts revealed long, shapely legs even Tina Turner would envy. She shared Gene Coon's wild, sardonic sense of humor. Long before Black comedians made it 'hip' to diffuse racially offensive terms by using them themselves, Andi could stop you in your tracks.

---

42 Nichelle Nichols, *Beyond Uhura*.

In a low, sultry voice she would answer Gene Coon's phone, 'Coon's coon!' If you didn't catch it the first time, she would not repeat it. While you were still asking yourself, "Did she just say what I thought she just said?". Andi would politely say, 'Yes, this is Gene Coon's office. May I help you?"

39

DESILU HAD BEEN DEVOURED by a corporate beast. The food was better but the atmosphere wasn't. It was no longer warm and family. Ernie Scanlon had left Human Resources; it's now Paramount personnel and they've heard about my miniskirts. I call to tell them I need a new slot. They are not happy. I'm obviously not executive level clerical support. Luckily for us they have a rogue producer that I'd fit well with. And he works from home. They are scandalized because that's nonstandard. They hesitantly explain I would have to go to his house. Fine with me.

The producer was James Poe, a descendant of Edgar Allan Poe. He was producing a feature film from a novel by Chester Himes who was a favorite author of mine, especially his crime fiction. His Coffin Ed and Grave Digger Jones books gave me great pleasure. When I lived in New York, I'd be cracking up on the subway heading up to Harlem and WLIB. I'd be completely unable to keep from laughing out loud at the behavior of the 2 Harlem Detectives, the crooks and cons and almost every day people on the street and in the clubs of Harlem. The movie would feature a near all black cast. Jobs for black actors! Halleluiah!

I would arrive at Poe's house in the morning with fresh orange juice and pastry. He would make coffee for us, including any overnight visitors. I remember Jay Sebring in front of the fireplace, just awake and wearing only his tighty-whities when I arrived one morning. He approved me with a smile that I returned. Jay was instantly likeable. He was quietly inquisitive and subtly haunting. We had a lovely day. I never saw him again. Jay was killed when followers of a mad man named Charles Manson massacred him and some of his friends.

It wasn't Coffin Ed and Grave Digger Jones' time. Preproduction on the film stopped. When the Chester Himes films finally got made, Godfrey was cast as the Detective and my fantasy mate Raymond St Jacques scored the role of the other Detective.

When James Poe left, I needed a new assignment.

The next Paramount assignment wasn't as much fun as James Poe. Although I was pleased to work with actor James Whitmore, I didn't have to wonder why they'd put me with him. He had made a film called *Black Like Me* about a white man who gets his skin tinted enough to pass as black and records his experiences. Maybe they guessed we'd work well together. And we did. He had experienced temporarily being black. I didn't have to educate him or wake him up. Jimmy had also been a Marine. I was still with my people.

* * *

Gene hadn't given me a date to join him. He was now producing a show at Universal Studios, but wasn't able to get me there yet. Soon, he promised, very soon. I knew

Universal would be different. Very different. Universal was a very structured environment. The men who worked in 'the black tower', the home of the execs, not the creatives, all wore dark suits and ties. A Hollywood story says: the head of the studio was in the elevator with another black suited executive whose black tie had a single small red square on it. "Going to a party?" he asked. Gene wanted me there with him, he just had to plot a way to do it. And I would cross Mulholland Drive. I was ready, I could do it when the time came! I had learnt a lot on TOS and at Desilu. I'd grown up there, Phaser on stun, seek out new, non-interference — except if necessary to howl.

When the Universal start date call came, I had a plan. I had been up front with Jimmy when I took the job that I was just waiting to join Gene and I told him my plan for a black woman replacement. He thought it was pretty funny when I explained how it would work and introduced him to my replacement, a friend I'd known since junior high. She was in need of a job and a single mom, glad to be there and competent enough to handle the work. Jimmy was happy to go along and if my plan didn't work, he would make a supporting phone call to Personnel.

My replacement shadowed me for a couple of days including what would be my last there. Just after lunch that Friday, I called Personnel and told them I wouldn't be in on Monday. I quit, and there was a person who knew the job and could take over. She was available to meet with them immediately. There wasn't much they could say when I told them how well she and Mr. Whitmore got on and that he was delighted with her. Done! My friend filled out the papers and would officially start on Monday. I had made sure there was going to be another black woman around.

PART III
GOING PAST OLD LIMITS

40

What I noticed about Universal Studios was what I didn't notice — Black people. Only a few outside of those working in the commissary. I'd seen one black woman a couple of times during my first few days there. She didn't return the acknowledge nod I gave her. She looked through me. We were not destined to be friends. She apparently worked in the monolithic black tower where 'the suits' lived. I heard later there were a few of us there. I was placed in a secretarial pool in the tower run by a dragon of an old school white lady.

She assured me that although I might think I was going to work for Gene Coon, I was hers. Gene couldn't protect me from internment with her. It will only be for a few days, Gene promised. I had to grit my teeth. I let him know it was a stereotype I didn't care for.

Universal wasn't much further away than Desilu but going there required my crossing my internal border. For the first time in my work life, I had to cross Mulholland Drive. Universal was in the Valley. At least it wasn't in Burbank. Going to work in the morning only took a little longer, if I went up Highland Blvd past the Hollywood Bowl, and the Pilgrimage Theatre, now the Ford. I preferred the back roads. The curves of the canyons were much more fun, especially in a sports car and even more fun when I bought a Honda 90 motorbike.

Gene was right, I didn't stay long in the pool. I noticed while I was there that I was constantly tested. I think 'The Dragon' who ran the secretarial pool thought I was a girlfriend being put on the series budget, which did happen. Evidently, I was the subject of gossip. My short skirts and Afro were not standard... anywhere. Luckily, The Dragon didn't have any dictation jobs for me.

The old dragon sourly informed me I would be going on assignment to *It Takes a Thief*. I'd be leaving the black tower to work over in the bungalows where the creative people lived. She made it sound like I was her property on loan.

Gene and I fit back in. Nothing had changed. Soon I was commenting on scripts, suggesting actors for parts, and making sure his ups supply was uninterrupted, that he had his hot chocolate at three and the Slivovitz was there for later if he felt like it.

I went back to the afternoon timetable, and cheekily interrupted a high-level administrative meeting to bring his afternoon drink. We laughed about it when he got back. Raising his cup to drink he'd explained: "my hot chocolate". Gene said the response from his boss Sid Sheinberg was "she didn't stay long".

Gene was lacking something. I know 'Thief' wasn't as exciting to make as Trek or as potentially pertinent. The positives were he now had less creative conflict and issues. Why was he still flat? I hated watching a Gene without any spark. A good friend of his came into town from Reno, even that didn't brighten him up.

40

Ken Kolb was a wonderful writer and a very funny man. He had an interesting mind and was company we all enjoyed. He also had great weed that he grew. Another friend of his, Steve Bochco whose creation Hill Street Blues changed TV forever, had an office just upstairs from us. He and I had also become friends. Steve was living with Barbara Bosson, who became one of Hill Street's leads. Ken took me to dinner at their place. He had a wife back home in Reno and I was never going to sleep with him. But he liked to imagine I would, someday. Barbara thought I was sleeping with Ken. She gave me dirty looks all evening. The next day I did a dramatic retelling of the evening for Gene, exaggerating Barbara's behavior only a little. He thought it funny but the laughter was weak. Nothing else was even making him smile. That would change.

41

EVERYONE GOT THE GENE and Jackie love story wrong. It didn't happen at Desilu. It was a nothing much going on day. We were in our little bungalow and Gene was going through the Academy Player's directory. It Takes a Thief wasn't casting anything at the time. But producers often had a look through the book for ideas before asking the show's casting director for suggestions.

Then Gene gave me some strange instructions. He showed me a photo of a pretty woman, Jackie Mitchell. "Call the agent and set up a casting interview. No need for casting to be involved." Ok, but unusual.... I was also to find out if her last name had been Owings. That was also unusual but it wasn't weird. I reckoned it meant he'd worked with her before and was verifying it was the same person. That was understandable.

Then it did get a bit weird: I was to say the name of the show and not mention the producer's name. Ok ... Then I started to wonder what was going on. Don't mention his name. Gene stressed that.

The appointment was before his afternoon nap so he had nothing else scheduled til later. Jackie arrived, bright smiling and friendly. When I opened his office door she seemed to brighten. I wish I'd seen his face when he saw her. Darn!

It was becoming a very long interview. Then it was a really, really, really, long interview. The change in him was evident when he opened the door to his office and escorted her out. He continued through my office. And then he didn't stop at the door. He walked her to the building entrance. He'd asked me to arrange a special drive on and she was parked right in front, so I left my desk and had a peek. He walked her to her car, took the keys and opened the door. Something was definitely going on. I was at the door when he came back and followed him into his office and plopped myself down. "Ok, what's going on?" The radiance of his presence said something big had happened. As I waited, he got himself together and began to tell me the story of how they'd first met.

They were young, Jackie just leaving her teens and they were in radio school, I think it was the Don Martin School in Hollywood or one in Glendale. He and Jackie, and his now wife Joy had been students, and were all friends. Gene had a special thing for Jackie. Unfortunately, Jackie was engaged. To Gene being engaged was like marriage, something to be respected and he didn't make his feelings for her known. He had loved her then and was too much of a gentleman to 'cut in on another guy'.

He had married Joy and through the years a bunch of dogs had connected them. Not a lot else. Finding Jackie again, and finding her single, he had a chance. Jackie didn't hold back. She told him she'd been married, had a daughter and worked as a model. She preferred runways, she liked the eye connections and strutting. And that she had cared about him back then.

The rule was women didn't chase men and he hadn't made the move. Gene wasn't going to blow it this time.

Within days he had informally ended his marriage. He moved out, and he, Jackie, and Kathleen, Jackie's daughter became a family. Gene quickly bought Jackie a new Mercedes-Benz, a boring white one. He wanted his love held safely. He bought a new dog and they found a house near me, off Mulholland and Laurel Canyon. 'Encino Fats' as Bob Justman called him, was no more. He'd moved out of the Valley and moved on.

Gene getting back with Jackie so quickly meant that Joy didn't see it coming. In the space of a week her decades-old marriage was over.

When Gene asked me to send Joy roses, I couldn't be bothered sending this wounded woman something so prosaic, so boring. She could use some cheering up. Something special, exotic, expensive, and cool. Show her how much he valued her. The florist agreed with me that the bouquet I choose was special and fabulous. I didn't get a chance to tell Gene. Since Jackie had come back into his life, he often left early.

I was sure I'd made the right choice of flowers. After all Gene was in his forties, he was so old. And so totally not with it. I had taken on the challenge of being a great PA. My job was to make it easy for him to do his job: writing and running the show. To anticipate and interpret what and ways, that helps him. Got it. I know what I am doing. I trust my judgement and my taste and I'm used to pretty much following my own lead. Great flowers ordered! All done, ticked off and on to the next thing on my super PA's list.

I am at work before him the next day and patting myself

on the back when he comes in. Something is very, very, very, wrong. His body has changed shape, caved in and his face; the way he looks at me. His face looked sad again. Grief? This look I haven't seen since Jackie brought him back to life. 'The flowers?' 'Yes, I got her something really cool. Not boring roses. I got her some...' Yes, she called and told me. You got her anthurium.'

He shares with me the story of a special time. Joy and Gene on a romantic holiday in Hawaii. She'd seen the flowers for the first time when Gene presented her with a vibrant bouquet of them. Anthurium come in red, pink, white and even green, and importantly, I didn't pay attention that they grow in the shape of a heart. A message. I wasn't expecting that. I had never before thought of him as poetic, or subtle. From his telling, I'm sure Joy reminded of that time, thought him cruel. Roses he'd asked for and roses would have been appropriate.

I have no words; Miss Dumb Bastard show off! I am supposed to make his life easy not more painful, especially at a vulnerable juncture. I have totally fucked up! It happens! Gene knows I don't mean to harm. He shrinks into his office. It's a painful lesson. I've hurt someone I care about. And the internal dialogue starts. Blame is a powerful doubled-edged shaming tool. First you should on yourself and then you put the should on someone else. It can take a while to stop should-ing.

We didn't talk about it again. I didn't try to make amends, didn't do something like call Joy and confess it was me. I was frozen. Joy shut down communication after the flowers. For years I felt guilt when that time was mentioned in interviews. Joy refused to see or speak to him even when she was sick, when she was dying. And, I felt it was because of the flowers.

Gene was so in love. And looked it. Jackie improved Gene's appearance. He was crisper, groomed. She'd suggested much shorter hair so he didn't have to fight his hair's natural tendencies to stick up. It suited him and might have reminded him of the corps. Her mother came out from Florida for reconnaissance. They got on well, she approved. The deal was done. Gene smiled more. I was happy for him.

★ ★ ★

I drove close by Gene and Jackie's new place every morning. It was the cool route to work because I headed up the hill instead of down Nichols Canyon like the majority of commuters. There was a narrow twisty road, known only to the locals which connected Nichols Canyon Road to Laurel Canyon Drive, and after crossing Mulholland I was more than half way to the studio.

Heading for work that morning on the Honda, I was wearing my racing jacket with the Goodyear winged foot on the back, and Indy 500 racing patches on the front. Robert Wagner had given it to me. RJ knew I no longer seriously followed the races but still loved fast cars. The jacket was his from the film *Winning*. He'd co-starred with Paul Newman. The rest of my outfit was minimal: my favorite black leather racing gloves, sandals and mini dress. No underwear. I was a liberated woman!

On the narrow road I go into race mode. The speedster in me loves the challenge of my little Honda 90 and me straightening out the canyon. I surf thru the turns of my favorite imaginary Grand Prix, taking each curve at maximum, leaning in, imagining I'm out ahead the pack. I'm quickly thru the esses and out onto the two lane busier, steeper, Laurel Canyon. I strain the little engine to match my previous speed and I'm doing quite well. I don't register how shiny the curve is as I kick into it and notice too late the luminescence rainbow sheen of oil spilled in my lane. Then I was too busy trying to pull my dress down to keep from flashing the oncoming traffic. I parted from my motor bike and skid uphill without it. Forget cool. I need to save my ass. I roll to my right not worried about how I looked, or what they saw. The bike came to a stop and the guy whose car had spewed all the transmission oil ran over to help me. I waved him away. "Go". I was worried! "Go check around the corner," I yelled at him. There was a guy that used to fake race me as he whizzed past my little Japanese 90 with his huge Harley 750. Him hitting the oil slick could be serious. And moments later, warned he slowly went past. I tried to bounce up, tried to pretend I was ok.

 I had a good deal of road rash, and a cut bleeding down my leg. It is my arm, luckily my left arm, that hurts. I don't think I flashed many of the drivers and I am grateful I didn't skid into the oncoming morning rush hour traffic.

 I adopted a no big thing facade while feeling guilty at blocking the road, embarrassed at my spill. I picked up my bike, rolled it to the side of the road and assessed my situation. The arm hurts like crazy. I don't seem to have broken it. The bleeding down my leg was clotting already. I was pretty ok. We exchanged details and when I could, I got back on my motorbike and continued to work, using one arm.

 When I got to the studio, the parking lot was full. Glad I hadn't driven my car. But if I'd driven my car I would have been early and had lots of parking and no injury. I notice scrapes on the bike as I fit it into a small space. I was lucky I wasn't seriously hurt. I limped over to our Bungalow feeling pathetic at my close call. Luckily it was nearby. The front steps hurt to navigate and my arm was throbbing. I cradled it to my chest, my bag hanging from my wrist.

In my office I dropped my bag on my desk and went into Gene's to tell him about my morning. His eyes raked me from head to toe. He didn't look happy. I didn't say anything, just let my appearance speak for me. I was thinking how grateful I was that I had been wearing the leather gloves--my hands would have been shredded. And even more grateful for the jacket, Indy had come through for me and the only cuts were on my unprotected legs, the blood down my leg by now dark and dry.

I look up at Gene, hoping for a sympathetic gesture, a soft look. He grinds his jaw and snaps: "Ande you'd do anything for an excuse when you're late".

His tone hides his understanding how close I may have come. He drives Laurel Canyon too. After I made sure he is covered for the day, I let Gene send me home. He orders me to see my doctor, get x-rays and get an orthopedist referral if there are any question. He gives me a blank check to cover everything. He knows, like too many others, I don't have insurance, couldn't afford to pay for it. I made a half-hearted gesture of refusal. My mother had taught me to refuse until they insist. I could tell the way he grumbled at me about that damn Honda 90, that he cared. I understood that the check was a gift. I didn't have to pay it back. And he never once made a reference to it. He wasn't looking for praise or payback. He just did what he thought was necessary. I didn't mention it because I was grateful and I know he knew it and because I was cool. Mostly.

42

Ros wasn't getting work, and she thought a Jet Magazine centerfold might help. Howard Morehead was the photographer responsible for many of those shots. His centerfolds were signature of the weekly and the first thing I looked at when I opened it—comparing myself, as usual. Howard had invited Ros to his place for drinks. She thought she had a good chance, but she didn't want to go alone. As I'd told her, the casting couch was real, and agreed to go with her.

Howard had a friend visiting, Don Mitchell, totally gorgeous and terribly sexy. Don was a co-star of the TV series, *Ironside* and his girlfriend was Judy Pace. Along with her sister Jean the Pace girls were two of the most beautiful women in Hollywood. Her sister was married to my hero Oscar Brown Jr.

Howard showed us some of his current work and then a couple movie clips. Then we were somehow watching porn—hardcore. I'd never seen any before and was fascinated that people could do that and that and THAT! I was desperately keeping a cool, nonchalant attitude. I needed to leave. I was aroused. Casually, I signaled our prearranged "Let's get out of here" to Ros. Soon we were saying goodnight, properly regretful, gently brushing away the invites to stay for another glass of wine, to stay a little longer. Perhaps all night. There was work at least for me the next day, and...when we got in the car, what we had seen and how horny we felt was all we could talk about all the way home—and what we were still talking about as we got ready for bed.

Ros stopped by my room as I was getting in bed, leaning near the doorway to say goodnight when we got a knock on the door. The gorgeous, smooth Don Mitchell wasn't letting us get away. Within minutes the three of us were in bed. He started on her. At first it was great. I loved the feel of Ros and stroking both of them. Then it was my turn, but that just wasn't working. A penis by itself without the rest of the orchestra wasn't enough to make me sing.

She and I didn't talk much about it the next day. We soon ended up in bed together again. I was dating my first European, a Frenchman, Francois a guitarist for the jazz singer Carmen Mac Rae. He liked Ros and suggested a threesome and she said yes. This was different: although he paid full attention to Ros, her attention was on me, her touch was so sensuous that just the feel of her fingers set me off. I could feel the feeling the next day. How did I learn about my vagina and the feeling connected to it? What was acceptable, what nice people did or didn't do.

Thing were going to change. Ros still wasn't getting work. Not much of her scenes made it onto the screen. She was a great beauty and a great cook and a great playboy bunny, but acting wasn't her thing. She couldn't afford the rent and I couldn't handle it on my own. She offered a substitute: her friend Pam would love to move in. Pam also was a beauty—as was Ros's friend, Francesca Emerson, another Bunny. In that company I felt like the ugly duckling. (Take a look at Franny's book.[43] It's a good read.)

Ros moved into a tiny place in West Hollywood, and her friend Pam moved in with me and my daughters. That was never going to work. Pam made her living from her looks. She was an 'escort' and thought highly of herself. But unfortunately, she was also dumb. And when we had a burglary at our house, she didn't realize the broken glass from the window that allowed the "burglars" in should have been inside the house, not outside in the yard.

★ ★ ★

It was time to leave Nichols Canyon. I knew Nichelle was the perfect person to live there. Not only would the location be more convenient to the studios, it had the cachet that went well with her growing reputation. It was simply appropriate. After I left *Star Trek,* we didn't see each other much. We drifted, still in the same circles, apart from each other. When she got together with Duke, who she later married and divorced, I stopped dropping by. I didn't like him very much and I couldn't understand what it was she ever saw in him. He must have been a hell of a musician or lover or whatever. I didn't think he was special enough for her. I guess my mother taught me that. Who'd taught her? Actually, I thought Nichelle's judgement failed when it came to men.

The man I met with Nichelle that I thought was special was her son Kyle. She had done well. When he starred in Gordon

---

[43] *The Chocolate Bunny,* Francesca Emerson

Parks's *The Learning Tree*, she was so bursting with pride that all her buttons popped off.

When I approached her about moving in when I moved out, she was hesitant. But I got her to come up and see the place. The master bedroom was beautiful, and the ensuite was luxurious, plus there were two more bedrooms. She liked it, so did her son Kyle who lived with her. And when I told her I'd already cleared it and the real estate agent was happy to have her, every black person's concerns about being denied accommodation was a non-issue. But the biggest selling point was when I said to her: "Nichelle Nichols deserves to live in Nichols Canyon".

A few years later my daughter Paula who had gone to live with her dad and Jeannie's kids, went with them to visit. Kyle was about to show her around when she informed him, no need, she used to live there.

★ ★ ★

Nichelle didn't let it show, but carrying out Dr. King's wishes to be a role model took a toll. She was valued so lightly that they dropped her contract and chopped her pay, making her even more absent from the screen. As Bob Justman said in a memo. 'It is already apparent to me that we have made a mistake in making a series deal with Nichelle Nichols'.

I'm glad he was never the *Star Trek* producer, not everything has a measurable dollar value. Had he monitored the cost of Bill Shatner's breakfast he would have saved a hefty amount.

The stars... I mean star, William Shatner was not going

to let Nichelle have any line that could be his, something Leonard Nimoy may have noticed. From the feedback I got, Bill counted and compared his lines to make sure he was the number one. She was lucky to keep, 'hailing frequencies are open, sir'. Today though there's a recognition of pay inequities few male actors have actively done anything to support their co-stars. much less taken a cut for a female co-star to get more. I think Nichelle's parting words at Bill's roast were more message than joke[44].

A Gene Coon today I hope would recognize gender discrepancies, some of the things Nichelle endured. His blind spot then was more in how he saw women. He was systemically biased. Like racism, the role of women was unconscious, accepted, and built into the system. The places where women fit, the roles they played in real and reel life.

I realized more and more Nichelle was the real deal. A lady, and tough as and talented as she was, she did a lot with a little. Nichelle took on NASA and let them know they weren't doing enough to recruit women and people of color. This was Nichelle who had been through the fire and forged her place in the world. This was the "No you don't!" Nichelle. The Nichelle who'd confronted NASA, let them know they had to do more and made sure they did by working with them through her Women in Motion company to attract new candidates.

Nichelle's work with NASA ran from the late 1970'until the late 1980's. Many of her new recruits were women or members of racial and ethnic minorities. The program was a success. Among those recruited were Dr. Sally Ride, the first American

---

[44] "You can kiss my ass."

female astronaut, Air Force Colonel Guion Bluford, the first African-American astronaut, as well as Dr. Judith Resnik and Dr. Ronald McNair, Lori Garver, a deputy administrator and, the first black woman in space, Dr. Mae Jemison, who appeared in a *Star Trek* episode. Nichelle's influence continues.

Woman in Motion: Nichelle Nichols, Star Trek, and the Remaking of NASA is an excellent film that shows her influence. Recently I saw a photo of a commercial flight with a load of women, crewed by women, on their way to visit NASA. We can't thank you enough Nichelle!

43

For a short while I lived with Ros in her little WeHo (West Hollywood) cottage while I looked for a place. Paula and Kandi were in Texas for the summer, so I had time.

I could afford either higher rent or private school. Beverly Hills had the best schools and apartments in my expanded price range. I focused on "the flats" of Beverly Hills, the less expensive area between Wilshire and Olympic and close to Robertson Blvd.

Up until the agent/owner saw my face things were fine. I got sick of their attitudes when I showed up black, so I started telling them, "I'm black, so if you won't rent to me, save us both the time." I was at home in the area; I was becoming assimilated. I didn't want to go back to the old neighborhood with mom. I think, unconsciously, I thought that white was better. What could have taught me that?

By now I'd gotten smarter about money. I had a business manager who gave me an allowance and budgeted for things like car insurance, rental deposits and dental work, which was handy when an owner said that he didn't have a problem renting to me. I was surprised. Then I felt concerned that my moving in might cause him some financial damage. I got over that quickly. My business manager immediately transferred a deposit. I didn't even need to see the apartment.

I couldn't believe my luck. And it was luck. After I got to know the neighbors, I found out the owner's wife had contacted each of them to say that if they didn't rent to me, they would be sued. If I'd talked to her instead of him, you know what would have happened.

However, I didn't know you weren't supposed to paint without permission. I disturbed the whiteness of every room by painting the girls' room a warm peach. I hadn't rented much before that didn't need painting when you moved in. Besides painting the room, I covered the new push button phone with printed contact paper. The first phone I'd had without a rotary dial. They had become standard, so I didn't have to pay extra.

The apartment was in a small L-shaped building and faced Doheny Drive in the flats of Beverly Hills. It was an easy drive straight up to Sunset Boulevard. People still acted as though Diahann Carroll's *Julia*, who lived in a white neighborhood and had white friends, was fantasy. Living in Beverly Hills meant different places for going out. I was now hanging out at Ye Little Club and Nate n Al's Deli instead of The Troubadour and Greenblatts. Both clubs had good music and both delis made great Reubens sandwiches. But The Old World remained my overall favorite restaurant and hangout. They had the best-ever Belgian Waffles and a hamburger with olives that I tried—and failed—to duplicate. There was also the ambiance of hanging out on the Sunset Strip.

We were all settled. Gene and Jackie were happy. I liked Jackie and became friendly with her daughter Kathleen as well. Jackie was beautiful and wonderfully natural and unaffected.

Gene thought it was hilarious that, in the midst of sex, she had asked why the act was called 86. Okay, 86-ed meant to throw someone out of a place and that's not what they were doing. I laughed. It was funny, mixing up the numbers. He just couldn't keep it to himself. I wish he had. And that intimacy shared with me made me wonder.

The Great Bird had done the same thing. What gave them the idea they could share intimate information about their sex life? What allowed that liberty? They had power over me as an employee. As much as we went to each other's special events, we weren't seen as equal, weren't rewarded the same, or received the same privilege. But, again, back then I laughed at blonde, writer, and Polish jokes, not considering the bias inherent—the "that's so cute" kind of unconscious put down, the racial prejudice reinforced. Once again Malcolm's words "Who taught you to hate yourself? Back then it was probably the projected image sold to me of the whites who were the only, the constant visual reminder of normal, and right.

44

I started out fine with the associate producer on *It Takes a Thief*. Glen Larson welcomed me. Glen had been a member of the just barely differently named Four Preps, a singing group who owed much to their resemblance to the very popular and earlier Four Freshmen. He wrote, or helped write, the Preps hit "*26 Miles*" *(Santa Catalina)*. Robert Wagner (RJ) the series' star was a Hollywood High School contemporary of his.

Glen became one of TV's controversial figures. Harlan Ellison called him "Glen Larceny," accusing him of taking film concepts and making them TV shows. An example: *Alias Smith and Jones*, a western about outlaw cousins that had distinctly familiar *Butch Cassidy and the Sundance Kid*-characterizations look and feel. Fox studios even sued Universal over *Battlestar Galactica*, claiming copyright infringement of *Star Wars*. The outcome was never made public.

As long as you did what he asked, Glen was nice. One day he asked if I would do him a favor, type up some pages. It wasn't much and wouldn't take a long time he said. Nothing on my desk was desperate, so I said okay. He brought the paperwork and put it on my desk and left. When I got to it, one quick look, and it was clear it was church business and he was an LDS member, a Mormon. It was for them. No way. I gave it back to him and said, "There's no way I'll do anything to help the Mormons. They discriminate against blacks[45]." He tried to explain, but I wasn't listening. I turned up my nose and turned him off. And when he got snotty and started being rude to me, I told Gene. Gene reamed him out. But my relationship with Glen was not going to improve.

Glen had a be-nice-to-Negros attitude. He was even mentoring a nineteen-year-old black singer who was cute—very. The singer invited me to see the newly released *2001: A Space Odyssey*. He had some really good acid and it had been a while. After the movie, I wasn't sure what had been in the film or if it was in my imagination. The ape threw the bone into the air, the acid had kicked in and magic happened. The steward walking upside down—or did that happen only in my head. I waited about ten years to see it again. It was still magic.

Glen's protégé and I finished the evening pleasurably. It was legal and consensual. I was twenty-nine; he was nineteen. It was a perfect ending to the night and a beautiful morning. Again, prohibitions: the tradition that women should be younger than the man. That a ten or twenty-year difference wasn't a problem as long as it's the men who were older. Glen went berserk when he found out.

★ ★ ★

Looking for love still, I met a couple non-industry black guys.

---

45 member of [The Church of Jesus Christ of Latter-day Saints or Mormon Church] at that time Blacks were not allowed to fully participate as members.

I was dating an *Ebony Magazine* "Bachelor of The Year" and a former Olympic sprinter who broke my heart. The dimpled-cheeked, Ebony bachelor had the possibility of being the one. He was from Inglewood, then a covenant-filled white suburb, which I thought was daring of him. They weren't "genteel" in that area. He also had a motorcycle; he was doing well and he could dance. It didn't work out with us when he resisted coming to *my* part of town.

The former "fastest man in the world" was my dream guy for a while. World class in bed, money in the bank and a bright future. He could definitely be "the one." I wanted that! But he had a live-in girlfriend and I gave up trying to get him to stay with me. That was painful. I was strongly attached and breaking up with him left me taking too many sleeping pills. I passed out in the backyard of a friend where I'd gone to cry on her shoulder. She came home while I was lying there and walked past me and into the house. The guy with her queried, and I heard her say, "She's done that before." And I had.

I tried to feel better with alcohol. But once again fell victim to the it-ain't-brown-so-it-ain't-strong myth that sake had shaken but not destroyed. Vic the bartender at Nate n Al's, said they were trying out some sweet stuff from Italy called Galliano. He liked me, and since they were introducing it, he kept the easy to drink concoction coming with no charge. It was sort of healthy since it was mostly orange juice. After a number of these new *Italian screwdrivers*, I left the bar feeling fine. I was close to home. It was an easy drive. Except I didn't understand who the hell had hold of the double white lines on the darn street. They kept moving them, back and forth, back and forth, to either side of my car. I was glad to get home and park safely. And Lucky! My guardian angel, again!

* * *

Mom was proud that I lived in Beverly Hills, in a white neighborhood. She loved staying overnight when she needed social security help, she claimed the people at the Beverly Hills social security office were much nicer than the ones in the black neighborhood.

I was sliding back and forth so easily that I was code meshing rather than switching. I'd been dating a talent agent, a sweet Jewish guy who'd been a bullfighter in Spain. He'd been lucky where he been gored. The scar was centimeters to the side of his penis. I also dated a few TV directors and a couple producers. But no one for long or for anything meaningful.

There was a sleaze in the bunch and he was the one who dumped me, to my daughters' delight. They had even hated the smell of him. We were in Malibu, just before sunset at a super-cool restaurant. When his friend who "had come along for the ride" headed for the toilet, he had flatly told me we were over. Great setup in that location—no loud voices, silent tears, no questions. That had been a first for me. I kept learning. I returned first to the lesson from Gramma Booker. Pay more attention to what they do than what they say. I'd overlooked. I'd made excuses. Wanting someone to be the one. And actually, I hated his cologne too.

In my research, I discovered that a back could be *that* hairy and a penis could be *that* small! And like an exorbitantly endowed penis, it made not one bit of difference if they were inventive. One of the production office girls was the one the "little fella" had set down. The new Mercedes convertible and engagement ring demonstrated how well he'd satisfied her. As I freely engaged sexually, I learned that when someone invested the time and attention to deliver great sex, they deserved endorsement and are the reason I've noted the good ones I experienced.

* * *

I especially remember a guy from New York whom I considered an ace lover. He was a member of Bobby Kennedy's staff and to my delight was coming into town for the California Primary and would spend the night with me. He asked if I'd be interested in joining the California team and invited me to breakfast with Senator Kennedy the next morning. No way! I'd experienced too many deaths of people I'd worked with or been close to. Medgar, then Malcolm and then Martin. I reined in my fearful imaginings and agreed to think about it. He sent a bunch of posters to me at work and I pissed off some Universal Studios folks by putting them up in our bungalow. Especially the big KENNEDY poster on the front door. I wasn't going to get involved with the campaign, but I couldn't resist a bit of showing the colors.

My NY friend came to pick me up from Nichols Canyon to take me to the Ambassador Hotel for what we hoped would be a celebration party that night. He loved that house — especially my bedroom, where we immediately and repeatedly renewed our acquaintance. We asked for election updates to be shouted through the door. When it was certain Bobby was going to win, we knew we'd better get up and get going down to the hotel. We were about to be very late when the news screamed that Kennedy had been shot.

My car license plate was RFK 605. Robert Fitzgerald

Kennedy June fifth. RFK was shot on 6/05, and I made a promise that I was never going to get anywhere near anyone else who might be a target for their beliefs and values. I retired from being involved. I was going to go for the drugs and fun. I dropped out again, but good acid was now harder to find.

★ ★ ★

The number of black faces at Universal increased with black Olympians who occupied the Black Tower for a hot minute. A couple of black women who came for just for show and publicity but had no substantial position anywhere. I never did understand what those top black athletes did in the tower. But my kids were impressed when their mom brought gold medalist Wilma Rudolph home with her. Both of my girls were runners and Wilma was a 'shero'.

Art was bursting out. Cousin Gil Draper was at Chouinard Art Institute and other friends were getting involved with creative stuff. Inner City Theatre Company was going even stronger, steered by James Birks while Barbara Ann Teer birthed Harlem's National Black Theatre. Frank Silvera, and Bea Richards stirred audiences with *The Amen Corner*. Plays produced by Nick and Edna Stewart's Theater on Washington Blvd and at Vantile Whitfield's PASLA, the Performing Arts Society of Los Angeles, were both drawing audiences. I'd met Garland Lee Thompson Sr on Star Trek and our friendship

44

held over the years. Garland later inject African Americans and women playwrights into the industry via the Frank Silvera Workshop. We were making it happen!

45

I would not have known about Melvin Van Peebles if I hadn't lived in Beverly Hills. I was walking home from the tennis courts and passed a cinema. There was a black man in the posters; so I checked it out. It was a French film. The cinemas in Beverly Hills, unlike the ones in my old neighborhood, didn't limit themselves to blockbusters. My interest in producing had increased my enthusiasm for films and especially storytelling from other points of view and countries. I'd started seeing more films where I had to read the subtitles. European new wave and everything Ingmar Bergman directed.

After seeing *Story of a Three-Day Pass*, Melvin Van Peebles was my new favorite movie-person—the one I admired more than anyone else in that industry. His was the first US black-directed feature film since Oscar Devereaux Micheaux in the 1920s. Micheaux made films that countered the white portrayals of African Americans, which emphasized stereotypes and inferiority. He created complex black characters of different classes. His films questioned the value system of both African American and white communities and caused problems with the press and state censors. *Within Our*

Gates 1920 was his answer to DW Griffith's overtly racist *Birth of a Nation*.

Days after seeing the film, on my way to the commissary to buy my own lunch, there was an unusual sight. Sunning himself on the low divide in front of me was a black man. That alone was enough to cause me to stop and stare. Lounging in the sun, on the brick "stoop" in front of the commissary, shirtless, wearing combat boots and cargo pants, totally at ease amongst the suited figures going past was Melvin Van Peebles.

I recognized the mustache first and then the eyes, and between his lips, the cigar that was being treated with a sensual delicacy. His feet, in unlaced combat boots, stretched out and crossed at the ankles. His army surplus fatigues stretching up from the boots to a khaki-colored undershirt. Things not usually seen out in public, especially a work environment. It's not even a shirt opened to expose it. There's no shirt I could see. It's like it was deliberate to get as much sun as possible. I could understand a former San Franciscan's appreciation of the Southern California sun, but you don't show your underwear at work. He was in front of the dining room where all the exec folks went for lunch, next door to the regular-people cafe where I had been heading. Didn't he know he shouldn't be dressed like that where they could see him? Image. Appropriateness. I felt like Stan Robertson, seeing a ragged, unkempt black person boarding his bus, his next "we ain't ready" column already being written before they're seated. What I was seeing was not how I was raised; I'm intrigued.

I stopped in my tracks, hungry not for food anymore but for the bewildering sight in front of me. I walked up to him, and my first words were, "I saw *The Story of a Three-Day Pass*, and I liked it." He took the cigar out of his mouth, and with it, gestured "sit," and I planted myself beside him. "Why?" he responded finally. Soon words were racing between us. Sitting on the brick wall, I forgot how inappropriate he was; I didn't care. We were absorbed in a conversation about film, about stories that needed to be told and images that must be shown. Melvin was the first African American to direct a feature film in fifty years, a man who was determined to do it his way and wasn't afraid of the men in black suits occupying the black tower. Melvin had no awe of anyone.

Melvin was ready when the film offers came. He figured out it was a game and he could play. They gave Melvin a deal to write a script. He didn't waste his time. He knew that the assignment was a gambit, it wasn't something that would get made. He outsourced the job to one of the secretaries who wanted to be a writer. He knew it wasn't going anywhere. It was a get-your-hopes-up-and-let-us-mess-with-you-for-a-while-and-pretend-we're-actually-doing-a-project-with-an-international-black-filmmaker.

Melvin, like the other creatives, was housed in a bungalow. It was physically close to Sidney Poitier, but that was all they had in common. I was there any chance I had. He kept me laughing, telling me about dinners with the executives, a life I wouldn't mind. But Melvin had no stars in his eyes, no need to become part of or equal to. He was already sufficient in himself. He wasn't interested in joining them. Melvin didn't even bother to impress me that he'd been to dinner at the NY penthouse of the top Columbia Pictures exec Stanley Schneider. He told me about the attractive white woman who couldn't get enough of Melvin. The exec she was with wasn't happy, but when Melvin and the girl started speaking French, it had been too much for him. Melvin's French was excellent. In order to make his film, he had to first be an author published in France. Typically, Melvin didn't write just one, he wrote several books. One of them, *A Bear for The FBI*, I later found in English. *The Story of a Three-day Pass* was published and he'd made it his first film.

Melvin told me that when he arrived from France for the San Francisco Film Festival the greeters looked all over for him before realizing he was standing right in front of them. They were looking for a white man. They assumed that he was French, and to them, that meant white. I always thought Van was Melvin's middle name, not part of his last name.

Melvin was comfortable letting me hang out in his office. I appreciated listening to his stories, asking him questions, visualizing his plans. He's in negotiation, lots of them. No firm deal but he's still in the bungalow, which meant Universal was still talking. Film wasn't his only focus. He had an album coming out. I was a bit doubtful. Melvin didn't sing too well. Glen Campbell was next door and I liked his voice a lot better.

I was now almost certain I wanted to produce TV. A couple of the producers hopeful of getting laid, regularly took me to lunch. The married one wasn't gonna get laid. No more married men. I picked their brains about how they got where they were. They didn't mind my questions. The path for most of them was assisted by contacts. Plus the ability to write or rewrite. Well, I had Gene. I had my copy of *Strunk and White* and was attending the Open Door, the WGAW's writing workshop. David Rintels, (later their president') was my mentor. He thought I might have some writing skills. The next step to getting to the Producers chair was an associate producer slot. It's often a learning slot. So, I didn't have to be good at writing then. It would give me the credibility to move up but not move so fast that it would scare folks. Or scare me. Glen was going to be moving on. When he did, it would be leaving an opening and I was going to go for it. I wanted to be the associate producer on our series. There were no women doing it and especially no black women, but I knew I could do it.

The associate producer was a below-the-line job. They were the producer's support and could be involved in the script at the earliest stage and postproduction, working under the supervision of the producer. It could be an entry-level gaining experience spot. From the position, they got more responsibility—skills and duties as they learn. They did the producing stuff the producer didn't want to do.

Gene was happiest in his office with his typewriter. It was his first choice for solving problems and making things work. He wandered around the set a bit and went to dailies, but almost never the dubbing stage or edit suites. At Desilu I had spent lots of time in the editing rooms and watching the scoring and the dubbing. Universal was more structured, but the work was the same.

A script was an ingredient, so were the actors. The directing was the measuring and mixing the major ingredients. Postproduction was adding the last seasonings, tasting and correcting as necessary. Making the dish ready to serve. Hell yes, I could cook. I could handle the job. But that wasn't the main point. Hollywood was about selling. Asking for the sale.

I wasn't much good at asking for what I wanted. The family practice had been to do such a good job that your work will demonstrate your ability and you would rise.

I'd been pathetic, timidly asking for a raise at Desilu and I'd got it, not because I sold them on the idea, but because I was looking for another job. I learned that I was worth more, and Gene knew that and wanted to keep me. Now I'd come under the sway of Melvin Van Peebles and I was ready to open my mouth and ask for what I wanted. I got the opportunity! Sooner than I thought, Glen Larson was going to be a producer. The associate producer's job was going to be vacant!

An internal *Star Trek* theme was silently giving me a goosey brave feeling when I went into Gene's office with a Slivovitz for him, and unusually, a Slivovitz for me. I needed it.

I was a little shaky. Gene noticed, his eyebrows raised, and the speech I'd planned to deliver evaporated, as my mouth delivered a news bulletin instead of a sales pitch: "Gene, I want the Associate Producer job!" He wasn't expecting that. He was taken aback, I could see. And sure enough he started grinding his teeth. I stopped anymore words coming out of my mouth. It took forever; then he finally responded, "I'll let you know".

I thought it would be a quick yes or no. I guessed he had to check something out first. I didn't know what. He knew me, my work, my abilities. He probably had to clear it with the black tower. That could be a problem. They were pretty conservative and would want someone with a university degree. I don't have any real training in post-production; I didn't study it. I argued with myself to be positive, that other people had taken on those jobs with less qualifications than me. Yes, and they were white and male. I had to be more positive.

After a nervous night and a miserable morning, the answer from Gene was no. No, I couldn't have the job. Sure, I sort of knew, but it wasn't what I wanted to hear. I had no words, making futile gestures with my hands. Okay, I hadn't seen or heard of any women or black person in the job. Could I crack it. And the over-thinking began. Okay, I didn't have a degree. Okay, Gene was no radical. Okay, okay, okay. I was moving toward acceptance. But Gene wasn't finished explaining. He needed to make me understand, to justify what he'd done, without making me feel bad. So, it couldn't be my fault that I hadn't gotten the job. Better to blame it on *them*. Make some bad guys. I think he was trying to sound serious when he'd said with a straight face, "The men on the dubbing stage would have to watch their language if a woman was present." Woman on dubbing stage? Language? Words spilled out. "Gene, I don't give a fiddler's fart about language! You know that!" They've never changed a damn thing because I was around. What the hell! "They've never watched their damn language." He had no response.

The decision had been made. Maybe I could have appealed, but at the time, there was no example to argue for. I wasn't turned down because I couldn't do the job—or couldn't learn. It wasn't for lacking the qualities that you looked for in a hire. Would I have gotten the job if I'd been male, white male? Yes. Had Gene supported me with the same energy as he'd fought for David Gerrold? Probably not.

I made an effort to move on, trying to convince myself it was only a delay. Gene and I were generally close, so I told myself he did what he could. Let go and move on. One day it would make a funny story. It wasn't what I'd expected from him. He could have come up with a more creative rejection.

* * *

It's not the individual that does dire damage. It remains the systems of laws, education, and finance that wields the power. Voter restriction does more lasting damage and is ultimately more painful than police beating.

* * *

Thief now was just a job. I was putting in time for a paycheck. Nothing more. No commitment, no passion. I needed to take the other path. Can't tell the color or gender from a script if you use initials like Dorothy had. I got deeper into the WGAW program and started to write a script. I targeted writing for *Ironside*. David Rintels and I had become friends. I liked what I was learning. The descriptive images... Maybe I actually could be a successful writer.

I was so pleased with my first writing effort that I didn't wait to finish the script before sharing it with Don Mitchell. By now many TV shows had at least one black or female co-star and I'd written an episode of *Ironside* to feature him. Don took it home to read and lost it. Maybe I should have been more enthusiastic in bed that night with the three of us. It had been my only copy—and when I tried again with my second effort, my biggest fear took over. The "imposter" fear. If at first I succeed, it was an accident and I was bound to fail the second time. The depression came back and I looked for reassurance from men. Repeating the same actions and not recognizing it.

If I couldn't get the career I wanted, then I'd look harder for love and someone to set me down. The next guys I chose were good-looking black actors who expected me to come when they called and leave after they did. One had a lead in a Blaxploitation film, where he proudly played a pimp and gave me a cast-off cape as though bestowing some great gift. Mom liked it a lot and wore it for years. Another asked me to show his out-of-state-visiting brother around. I didn't realize the brother was expecting sex as well as the tour. I was treating myself as worthless. Why shouldn't they? I seduced men and tried to make from their raw material my ideal. I guess that's how I became most anybody's most anyplace. On the other hand, I bedded some very interesting men, some most attractive men, some very good lovers, some who enriched my knowledge and my spirit. Seldom did I find a combination that was totally satisfying. I was looking for my prince and medicated myself doing enough to keep on looking for that magic man that would fill up all the corners. Or, at least the vital ones. Which of course were constantly shifting.

* * *

Being around Melvin created a little hope. The two of us were now hanging out away from the studio. He didn't have a car. To pick him up, I just drove straight up Doheny to where Melvin would be waiting on the corner at Sunset wearing his long leather coat. I was curious the first time when he ducked down along the curb before getting in. What was he doing? "Getting my knife." He'd hid his switch blade in the sewer grate so he wouldn't have it on him in case he was stopped by the police. Melvin was Melvin; it was not a front he put on and I was grateful for his company.

45

Melvin's album had arrived. He played it for me. After having talked about it so much. I wasn't exactly expecting what I saw and heard. On the cover was Melvin looking like a dirty, share cropper/construction worker with a head rag. Where was the fukin' cool, the glamour? I was disappointed. It was not what Johnny Mathis's album covers looked like. And...he wasn't what I thought of as a singer. Although interesting, it wasn't Glen Campbell. It wasn't jazz as I knew it. It was absolutely nothing I'd heard before. I hid my disappointment, congratulated him and wondered was going on. Years later I came across *sprechgesang*. A German word literally "speech song"—a style of dramatic vocalization intermediate between speech and song. Melvin's album was sort of like that but more like shouting. Why did I think opera was right and this was wrong?

Melvin was an insurrectionist and I was a house nigger. Structural racism affected everyone. We learned to look down on ourselves and each other much like Stan Robertson did to those who didn't aspire to or failed to copy his role models. Malcolm again: "Who taught you to hate yourself?" My hair, my nose, my skin color... The shackles had been physically removed, but mine were invisible and mental. But give me a break—I wasn't the only one raised that way. Although it took me a long time, eventually, I got free. Back then I was still captive and unaware. I was a Medgar Martin Malcolm radical, not a "straight razor" fighter like Melvin. Or even an intrepid Ewart Abner or Clarence Avant. Melvin could see that I was still sticking to the rules. The white rules. He treated me no less kindly. He kept trying to teach me.

On one of my down days, Melvin took me to lunch with dessert back at his suite at the Chateau Marmont. Afterwards he pulled me out of the bed and dragged me to a mirror. "Look at yourself," he demanded. "Do you see how beautiful you are? Don't let anyone dog you." I passed that advice off. I wasn't really. It was the make-up. I was fake. I was worthless. I didn't consciously say that to myself. But my actions, my choices, showed it and I interpreted things through that filter.

Melvin eventually got a movie to make. *Watermelon Man* was about a white man who wakes up black one morning and his life and attitudes change as a result. The writer had written the script on spec, after realizing that several of his friends who espoused liberal sympathies still admitted to holding on to racist ideologies. Wonder where they'd learned that? Columbia Pictures liked the script but were afraid to make the film without a black director. I was glad when they hired Melvin. It meant he'd be around longer.

For the lead the studio was looking for an Alan Arkin-type character that they would darken with makeup. Melvin said "Lawdy, still got them minstrels' thinking" and he quickly changed things. The character was only white for the first few minutes of the film. Melvin suggested that they cast a black man and paint him white. Would save a lot of time in makeup on a daily basis. That made budget sense.

Melvin and the writer didn't get along. Melvin was going to make the film his way. There was a lot of discomfort. People were used to blackface but not a whitened face. The writer intended the movie to be a satire of white treatment of blacks and show the bias hidden by white liberals who were unaware of how they treated blacks. Melvin didn't give a damn about white people. This film was going to be about the recognition of a formerly white person and the injustices suffered only because his skin had changed color and his anger about his treatment.

Godfrey had gotten the lead role. Before they started shooting, he took me with him for a friendly dinner at the Cathay Circle home of the film's producer. We were still dating casually when he was in town. Godfrey was comfortable with the film's concept which included an ending where the character woke up white again.

God and Melvin had lots of hiccups. They couldn't have been more different in superficial things and they fought. I cared about them both and couldn't bear their misunderstanding. And I tried in the best *Star Trek* tradition to be a peacemaker with two men who had satisfied my curiosity and showed me options, and in different ways, had tried to help me recognize I was deserving.

Although the *Watermelon Man* writer wanted the film to end with the character again waking up. This time, to discover that the events of the movie had only been a nightmare and he was white again. Melvin convinced studio executives to allow him to film an alternate ending as well. His ending was the character, still black, is now super fit and is leading a group of other extremely fit black men in training, getting ready for battle.

Melvin was already at work with *Sweet Sweetback* when they called him looking for the "white" ending. But Melvin had "forgotten" to shoot their wake-up ending. Godfrey approved and was proud of the ending. They were different in dress, attitude, humor, and speech, but both were men, black men, both creative and in agreement on the ending. Godfrey bragged about it. Feeling a new overt militancy, he even took me to a fund-raising party for the Black Panthers, and of course, it was in Beverly Hills. Black Panther activist and writer, Eldridge Cleaver, was the guest of honor. All of us were in awe of and paying homage to a convicted rapist who had served time for it.

Columbia was happy with the finished product; the film was a financial success and they offered him a three-picture contract. Instead of accepting their offer, Melvin used the money he'd made on their film to start work on his film *Sweet Sweetback's Baadasssss Song*, which later turned out to not only be the highest-grossing independent film of 1971 but also the highest-grossing independent film up to that point.

Typically, Melvin named his production company "Yeah." He said it made answering the phone easy. Melvin was a true auteur, the film's author. He wrote, produced, starred, edited and scored the film. Melvin gave his all.

He told me he got gonorrhea on *Sweetback*. He was told not to put it in, but Melvin kept things simple. They were supposed to be having sex. He said he filed what may have been the first worker's comp case for the clap and won. The sex was deliberate and all about misdirection of attention. He knew the eyes of the studio were on him. Melvin was on hostile ground, under the microscope for any reason to shut him down. He got around the lack of union participation by pretending to shoot a porn film. He knew that there would be spies in the projection room watching the film so he made sure to maintain the fiction by shooting those sex scenes early. The spies came and left, convinced that what he was making was porn.

Columbia took back their offer of additional films. He couldn't be handled. It pissed off a lot of important people that

Melvin managed to get a goal past their defenses. He knew they'd be waiting for him, so he didn't try to do another film right away. Melvin went to Broadway, successfully turning *Ain't Supposed to Die a Natural Death* into an award-winning musical. The album that I thought not good enough.

1. Melvin Van Peebles on the phone. He named his company Yeah because it made answering the phone easy.
2. Gene Coon visiting the It Takes a Thief set.
3. Out on the town in my designer duds
4. Mark and me. I have his attention
5. A 60's Wedding
6. Mark and me, honeymoon.
7. Joan Pearce at my baby shower
8. Post-production The Spook Who Sat By the Door.

46

I'D HAD A GOOD time working with Joe D'Agosta at Desilu and we remained friendly when I left *Trek*. I didn't get on well with the casting director at Universal. He had a southern, good-ole-boy vibe, and his attitude was that I was somehow beneath him. He didn't like that I had casting suggestions—always suggesting black actors for white roles.

Once there was a part that would be perfect for a high school friend who was acting and represented by David Moss, an agent that I'd dated. She was very dark and very beautiful. The episode was set in Africa and for that reason was specifically written for a black woman. She was perfect. The casting director dismissed her and insisted on another black actress who was so fair skinned that she could have been white. They had to Max Factor her with 665 or negro #3. Whatever the darkest make up shade was. He knew I was pissed off. But so what? I had no power. Today there is not much comment when someone makes money insinuating or replicating a person of color with something that comes out of a tube. It's been happening. Love the culture enough to copy it but not enough to acknowledge it or quit exploiting the people.

The casting director was particularly angry with me when

Martin Luther King Jr was assassinated and I told Gene if the funeral was televised not to expect me at work. It was and Gene insisted I had to be at work because they were casting. A bunch of people would be coming into his office that I had to ride herd on. I think he was worried about my sadness and didn't want me home alone. I insisted that I had to see the service. I had expected it, I had known it could happen, but the news slammed me anyway. I was angry, with the shooter, with racist white folks. A sniper had killed him. Someone blocks away.

The mentally ill black woman who had earlier stabbed him did it up close. She wasn't a coward, like the Klan hiding behind hoods. We just sat there, then Gene talked about his dad having been a Klan member back in Nebraska. Gene was born just as the KKK began to decline from its high point in the state. It wasn't a particularly anti-black Klan like my ancestors knew. It was more anti-evolution, resist immoral practices and most of all block the Pope's influence. Don't let the Catholics take over the country[46]. There were probably more Catholics in the state than there were black people. Gene didn't carry much race baggage and I didn't get any bias about black people from him. He felt shame about the treatment of First Nations people where he was born. He wanted to contribute positively. He did.

Gene had a huge, as they were in those days, TV brought into my office so I could watch and I agreed to work. The

---

46 "We are an organization of Americans. We are non-everything that is un-American ... We are a secret organization of Protestant, white, gentile Americans, ready to uphold the constitution. " Edward Young Clarke, worked with Mrs. Elizabeth Tyler at the Southern Publicity Association which made the Klan's positive image,

casting director was ropeable. He told me it was most unprofessional that my attention was on the screen and not his wishes. I told him to get stuffed.

* * *

Finally at *Thief* I got a win. I finally scored with casting. Bill Russell was coming in to read for a part. My teen dream-hero. I used to spend date night babysitting my little cousin, stuffing my fat face, and watching Bill play basketball for the University of San Francisco.

On his audition day I checked my to-do list a hundred times. I went back and forth to the bungalow door to check that the reserved parking space was still empty. Then I saw a Lamborghini heading towards it. I held my breath, hoping. It glided into the space right in front of our office. Beautiful! One more look, and I scuttled back to my desk, trying to be cool. I have to tell you, if you haven't understood by now, I'm a bit of a rev-head as well as a basketball fan.

Bill Russell had changed basketball. He'd made more than balls flying through the air because he'd busted the theory that players had to stay flatfooted at all times to react quickly. Bill jumped in the air to block as well as score—and others quickly emulated. I do so miss the tight little shorts they wore then! I never figured out why the shorts had to get long and baggy.

I heard my hero come in and tried to look busy. Then I couldn't help it. When I tilted my head and looked up into that grin, I was gone! That wasn't the ferocious face of the fierce competitor I'd seen on the court! It was smiling and friendly and I didn't know what to say. All the things I was thinking were scrambling around in my head, elbowing each other, trying to be first: *What is it like to... Do you ever... What does Wilt... Where do you... Are you single?* How had this incredible thing happened to me? Words managed their way out of my mouth. I have no idea what I said but he laughed the silliest giggly laugh ever. WOW!

Gene heard him and came out of his office, not waiting for Bill to come in. I gestured "Mr. Russell, Mr. Coon." They shook hands and as they turned to go into Gene's office, the words slipped out so easily—I didn't know from where: "Hey, Bill, can I drive your car?" My lips must have moved on their own, there's no way I would have asked to drive his expensive car, but Bill tossed me the keys and, with another smile, followed Gene into his office.

I jumped up and almost instantly was inside the car, examining the dash of what was called the most beautiful production car ever—the Lamborghini Miura. I was in fantasyland, examining the steering wheel. There was a raging bull in the center of the steering wheel with the spokes set at two, ten, and six. The round eyes of the speedometer and tachometer looked through the steering wheel, looking right at me. At *me*! I was in the driver's seat and the key fit. It wasn't a dream. When the key turned, the thrumming of the engine replaced the thumping of my heart. I was in heaven. A single moment of fear intruded but didn't last.

But something was wrong. I couldn't reach the pedals. My brain finally registered that I was 5'7" and he was 6'10". I reach for the seat adjustment but can't find it, desperately feeling around, everywhere. There didn't seem to be a way of adjusting the seat. Then reality hit, slamming me back against the seat, smashing my dreams. Of course! Dummy! A car like this was custom. And there was no way I'd be able to drive it. Of course, it's a joke. Why would someone actually let a stranger, some woman they didn't even know, drive their luxury, *made for them* sports car. My heart was broken, then the sadness was replaced by blame and shame. And resentment! How stupid could I be, him making me believe that I could? That's a dirty trick. He's going to get the part and then I'll have to see him again.

I'm a Booker; my mother's daughter! I couldn't hold it in. I went into Gene's office and confronted him. "You knew I was too short to reach the pedals." There's that laugh of his again, but at that moment I was not amused. "You don't have to laugh at me." I was getting angry. He had already shamed me by giving me the keys.

"It's just a normal car seat, come on." Gene didn't say a word as Bill walked me back to the car, giggling. I sat in the driver's seat, and he guided my hand, holding it for an extra moment. The junk-food stuffing babysitter was now slim and sexy. Then he showed me how to adjust the seat and finally I could reach the pedals. Bill made sure I was okay and then stepped back as I drove off slowly, carefully navigating my way to exit the Lankershim main gate. Hoping, praying, begging that I'd see someone I knew as I drove by. When you've driven winding Mulholland Drive and the canyons on LSD, you know you're good and I roared up the on ramp of the Hollywood freeway.

The Hollywood freeway, as usual, had been too crowded and I hadn't been able to get out of second gear. It was a good thing, because if I coulda, I woulda. I was okay because I had actually driven a Lamborghini. Reality dictated that I didn't go far. Too soon I was back in the parking spot where I slowly pulled the hand brake up, click by click, stroked the steering wheel and rubbed my bare legs against the leather seat one last time. I took a farewell look when I finally got out! Compared to that work of art, Mustangs and Corvettes looked weak and incomplete. Bill was now more than my hero. I could tell he was gonna be my friend.

I contacted the publicity department and arranged for the whole Celtics team to come for lunch in the executive dining room and then have a special studio tour, most of the players showed up. Word got around about their coming visit, and I was pretty popular/suddenly getting lots of phone calls and requests to join us. I turned them all down and had the team to myself. Yup, spoiled brat, only child, doesn't play well with others.

I dated one of Bill's teammates for a short while. Switching an actor for an athlete wasn't any more successful. After a game, I was waiting with the wives and girlfriends when someone dropped a clue that my Celtic had a wife at home. It had hurt. We had been about to move to a more intimate level. If I'd known he was married I might have anyway, but hiding it from me was a foul and I kicked him out of the game.

I'd had a casual friendship with Bill. He tried it on me once asking if he could send me a ticket to meet him on the road. I declined. He and I became more comfortable with the friendship, especially after I'd met Sandy, his girlfriend. After that—no sexual tension; just Scrabble and hanging out.

Bill also took the fierceness he displayed on the court to the Scrabble board. My pride in my vocabulary did me no good. Knowing what a word meant was less useful than coming up with one that scored big. I didn't have the visual dexterity, didn't see what could be. I hated things I wasn't good at. Bill had total concentration. Playing Scrabble, he was invincible! I could understand that after what he gave to the fans on the court, he didn't see the need to curry favor by signing autographs. He wasn't intimidated by the Celtics fans who loved the championships he'd brought them but hated him for being black.

He had moved to a nothing-special apartment in Hollywood near Fountain. We didn't see a lot of each other. He was trying to get a travel agency started. It wasn't an area occupied by many blacks and I don't think they ever let him in.

★ ★ ★

I was about to get my own audience. An unexpected performance opportunity happened. The idea came from one of our series writers, Elroy Schwartz, brother of the *Gilligan's Island* creator Sherwood. Elroy had noticed my long legs and bouncing boobs and offered to train me for a new career: stage hypnotist. Pat Collins, the Hip Hypnotist, was big, and a black woman would be novel. I thought, *why not?* I was hip and now I could be a hypnotist too. I'd had mic fright and failed as a DJ, but with people in the room, everything was different. I loved showing off. People paying me to run my mouth and show off would counter my mom's "sit down and be quiet." Yes!

There was, however, one concern on his part. The last person he'd trained had suddenly gotten married and her husband hadn't approved, so she'd stopped training with him. All the effort he'd put in was wasted. Ha! I reassured him there was no one anywhere in sight. He needn't worry.

Elroy was married, not attractive and sneaky. He insisted that my being hypnotized was necessary, and he would put in a post-hypnotic suggestion that I kiss him when I woke up. That wasn't gonna happen.

I became good at hypnotizing but not at being hypnotized. I worked hard and learned well. Things were positive. I gave a show for my friends. I was a hit. People got a good laugh when the person who wanted to stop smoking reacted on puff number three to a posthypnotic suggestion that he could have two puffs but the third would taste like horseshit. He couldn't stop spitting. My 'disappearing' June was a success with only one hiccup: I'd forgotten to take her friend out of the trance that made June invisible to her. June was driving and her friend would have been pretty upset when the car started driving itself. It was fun and I was invited by the USO to visit troops in Vietnam. I was against the war but if I could bring something to the brothers serving there I would. It turned out Elroy was right to worry.

* * * *

Bill picked me up from work one evening so I could go with him to a taping. He was doing a show produced by Allen Ludden, Betty White's husband.

Mohammed Ali was another show participant. Ali was polite as usual. We'd been introduced a couple of times, Once at WYNR in Chicago when Bruce Brown our DJ had challenged him for the Heavyweight Championship of the Word. And when Malcolm had brought him to WLIB, the radio station I'd worked at in Harlem. I didn't expect Ali to remember me. He didn't. Another guest along with Bill and Mohammed Ali was General Daniel James, a four-star general, one of the Tuskegee Airmen. "Chappy" James was the first African American to reach that rank. I am ashamed to admit I gave him no respect at all. My anti-war biases were obvious. I was deliberately rude. The topic that evening must have been something racial. Why else would there have been three black men on the show? Funny, if it had been three white men, I wouldn't have even noticed. That would have been business as usual.

I politely chatted with Mark Reese, a young white guy who introduced himself as the associate producer. And then I couldn't get rid of him. He had a girlfriend there and I wasn't interested. She was giving me lots of dirty looks every time he came near me, which was often. I was no threat, I thought. She was blonde and very attractive and had that RWL attitude. Finally, I gave him my phone number. He was persistent and persuasive By the time the show wrapped, I'd agreed to let him drive me back to pick up my car. I thought that was that. I wasn't interested in seeing him again.

He was very persistent. After several rebuffs that week, I finally agreed to see him again. Then again. I took him to visit my friend/cousin Gil, the artist, for a covert assessment. I needed another opinion. Was I being silly? There was something off. I dismissed the feeling when they got on well. Gil liked Mark, and they talked art. I found out Mark was a painter as well as a writer.

Mark had good credentials. He was a graduate student at UCLA. Mark had graduated from University of Washington, The "Harvard of The West" he bragged. This annoyed David Rintels, my writer's guild friend who had graduated from

Harvard. Mark's dad was an architect, and his uncle was a John F Kennedy speechwriter. Another uncle was a linguistics professor at UC Berkeley, and his aunt Suzanne was married to *Get Smart* actor Ed Platt. At the top of the tree, Mark's grandparents—an opera singer and a former Washington state Supreme Court justice. But still...something wasn't right about him.

A couple of nights after the visit with Gil, Mark was at my door. Frozen. He said he had gone on a long motorcycle ride to clear his head and think. He'd run out of gas out in the boondocks and had to walk for miles, pushing this motorcycle to find an open gas station. He'd left home when it was hot, he didn't have a jacket. LA always cooled down at night, and it was cold. He bought a couple newspapers and stuffed them inside his t-shirt to try to keep from freezing. He looked absolutely pathetic and I always fell for the guy-in-need thing. He got out the words that his girlfriend was visiting family in Seattle. He didn't want her to come back. He had come to tell me he wanted to be with me. Stunned, all I could say was go get in my bed and get warm. I'd known him less than a week.

I regretted it the next morning. I'd totally forgotten, with the kids away on vacation, mom was having a holiday away from her mother and staying at my place. She still insisted the people at the social security office in Beverly Hills were much nicer than the ones near her home. Before I could say anything, make up an excuse, drop him out the bedroom window, Mark came out. Mom's eyes bugged. She was always good at passing out shame and she was on her game. I felt her disapproval that a man I was not married to had spent the night in my bed—and a white guy on top of it. Where was that nice *Ebony*

Magazine bachelor? Mark and I couldn't even claim a close and long-term relationship. On our one-week anniversary, a few nights later, we went to a play at Inner City. At intermission Mark asked me to marry him. Had Elroy wasted his efforts again? It looked like it!

A proposal and a ring on my finger offered recovery from my mother's shaming. I said yes and agreed to marry him in a week. Within a day I came to my senses and suggested that we think about it a bit longer. Mark was determined we were going ahead and had made an appointment with the marriage celebrant. I went with him. It was really happening.

I was dithering still. Either do it right away or he'd go back to the blonde, he insisted. I was thirty; I wasn't in and hadn't been in, any long-term, serious relationship since Jai. Mark would be a good partner. He was the power symbol of America. White, educated and from a powerful background. I could get a jet-assisted take off on my hopes and dreams. He could set me down. I could choose to work. He could protect me. No cop would mess with him, like the last cop who'd stopped me had. He could deal with the real estate people. He was adequate in bed—even if he did smell a bit, sort of like a wet dog sometime when he'd put his arm around me. (I think it was his sweaty leather watch band.)

But more than anything he wanted me. Valued me. Wanted to marry me. No one else did. I was afraid no one else would ever want me as much as he did. The wedding was planned a week after the proposal. June was making a dress. It would be at Francesca's house in Laurel Canyon, the Genes were invited and Mark's mom was coming from Seattle. Most of the family thought I'd lost my mind. I was the first to 'marry out' and some family members weren't pleased. Inter-racial marriage, especially a black woman and white man wasn't common.

I got shakier and shakier as the day got closer. I tried to postpone, but Mark wouldn't budge. It was going to be Friday night or not at all. I folded again. The night before I got the courage to say no and seriously tried to cancel. Mark had a tantrum. My last stab, minutes before the guests arrived, I became Bridezilla! There were no strawberries for the champagne punch. I couldn't get married if there were no strawberries. His mother and mine were helpless. They tried to calm me. I was desperate to find a way out. There I was in my new dress, makeup and all, and I told them no strawberries, no wedding.

They sent me upstairs to Franny's bedroom to chill. It was a lovely room; Francesca has excellent taste and decorating ability. It was in the front of the house. Down below some work going on had left piles of dirt, and I thought seriously that maybe if I jumped and landed on the dirt it would be softish and I could tuck and roll like I saw the stunt people do. I could get away. Had I been hanging out with Ronnie Rondell, Eddie Smith, or some other stunt person to even consider that? Besides, all those people were downstairs. Even Chuck Barris, the *Dating Game* producer and host, had showed up with my friend Cassius Weathersby.

So I did it. I walked down the stairs, wishing it were a burning building so we could all run. My life changed drastically again.

★ ★ ★

Mark moved in with me. A week or so later, gathering clothes for the cleaners, I found a receipt from UCLA psychiatric department in Mark's pocket. "What was that about?" I asked him.

"Oh, just some identity issues." I had no idea what that meant, but he said there was no problem. People I knew had lots of identities—they called them roles.

My makeup went first. Mark said he liked my natural look. I missed my eyelashes but kept lipstick. He didn't like my male friends, and soon Melvin, God, Georg, Max, Len, and all "my buddies," with benefits or not, had to back up. Mark was concerned and protective.

When I unintentionally demonstrated his Firebird convertible was overpowered and under braked, he researched safe cars and came up with an obscure German car that had recently started being imported. It came from the Bavarian Motor Works and was called by the initials. It was an extremely safe car. We were talking about having a child, so it would be a Mercedes Benz or this BMW. The BMW we chose had a sunroof. We added a Jensen ignition system, eight-track stereo player, and an Abarth exhaust system. It didn't handle the curves as well as I liked, but it was okay to drive, and I appreciated the music, comfort and everyone wanting to know what the hell kind of car it was.

Paula and Kandi came home from their gramma in Texas and I was still on Doheny, so they didn't have a new school, but they did have a new stepfather. They liked being back at their school. But not the new stepfather. Paula especially didn't like Mark.

Gene was taken off *Thief* and put on to produce *The Name*

of the Game, another series. We moved from the bungalow. Larson had taken over that as well as *Thief*. Gene decided to leave and I did too. This time I made sure I left two new black women to replace me at Universal.

Mark set me down. I didn't have to work and was getting more involved in writing. I was better at it than I'd thought. We converted the dining table into a partner's desk so we could both work at the same time. He was finishing his MFA thesis. It was a screenplay to star Bill Russell. I discovered Mark was an adequate writer...for the game shows Allen Ludden was producing. But at least Allen and Betty White loved Mark and his work paid the rent. We went to their place for dinner. They obviously thought a lot of him and were both very welcoming. He was in solid. We decided to make a child.

I'd never thought about what I ate. I was eating differently only because the food where I lived was different. it. But Mark quickly introduced new words like organic, natural, raw, unpasteurized. I learned to like smelly cheeses and to pay attention to and recognize the healthy things I liked. The concept of fasting was new. I didn't understand breaking a fast properly. When it was over, I shoveled in everything I'd missed. And vitamins. Thanks to Mark, I rattled like a maraca.

A doctor who knew me had once said that if I was anywhere in a room and someone ejaculated, I'd get pregnant. It didn't matter what contraceptive device or potion I was employing. And I had. Several times. What a relief when the pill eventually came. Terminations were illegal, dangerous and faced only in desperation. A woman in the back alley had shoved a straightened wire coat hanger up my vagina, and I'd only barely survived.

Given my history, I thought getting pregnant would be effortless. It should have been, but it wasn't. It was work. Mark was fine with my temperature taking and recalls to bed. "No, dear. The boy-making position." Mark was delighted when our effort finally resulted in a positive test. Finally! And Mark took charge. For the first time I suffered morning sickness. And it was the worst. Mark wanted out of the city to a cleaner atmosphere. He said the beach and the sea air would make me feel better.

Paula didn't want to go. Tensions had been growing, and a solution that satisfied was that Paula move with Jeannie, Jai, and her two stepsisters, Lisa and Debbie. Selfishly, I begged Kandi to stay with me. Being the kind, sweet kid that she was, she did. Then I betrayed her and moved her out of town, far from her sisters and other family into a total world of white.

47

AT ONE TIME RESTRICTIVE covenants, of different kinds, covered over 80% of Los Angeles County. That meant there were no black communities anywhere near the Pacific Ocean. There had been once.

Willa and Charles Bruce had bought their first beach lot in 1912. They added on three lots and developed a beach resort in what is now Manhattan Beach. They were joined by other black property investors. As their area grew it was called "the Inkwell." Then came the pushback.

In Huntington Beach the newly built, black-owned Pacific Beach Club burned down the day before it was scheduled to open. The Klan had arrived. Then city officials seized more than a dozen black-owned beach properties through eminent domain because of an "urgent need for a public park." The black property owners sued and were given miniscule sums after years of battle and recently a token acknowledgement was made. It took over a hundred years before any move to recognize the injustice. This happened in several places around the country. California wasn't alone. At least there wasn't the loss of life there was in Tulsa or Rosewood Florida.

Black people weren't the only ones. Los Angeles had

done it to the Japanese they'd sent to camps. Latinos were removed by police, stripped of a neighborhood, ostensibly for public housing, only to end up housing Dodger's Stadium. These occurrences, along with red lining and discriminatory financing practices, may link to the low levels of black generational wealth. Okay, I'm being sarcastic.

Actor Lou Gossett lived near the beach at Point Dume; so the people in the area had at least seen a few black faces, and we liked it around there. Nice beaches and a supermarket. I wasn't game to go through the rejections, so I told Mark to go pick out a place. I was staying home. It took him no time. The guy that rented him a townhouse had questioned where his wife was. Didn't she need to see it? Mark told him he made the decisions, and that was that. Nothing abnormal about that—back then. I didn't care. I was relieved not to go through the crap.

We were moving to Trancas a bit north of Malibu proper. I had to pack, so I threw away all those Star Trek Tribbles. After all, who would ever want them? And all those scripts. *Trek* was cancelled, over, and firmly in the past.

We were moving to a hill with a superb sunset over the beach view. One of several townhouses side by side that staggered up from the Beach Club where I would feel so unwelcomed, that I went there only once. There were a couple of jealous glances, but for the most, the stares and hostile looks were a bit intimidating.

I was pregnant. The hard work had paid off and I could keep the promise I'd made after Malcolm's assassination. He and I had both wanted to have at least one boy. I would have a boy and Malik would be part of his name.

Bill Russell was a real friend. A helping-us-move-with-a-U-Haul-truck-to-Malibu kind of friend. Unmistakable on the court and a stand out anywhere, Bill was noticed by the neighbors. Through the next-door fence, I heard a strongly accented male voice loudly inquiring of someone: "Are those niggers moving next door?"

Mark finished his MFA-degree screenplay and tried selling it. No buyers, even with Bill Russell in the lead role. A comedy western with a black hero was years off when Cleavon Little would do great job in Mel Brooks' film, *Blazing Saddles*. David Rintels put us on to a producer and we had our first writing assignment. When I wasn't vomiting, I joined Mark working on an "end of the world" movie. The morning sickness seemed to never end.

The most direct route back "home" was at least a forty-five-minute to over an hour drive down Pacific Coast Highway and onto the freeway. PCH was only two lanes and there were no guarantees that there wouldn't be a landslide or an accident. The other way, through Malibu Canyon and then the freeway, was longer and could also easily be blocked. That also could be an hour plus. I felt stuck out there. Kandi hated it. Name-calling on the school bus, looks in the market, stares on the beach. All from whites. I didn't see color. There wasn't any. Except Kandi and me.

It was a beautiful place to live. The rooms were large and the bedroom filled with built-ins and a mirrored closet/dressing room. It had a no-waiting two-and-a-half baths. There was a pool and incredible views. Those sunsets! It was a wonderful world. I'd never lived in such totally gorgeous accommodation.

Kandi was learning to swim and the swim school was the least hostile place around.

We loved the beach, finding shells and bits of sea glass. Mark looked very sexy in a swim suit. I was especially affectionate when I got dirty looks. That got more disapproving glares as well as some envious looks. Mark welcomed and appreciated the exaggerated affection. You get what you give sometimes and when the morning sickness ended, he got much more of my attention. And so did the script assignment. We had agreed on the broad outlines of the story. Apocalyptic couple, island, survival. Mark had gone ahead while I vomited. What he'd written had structural problems. It needed work.

Mark managed to hide from me that he was staying up late after I'd gone to sleep to create a piece of art for me. It was to celebrate our first anniversary. I was loved by the first man who had rejoiced when my period was late. I felt happy with him.

But it wasn't enough to stop me ending up in Gestalt therapy, first as a participant and then asked to co-facilitate the group when, during a session, the therapist was accused of becoming involved with a couple of the women. More racial blinders off. Wypipo! Realizing their tone deafness. Just not as aware, open, or flexible. So many subtle clues were missed. They didn't have to be hyperaware. They were the norm, the role model for everything. They were in and they didn't have to fit in. I became aware that I was now code switching when I made the long trip home and relaxed.

The screenplay was finished. I wanted to show it to David Rintels before we submitted it. We'd got the assignment through him and I didn't think the script was that good. Mark

47

didn't agree. He wanted the check. There was an expensive IBM electric typewriter calling to him. He thought he was climbing the Hollywood ladder! But he wasn't. The producer hated the script, and the guy who'd recommended us for the job wasn't happy either. Almost immediately after, Mark's workload and salary decreased. We weren't going to be able to afford Malibu on only Mark's salary. I was glad. I hadn't enjoyed the Malibu divide. Yes. It was time to go. Besides it was too damn far from Pink's chili dogs, Lucy's chicken tacos, Johnny's pastrami, Phillips BBQ, sweet potato pies and candied yams.

48

I went with Mark to look at one rental apartment. It was on Olympic Boulevard in Beverly Hills, a busy street, but it was set back and in a great building. We could afford it, and we'd be back in the Flats of Beverly so Kandi could go back to her old school. Mark didn't believe my presence would make a difference, but I saw the signs immediately — the looks, the attitude. I could smell "you ain't coming here".

Mark said, "And I could put my typewriter here," indicating a space front of a window with a lovely outlook. I watched the guy seize on that.

"Typewriter? No. No typewriters. Too much noise". Mark got it. He woke up to my reality. For the first time in his privileged life, he was being denied simply because of skin color. It wasn't even his, but he was married to it.

Mark's work had dried up completely. Allen wasn't doing any pilots, and I was too pregnant to get a job. We moved around the corner from the Chinese Theatre into an old rambling strangely altered Craftsman house that had a guest house in the back. We were down Franklin from the motel where Janis Joplin had died, there were Earth Wind and Fire members living around the corner, and Ellen Burstyn was across the parking lot.

We applied for food stamps and public hospital for the birth. Yes! Married to the power symbol we went on welfare, and no one in my family had ever been on welfare. Mark was steadfast. He had two degrees and wasn't pumping gas just to take care of a baby.

To Mark welfare was a right—something he could temporarily use to prevent the necessity of him taking a job he didn't want. To me, to my family, it was shame. People like us gave to others. From emancipation we had managed without it.

They never call subsidies and benefits like the ones Amazon and other corporations get welfare. It's only welfare, as a negative thing, when people who are receiving it, need it to live. For a billionaire it's called a tax loophole. To the head of a Wall Street firm it's a tax break. The only one looked down upon for government relief is the person struggling to feed a family.

We almost missed out on the relief when it was discovered that the value of our BMW was too high. If we had bought the Mercedes Benz we'd considered, our application would have been turned down at once. But since no one knew BMWs that well, Mark told them they were wrong about the value and that it wasn't over the limit. He got a quote from a dealer to prove it. Mark got the lower quote by telling the dealer he was ripping all the extras off before selling it to them.

1971 was a year of change, political and cultural upheaval, and some great music. Marvin Gaye asked *What's Going On*, and there was a lot. The year started badly for us. For some insane reason, I was probably manic. I was still not diagnosed, and who knew about Mark? We decided on a last-minute New Year's Eve party. Nobody came. Well, people came. Melvin dropped by, and I think Georg, and a few others, but not at the same time and didn't stay for long. It was a boring, frustrating night.

★ ★ ★

The baby was due around the fifth of February. The name was picked out. Tamerlane Adam Malik— Adam, Mark's grandfather, Malik, for Malcolm, and Tamerlane, a super bad ass military strategist and leader, who built a tower from the severed heads of the crusaders he'd killed from which the muezzin called the faithful to worship. A couple days after February fifth, an earthquake came instead of a baby. At 6 a.m. the house was shaking, and the dog, a highly strung Saluki, and Kandi jumped into our bed. In the dark Mark felt his way to the fireplace to get the box of matches and stepped into the very nervous Saluki's poo. He hopped all the way back to the bedroom on one foot, swearing. The Sylmar Earthquake brought down a hospital and a freeway but not my kid. It was 6.5 magnitude, killed over sixty people and when I went to the obstetrician, the building was still swaying. I would normally have been too terrified to go in the elevator, but I wanted that baby born, wanted it out.

The doctor told me that, even though overdue, the baby was fine and allowed to pick its due date. He mentioned that the cramps that moved the baby out were the same, only stronger than the gentle ones from an orgasm. Mark didn't get much sleep that weekend, but something worked. Around 2 a.m. that Sunday morning, I could feel the right kind of cramp, it was happening at last. Two weeks late. It was my third child; things should go pretty fast. They didn't. Finally, it was time to head for the hospital. And pain after pain. Mark was determined the child would come in its own time with no drugs. The doctor was a bit concerned with my narrow hips. It was a big baby. A caesarean might be necessary. Mark was there in my ear every minute, coaching me through the breathing exercise when the contraction came, telling me what a magnificent woman I was, how heroic and amazing and, of course, that I could do it. Mark prevailed. I pushed and pushed, and the baby came out. Ten pounds, two ounces. But Tamerlane hadn't arrived. Malika had! It wasn't the boy I'd promised Malcolm.

Steve Bochco had turned us on to the best obstetrician in town. He was flexible and went with our desire for a no drugs, natural birth with Mark in the room. The nurses hadn't liked that at all. Not only was the husband wrongly in the delivery room instead of down the hall in the waiting room smoking lots of cigarettes, Mark had grabbed a couple of photos of Malika being born. One of the nurses had threatened to take his camera away if he did it again. We had arranged a private room so that we could bond with our baby immediately. When Mark was told Malika was in the nursery and the head nurse, who was on a break, would speak with us when she got back. He told them go and tell her to get off her butt and get her ass get back there now. While we waited a nurse brought Malika in for a brief uncovering to show us that she had all her parts. She started to take her away but Mark stopped her. Malika wasn't going anywhere; she was staying with us.

We weren't popular before and the uproar he caused meant I went home from the hospital a few hours after giving birth. No rest and recovery for me. My dream of a week in bed with a clean, diapered baby coming for feedings and having help looking after her...evaporated! As a final battle, they insisted we could not leave without filling in her race on the birth certificate. It had to be black or white, they didn't think our choice of "human" was good enough.

The birth certificate said she was Malika, in honor of Malcolm, and Insha'Allah to signify we accepted it was God's will that she was a girl born on Sunday February 21, the same day and date that Malcolm had died—and at almost the exact same minute. The cake for the baby shower, directed by Mark, had written on it "For He Who Has Come to Save The World." The Jewish baker added a postscript at no charge: "I hope." She was a very wanted child.

I didn't get much sleep and I was immediately trying to breastfeed, exhausted and in pain. The child I'd wanted so much was there and I didn't feel any joy, just weariness. She didn't sleep; so I didn't either. I wasn't happy. I was depressed as hell. Black women don't get post-partum depression. It's not in our DNA. Tote that barge, lift that bale, pick that cotton with the baby on your back, while smiling and singing. Where did I get that?

I was pissed off with everyone. I couldn't sleep, couldn't eat. My one success, finally being able to breastfeed, became a shackle. Wina Sturgeon, Ted's wife, suggested I had post-partum depression. As soon as Wina had said it, I slapped it back at her. Maybe she had everything under control with Andros only months older than Malika. Maybe she was already preparing to win more blue ribbons at the LA County fair for her growing, baking and canning. But maybe she was hiding feelings like those ladies did in the Gestalt group. She could stop hinting about post-partum depression. Black women do not get that. We are extra tough. That's something white ladies get, the only vulnerability of the omniscient RWL.

Just because I got into arguments, was irritated by everything, was having difficulty accepting that I hadn't totally screwed up and that I'd been given a miracle, it didn't mean anything.

49

Wina, the wisest woman I knew, sent me off for a week. She looked after Malika, breastfeeding both babies. Andros and Malika became bosom buddies. They are still friends.

That much needed break that Mark and I were gifted with was gratefully devoured. We drove up my favorite Highway 1 and sat on a beach in Big Sur watching waves come through a huge hole in a giant rock. It was a private beach with people who were warm and welcoming. My brain asked silly questions: Where was Kim Novak's house? On the beach or in the redwoods? Did she miss Sammy Davis? And why did people think I have PPD?

The holiday was great; the effects didn't last. Taking stock, all my fantasies had come true! I had a cool husband with all the credentials I asked for, who adored me and was at my beck and call. We had a great place to live, my children were adorable and everyone was healthy and well. Why didn't I feel pleased or satisfied? I was argumentative. I had what I thought I wanted and was still depressed. The one good thing was that Mark and I had begun to gel as writers. We were in agreement on our new script and we worked well together, which was good. Everything else was starting to crumble.

We were both against the Vietnam War and showed our anti-war support. Mark's old Navy dog tags hung from a coffin on the front porch which we used as a prop when we did street theater. Kandi took the part of the weeping kid sitting beside it. When Mark joined Entertainment Industry for Peace and Justice (EIPJ), I got left at home alone with the baby. EIPJ was an anti-war group created by Jane Fonda and Donald Southerland who were a couple after co-staring in *Klute*. They'd united and gathered friends and friends of friends. Many were entertainers and prominent, if not downright famous.

Mark now came home to a sleepless, resentful and depressed me. Mark's identity issue, which he casually mentioned a couple days after we married, was getting stranger. He was personally taking responsibility for ending the war—as though he could. I was lucky when he brought a new arrival home from EIPJ. She was a Jersey Girl and another Rosilyn. Roz Heller was a stranger to the LA streets, and we shared 'LA is not New York' stories, and we bonded, discussing the changes in our lives.

Roz was a person that didn't suffer a fool within a fifty-mile radius much less gladly. I think her friend, another film executive, Julia Phillips, was the only person who seemed tougher than her.

I got a publicist job at The Troubadour, a nightclub in West Hollywood. Hated it. It was a place that was supposed to be cool and hip and welcoming of others, but I'd found it fake. I complained to Mark and Roz that I was a token, that I was only there for show. Roz's job at Columbia Pictures had no name. She was an executive, and she was a token too—as much as she would allow.

I clash with Melvin over using his young son Mario in a

sex scene in *Sweetback*. He stops visiting. I'm busy with the baby anyway. Much too busy. I forgot babies were like this. This wasn't what I planned. Shit. Once again: Black-women-don't-have-post-partum-depression. That's for RWLs. We're strong. I've got everything I thought I needed, so why the hell am I not happy?

I tell Ted Sturgeon that calling a black male "boy" isn't permissible, unless he is or a member of his family. He says of the old white lady who we're talking about, "To her he is a boy. He's twenty. She's eighty." I don't yield, he doesn't either. I shut up. He shuts up. We never spoke again.

I fight with Harlan. He's gotten one of the secretaries at the studios pregnant. I say he should pay for the abortion. He says they should share it. I point out the disparity in income—not just for her but for all women. He disputes and points out the writer's guild pays men and women the same. 'Yes, just how many women are members? I ask. He shut up. I shut up. We never spoke again.

1. *1971. Sunday, February 21st 2:50 pm. Malika born. 1965. Sunday February 21st around 3pm el'Hajj Malik el-Shabazz assassinated.*
2. *Home a few hours after birth. I'm already sleep deprived and weary.*
3. *Beautiful Malika and me. I survived and go back to work.*
4. *But, no more Fred make-up.*
5. *Me at work*
6. *Godfrey and I seriously.*
7. *Max Julien and Wendell Franklin and the newlywed.*
8. *Ros returns*

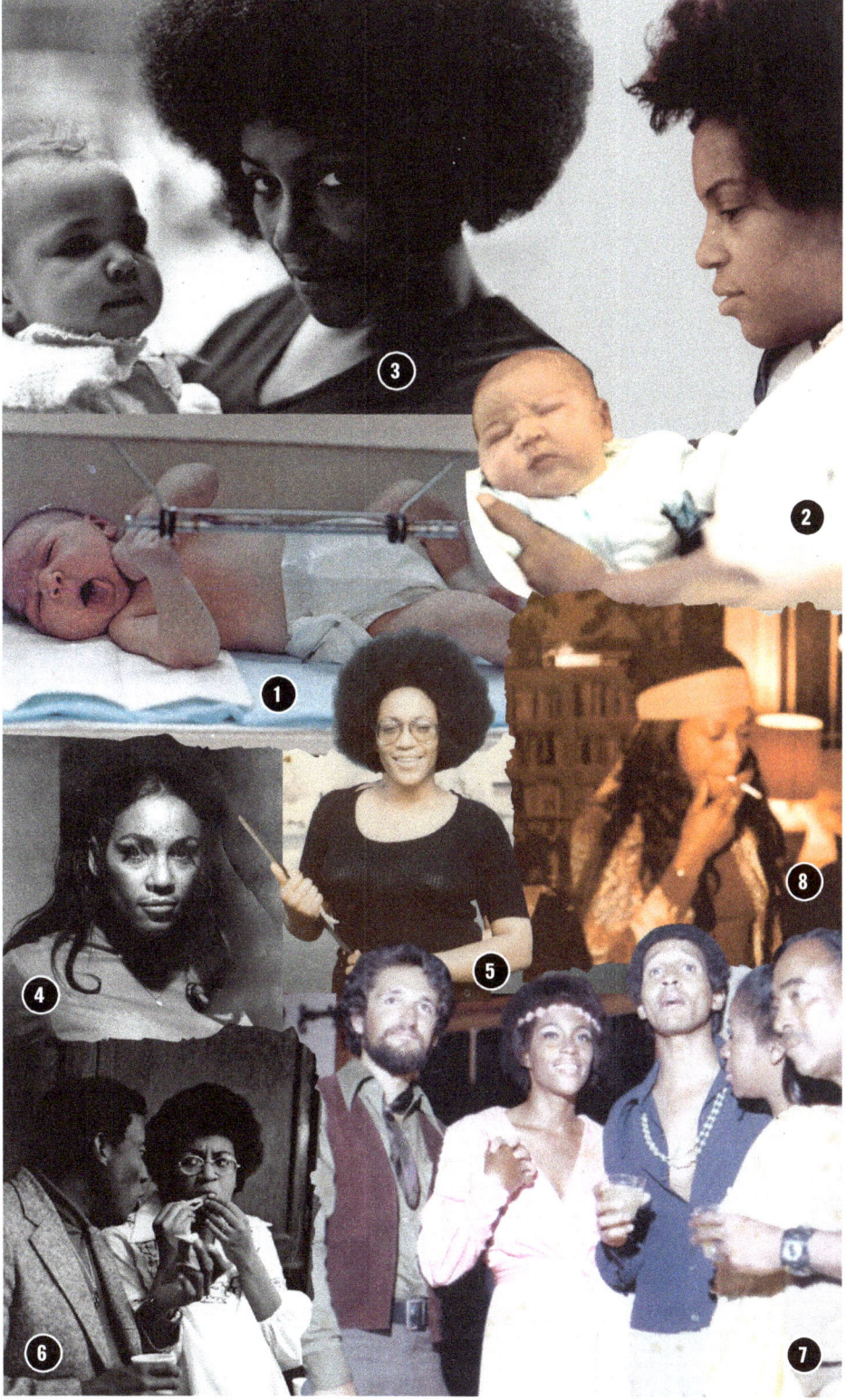

50

***BLACKSMITH*, THE SCRIPT WE** are writing is a Blaxploitation film and Mark's bringing some positive ideas to it. His language and conversation have changed. He's taking on the burdens of a black man's history as though he is trying to turn black.

It was our first script together that showed with Mark I'd found someone to howl with. The script was wonderful. It was my favorite and what it had to say was as topical now as then. It was just not the usual black folks and police. It was about a cyber-savvy, black industrial detective agency. The criminals they hunted stole ideals and methods, formulas, and practices. The crimes were non-violent, the criminals were highly intelligent, and so were they. The agency charged lots of money. It was also high tech. The IBM System/370 had recently started the trend to a smaller and faster computer. The computer person at our agency had a degree from the streets, a quick and agile mind and keen intellect who had picked up coding as though it was only a way of talking to some different friends.

We had written *BlackSmith* as a fast-paced, action film which demonstrated that a black man with a mop in his hands and a black woman in a servant's uniform were invisible. It was filled with high tech equipment, high-speed cars and an ironic sense of humor. The script gave a serve to the white establishment, while sharing a side of black people seldom seen at that time. It was not the lone hero but a group of people working together to enhance the skills and abilities of each other. Excellent people who were good at their job and operated with integrity and humor.

The plot involved health disparities in a poor African-American community where volunteers were paid to participate in the trial of a new drug and racism allowed the company to get away with experimenting on them. The villains were a multinational drug testing pharmaceutical company operating in the black community behind a front of doing good.

With much hope, I gave our precious script to my friend Roz Heller, who by then had a title. She'd demanded better treatment at work, including a title equal to that of the men from other companies that she was dealing with. She became the first female executive at a Hollywood studio and vice president at Columbia Pictures, which meant she was in a position to get our script to someone who could make it happen.

She told me that our premise was preposterous—a pharmaceutical company wouldn't be that deceitful in the chase for profits. No unethical medical study would ever be allowed. She and whoever else had seen the script had never heard of the ethically abusive medical study conducted between 1932 and 1972 where the study's African-American participants experienced blindness, mental impairment and death. It was a mild example of today's Sackler[47] family. The

---

47   https://www.npr.org/2021/09/01/1031053251/
     sackler-family-immunity-purdue-pharma-oxcyontin-opioid-epi

white view of a black script also wouldn't pick up the subtle references, the inside jokes. The pride and light it shone on black accomplishments, ability and unfettered initiatives. I swallowed Roz's disdain, blaming myself all the while for the anger I tried not to feel against a film she *had* helped get fast tracked to production. Columbia's Steve Tisch's *Cleopatra Jones* was easier to understand. "Cleopatra...Jones? Ha-ha—what a funny juxtaposition! And it's about black people and drug dealing. Now that makes sense!" The writer was an ex, Max Julien. I'd introduced him to Roz and they'd gotten on very well. The film got made and proved to me that Melvin had been right. He'd said Hollywood was a "plantation". The people who chose which film would be made, 'The Massas,' were never black and yet they thought they knew everything about how we talked, walked and lived. They even thought they were free of bias, claimed not to see color. They were blind...to their bias.

In my family the most important thing is getting up again. Resilience, rebound, reset, retake, repeat, reevaluate and reinterpret. It's the ability to take shit and turn it into something fantastic. Chitlins, hog head cheese, hooter and tooters cast off pieces of pig made more than palatable. Made delicious and sought after.

Mark had complained of not being taken seriously at EIPJ, not being invited onto committees. I laughed. I'd felt that way too many times to count. Cynically, I told him that as a black woman, a 2fer, I could do just about anything I wanted with that group of rich, white, bleeding hearts. And so I did. Soon I was a visitor at Jane Fonda's "little" house off Cahuenga, a few blocks away. Lounging around, envying the swimming pool, still carrying extra pounds from the pregnancy and discussing issues like discrimination against "larger women" and acceptance of self with a Jane Fonda that I read was bulimic at the time she was being at one with me. It was a drool-able lifestyle. Yes, I had drooled. It was my dream! And it was what I thought I'd get with Mark. I was aware how lucky I was to have the connections at EIPJ.

Soon I needed those connections. Mark was getting even more strange. It was a little scary. He was considering medically changing the color of his skin to look black. He had consulted the doctor who'd advised James Whitmore for his transformation into a black man in the film *Black Like Me*. He was like another person at times.

Our ending was as spontaneous as the beginning. I'd quit the job at The Troubadour, and Mark decided to take it. We were talking about the job over dinner at a favorite restaurant in Echo Park when suddenly I asked, "Would you like a divorce?"

He thought for a moment, then responded, "Okay, sure."

And the marriage was done.

51

I had so fucked up my life. I only had two children with me instead of three. I had no career path to producer. I'd lost some of my best friends. I could make an excellent Alfredo sauce, but I was twenty pounds overweight, plus I didn't have a job and I was broke.

With Mark gone I discovered that the guy who rented our guest cottage was not only an excellent German car mechanic but was also excellent in bed.

It was because of the renter/lover that my hunger for film came back. Extraordinary sex can make everything brighter and better. When there's a total effortless fit that hits all the spots, joy can come back into your world. He revived me.

I came outside one afternoon to find him working on a 1954 Mercedes Benz. It was the 220 or 300 Cabriolet. Not only did that car take my breath away then, but I still want one today. Anyway, I stopped drooling and recovered enough breath to chat with the old Chinese dude sitting in my drive waiting for it. His name was Jimmy. The car was his and he'd had it since it had been brand new. A bit later I finally got to the required "What do you do?" Jimmy said he had worked in Hollywood. Camera. And it hit me.

Jimmy was James Wong Howe, a cinematographer who'd shot over 100 films, an innovator nominated for several Oscars and had won two. He was a cinematic genius and master who, during WWII, had to wear a badge that said, "I am Chinese." Although he'd married his wife in France in 1937, they couldn't legally marry in California until 1967. Also, she was a writer and was white and, under terms of his Hollywood contract, that violated the morals clause.

We talked about the barriers, the joys and disappointment. The stupidity of denying people with ability to function in the industry simply because they were not white. This man, who had accomplished so much, put the spark, the desire back into me. I needed to get going and get a job and get back in the race.

Francesca was also ready for a change. She was still with the Playboy franchise but was no longer a bunny. She was ready to do something else and she wanted to be taken seriously. She had loved the life of being a bunny and has recently contributed a fascinating, engrossing, and pacey memoir, *The Chocolate Bunny*[48] that is a must read.

The unions were starting to open and the DGA was still running its program. The Writers Guild of America West also. The film editor's guild was accepting apprentices and encouraging people of color and women to apply. It was perfect for Francesca but she was worried that being a Playboy Bunny wouldn't give her the right background. So we decided she should take mine. I called Gene. He also liked Franny—everyone did—and explained what she needed and why. If asked, would he vouch for her and say she'd worked for him? Sure! And it worked. Despite her being shorter and

---

[48] The Chocolate Bunny by Francesca Emerson.

much better looking than me, one of the interviewers from Universal Studios couldn't tell us apart and told her that he'd often seen her on the lot.

Franny joined Academy Award-winning editors, Dede Allen and Verna Fields and my friend Marge Fowler, at Film Editors Local 700. Franny also had an application for a Fellowship at the AFI Centre for Advanced Film Studies. She gave me her application that she'd already filled in and I whited out all her info and filled mine in. They had an excellent program there, including one for producers. It was a long shot but might as well check it out.

52

BECAUSE OF MY "FRIENDSHIP" with Jane Fonda and actor Ellen Burstyn and some others at EIPJ, I got a job at the most politically correct independent film production company in Hollywood: BBS Productions, creators of *The Monkees* TV show, Oscar nominated *Easy Rider* and supporters of EIPJ, the Black Panthers, and other civil rights groups.

It was Hollywood. I knew the right people and I got the job. I loved that I could almost walk there. It was in a small building on La Brea, not that far from Pink's hot dogs. Redd Foxx bought it later. BBS also rented space to other producers, like Michael and Julia Phillips. Michael and I got along well and he was always willing to talk about producing with me. Julia didn't much like the information that Michael was happy to give me about funding films and making deals. He was an absolute delight! She wasn't. But credit is due. I admired her. She was the first woman to receive an Oscar for best picture and produced *Taxi Driver*, *The Sting* and *Close Encounters of the Third Kind*.

Bert Schneider was the first "B" in BBS. Bert was incredibly sexy, in a relationship with Candace Bergen and, according to gossip, screwing everybody he wanted. He was lean and tall with mop of curly hair, sexy eyes, and a sweet smile and an attitude that sent me messages radiating from below my belt whenever I saw him. While Huey Newton was on trial in San Francisco, Bert would attend court every day, flying up every morning and back every evening. I used to stroll past his glassed-in office whenever I had an excuse. He was just so darn cute! If I'd taken the job with *The Monkees*, I would have worked with him.

Stanley Schneider, the Columbia Pictures executive Melvin Van Peebles dealt with unhappily, was his older brother. The younger brother, Harold, was his production man on all his projects. Their father, Abe Schneider, succeeded Harry Cohn as president of Columbia Pictures. They were Hollywood royalty although BBS was an independent, they had close cultural and financial ties to Columbia. I'd be working for brother Harold. It was all good!

Bob Rafelson was the second "B" in BBS. He was the film director. Bob was married to Toby, his production designer. I think he enjoyed being called "The Welder" because of the design of his eyeglasses. He was a new wave wannabe...

The "S" was Steve Blauner, who didn't make much of an impression on me except that he was the first "suit" (production executive) I'd seen that didn't wear a suit. He wore Levi's and drove a Porsche in violation of the hierarchy code. I loved when he got stopped by a cop who thought he was a hippie in a stolen car.

Hippies were now getting the pushback black people were familiar with. They were being judged by the clothes they wore and the length of their hair. Cannabis was being called a "gateway drug," and they were going to jail for a joint. The police were learning to be cautious; some unlikely looking people were influential. We'd heard that the police who stopped music conductor HB Barnum for 'driving in Beverly Hills while black' were surprised when he pulled a small suitcase out of his car that was a new kind of phone—cellular. The number he rang connected him with a VIP who ended the harassment by speaking directly with the cops.

BBS was fantastic. I loved it there. I was with my people. Everyone was hip and aware; it was a perfect fit. And then when casting started for the film I'd be working on, Harold Schneider reported in. Harold would be the production manager and I was the production secretary. *The King of Marvin Gardens* would be shooting on location in Atlantic City, New Jersey in the winter.

I could tell Harold was not happy to find me in the production spot. He had his favorite, who he most often worked with, and especially didn't like having someone thrust on him. I could relate. I was not even his last choice for the job. Still, I needed a job. And it's one that paid a location rate and a per diem. It almost doubled my last salary.

We weren't gonna get along and be friends like me and Gene or the others I'd worked with; but that was okay. I would hopefully do such a great job that I would win him over. I knew I was good at running a production office and capable of multiple ball juggling while not breaking eggs.

An empty bag addressed to Harold arrived from New York. Harold asked me to follow it up and find out what it was about. It was before internet, so I called directory assistance, gave them the name of the company, got the number and called. It was a yarn shop. Nothing to do with production. After being shuffled around, the mystery of the empty bag was solved.

Harold's very rich mother had purchased some knitting wool and, to evade the NY sales tax, had it sent out of state to Los Angeles. Since the yarn was for her, she took it out, and the shop mailed the empty bag. That way they satisfied the law—evaded it, rather. It was all about not paying the sales tax. No wonder they were so rich. Good thinking. The Long Island Ice Tea also came from around there. They were swift RWLs. To Harold the empty bag made sense—a normal thing to do.

He had disdain for people who didn't understand his world for example the woman at DMV where he registered the classic gullwing Benz he'd bought. She'd remarked that he'd paid a lot of money for a used car. He'd thought she was an idiot.

He let me know how he felt about black people as well. He criticized that we complained about discrimination without doing anything productive. He bragged that Jews didn't ask people to let them in, that they got their own. If we wanted to play golf, we should build our own country clubs as they had.

Harold had no understanding of systemic racism. The prism of his privilege had normalized his world to show an even playing field that was no more favored than anyone else. In case he was right, I upped the stakes: I'd do the job and make it look easy.

Things were comfortable at first. I knew my job and did it well, but the treadmill kept getting turned up a notch. I'd never worked on a feature film before, so I didn't realize that I was going to do the work of many. There was one production assistant that the Welder had hired as assistant to the director. She had a similar upbringing and background to Harold and got on well with him. She quickly let me know that she would be no help to me. She was strictly there to look after the director and any of his needs on the set. The office was mine. I was there alone.

The first and major difference in location vs studio for me was being in the office before the crew arrived and there when they returned. I wouldn't see them again until they wrapped for the day. A 7 a.m. call meant I had to be in the office by 6, and 7 p.m. wrap meant I was in the production office 'til 9 or 10 at night. Instead of only me, there should have been at least two or three people to run the office. But Harold was like his mom. I put a smile on my face in the morning and one for good night in the evening. What there was to do during the day I handled easily. Making friends with the staff gave me access to a vacant suite with a kitchen where I cooked my food. It was an Atlantic City winter and I kept the cooked food on my balcony packed with snow. My per diem food allowance, along with most of my salary, went to my mother for looking after the kids and the new laundry appliances she required.

A couple of cute black guys came down from New York for small parts, luckily at different times, so I dated them both and there was good fun and adequate sex. My good friend-with-benefits routine meant that we stayed friends.

When Bob and Toby found out I wasn't going home because I couldn't afford the airfare, they bought tickets for my kids to come to the location to be with me for Christmas. I think they guessed if I'd gone home, I might not have come back.

Christmas stretched me, booking everyone home and back in for shooting, knowing their preferences and needs, and what affected the time they could leave. I timed all the flights to perfection! Sent them all off for the holiday and was patting myself on the back for a job well done. Part of me was wishing for some acknowledgment, while recognizing what I had pulled off was still not good enough for Harold to show any appreciation.

53

KANDIS AND MALIKA ARRIVED, Harold left, and we had a great Christmas with a local Atlantic City family I had gotten to know. They were Catholic, and the father was on the Howard Johnson hotel staff where we were based. He was kind and drove us to New York City.

We connected with Mark's brother, Gregory, who had a toddler Malika's age. He was a very talented actor. I saw an episode of *Naked City* and he was brilliant. However his behavior was so difficult, that the Actor's Studio had to reluctantly throw him out. He had some mental health problems. Like Mark.

The holiday offered me more gifts after the kids left. One was the possibility of attending a new university in New York that had places to live for single mothers with families. So novel and new an idea that the future homes I walked through were still under construction. A university degree. My mom would love for me to do that.

Another was a kind of mystical experience: looking up the stairs, while changing trains in the subway. For a moment, I thought I was seeing Malcolm. It took my breath away. When the stranger reached me, he took my hand and with those

Malcolm lips said, "Come with me to church," and I went with him. It was a Religious Science service at Lincoln Centre. I'd never been there. It was the perfect place to receive a message that enlightened and uplifted me. I'd loved being with him. He wanted me to go home with him to Boston where Malcolm had lived. It seemed a good idea.

Melvin Van Peebles talked me out of it when I met up with him later that day to see his play *Ain't Supposed To Die A Natural Death*. After producing *Sweetback,* Melvin had taken on Broadway. He'd gotten three Tony nominations for his work on it. He then became a Wall Street trader and wrote a book on how to do it, ran the New York Marathon, and wrote more and made more movies. The French government awarded him the country's highest award, The Legion of Honor.

Ain't Supposed To Die A Natural Death was a wonderfully happy surprise. As with so many things, once I saw it, I understood and appreciated it. Utilizing a flexible bare bones structure, Melvin had showcased on stage a community, baring their longing, pain, joy, and grief. And a strong desire for retribution, for payback. I knew the people he was singing about. The characters showcased reminded me of my San Diego family. They had the most siblings and stories filled with love and jealousy, pain and joy, fame and Uncle Frank, the wino who hung out in the alley off Market Street. Like the characters in the play, everybody knew everything about everybody: who won the lottery, played the horses, or "went to the dogs" (the kind you bet on). Be yourself was the only rule. They did nothing for show. Gram Percilla, on only my request, gave shelter and another chance to the struggling Catholic Atlantic City family when they moved to California on my recommendation. She took them in, the whole family, and when they moved out of her house, they moved into their own for the first time. She looked severe, but she gave generously.

★ ★ ★

Back in Atlantic City, Peter Sloman from de Forest came for a visit. He was serving in the Navy and stationed on the East Coast. We were both so far from family and home that I insisted he spend the night. To save money he would share my room with me. I promised I wouldn't. And I didn't, but I offered. We'd been friends for too long to change the status. Besides, Peter was waiting for a special person for sex to be special for him. I was reminded that relationship-free sex wasn't for everyone. Peter found Eileen. She was the one. She had been his wife now for almost thirty-three years. I envied them. I was eventually married that long, but it took three different husbands.

54

WELL, I ALMOST MADE it through the whole shoot. In a few days I'd be free of the whip-cracking Harold. But about three days before the production finished shooting and wrapped in Philadelphia, I cracked. The fractures in the production office that were apparent before the Christmas break widened when shooting started again. Several of the crew stopped by to say thanks for getting them home as soon as they'd wrapped and back just in time to start work again. Not Harold. He found a nit to pick and went into a rage over it. This time his screams, threats, and belittling were more than I could handle. I was proud of what I'd accomplished. I started to cry.

Harold misinterpreted the tears, thinking perhaps they were wimpy tears, and started telling me not to cry: "Keep your tears. That won't do you any good." My earliest-remembered childhood admonishment was "Don't cry. Whatever they do, don't let them see you cry." And here was this asshole... He didn't realize that the tears were an admission wrenched from my connection with the earth, how much I truly wanted to see him dead, and I was willing to do it myself.

By holding on tightly and not picking up any sharp or blunt instrument, Harold lived. I finished the last few days of the shoot. I was out of money from the visit with Kandi and Malika, and without connections to a place I could cook my meals as I had in Atlantic City. I accepted the gorgeous room service guys offer to charge my food to another room. A political act was how I rationalized it. Michelle Phillips, Jack Nicholson, Ellen Burstyn or Bruce Dern wouldn't notice a couple of small menu items. When he got caught, to my disgust, I pretended, to know nothing. I had lost my moral compass. My integrity took a hit. I broke my contract with myself, and I also quit the job, further betraying my code of responsibility, keeping agreements. I'd hired on for the entire ride, and there I was, walking out.

The trauma was shoved deep down and I was surprised years later when, seeing Harold Schneider's producer credit on a really good film, I found I was suddenly in a rage. It took more years before I could even see his name in print without that response. Reading the description of him in the book[49], that he was called a mad dog, and his nickname was The Doberman, I appreciated that he was as bad as I thought. I know people said he got over his rage quickly, and maybe he did. Still, it's not surprising he died at 55 of a heart attack.

Back to LA and West Boulevard. Back living at my mom's again and looking for work. The good thing was that the BBS-Philadelphia waiter-horror somehow was a benefit. I'd gone to a church for the first time in a very long time and I had felt connected there. Melvin's play was a wonderful experience and, despite everything, I'd done a damn good job in the production office. And, like they did on *Trek*, I'd interacted with a new life form because to me, Harold wasn't human. I

---

49   Easy Riders Raging Bulls? p. 76

had got through it and I was okay. I was looking exceptionally good and I felt it. I was finally accepting more parts of myself, loving more of myself and accepting more of imperfect me. At least a little bit more.

*   *   *

A temporary PA job with Ivan Dixon helped me out. He had finally gotten a directing break. He'd directed some of the *Hogan's Hero's* episodes and now he'd be directing his first feature film. It was another Blaxploitation crime movie. A sort of *Shaft* clone. Wonderfully, he was making it with a magnificent stage actor, Robert Hooks, a friend of his from way back. "Bobby Dean" was one of the founders of The Negro Ensemble Company, a well-respected theatre company. *Superfly* was a hit and the genre was making so much money that white producers and directors were teaching Yale-trained black actors and those from the actor's studio how to move black and speak ghetto. Like actors everywhere, black actors wanted the money and the work, so they did the *"Hollywood Shuffle"*, just like the Robert Townsend 1987 film.

In order to handle the early starts and long days required by a feature film, Ivan needed to be close to the studio. He gave me his requirements and I found exactly what he asked for—close to the studio, private and quiet, off-street parking and enough room for company. I was proud of what I'd found. A little house hidden down a long driveway, behind a large house and two blocks from the studio on a quiet street. And for the race-conscious Ivan, and a very big deal for me, it was owned by a black woman. She was fair skinned and may have "passed

54

for white" at some time in her life. I wonder what her neighbors thought she was. It was a win. She was thrilled when I told her who I was getting the place for and Ivan liked that it was hidden away. No one would know if someone visited or came home with him. He gave me a nod and continued his inspection. This was a place where he would have total freedom. No long drive home or excuses for his lateness.

I think he thought he'd start with me. "Hey, little girl. You want some of this?"

When I looked up, Ivan's penis was out, and he was refreshing it with a damp towel. I gave him ten points for the gesture. But only five for his assumption that I was itching to play his game. Getting on my knees was a position I was no longer interested in. He looked at me, and I looked back. I didn't move. I wasn't aroused, interested, or inclined. "Nah. Thanks." The person from the back seat of his mustang in the parking lot at the beach wasn't me any longer.

The accommodation turned out not to be so perfect—a disaster, actually. Each evening when Ivan got home, no matter how late, the landlady waved from her kitchen overlooking the driveway. No matter how early he'd left for work, she saw him off.

He was well brought up. Respect for elders trapped him into accepting one of the gushing old lady's numerous invitations for a cup of tea. She really did gush. Ivan told me he was desperate as he tried to deal with the olfactory evidence of her incontinence. Every time he took a sip of the peppermint tea, the rising steam cleared his nose for another assault. The odor eaters didn't even try to challenge the piss, much less the Taboo, her favorite scent since the 1940s.

I had stopped by the set to say hi and to tell him I'd been offered a job on *Mod Squad*. *Trouble Man,* his feature film, was shooting in the neighborhood at a pool hall on Western Avenue near Jefferson, opposite the best burgers in town. I admit I had to hold back a laugh at the way he told the Old Lady story. I quickly shifting into apology mode, "I'm sorry about the old lady. She was so excited. It meant a lot to her for you to be there". And I reminded him the place was exactly what he'd asked for. Sure, the apartment was everything that was on his list and I wasn't surprised about the landlady.

I changed the subject. Lunch was almost over and people were starting to wander back. A substantial number had gone across the street to Fatburger and paid for their own lunch instead of eating the free prime rib and goodies on the set. They were the ones who knew Los Angeleno insider food secrets: Philippe's French dip, and The Pantry for breakfast at 3 a.m. For burgers, a Fatburger was the burger. No in and out about it.

A Fatburger was cooked on a grill that was never ever empty. Generation after generation of flavor seeped into every molecule of the patty, the bun beside it, sizzling gently, giving the first bite an orgasmic crusty crunch. So good they franchised it. It was never the same. Snatched from its homeland and its whole being monetized, it became a different thing. Like slavery.

When I walked back to the car with a bag of Fat Burgers for the kids, the smell driving me crazy, I felt a little guilty about Ivan and a tiny bit ashamed. My blame-yourself-then-blame-them strategy was almost automatic. I ran through all the should haves and when I stopped blaming myself, the passive-aggressive me had to admit it was what he deserved.

54

I recalled every slight, real and imagined, that I had suffered from him. Calling me "coon's coon," telling me my skin wasn't dark enough, that I was shit brown, and my feeling I had no choice but the back seat of his car. The sex part wasn't a big deal to me and I recognized that, more than anything, what I was most resentful of was him not giving me a break, of him keeping the status quo: women equaled secretarial support. He kept me in "my place" as much as the white producers and directors I'd worked for. By not taking responsibility for my needs, by not maintaining my boundaries and not asking for what I really wanted, I was taking out my frustration on him. It took me a long time to realize that asking makes life a lot simpler, especially if you knew not to take 'no' personally.

55

I took the job on *Mod Squad* which was shooting at 20th Century Fox Studios. No need to cross the Mulholland divide. Drive 3 blocks up West Boulevard, left on Pico, and straight ahead. On the lot we were located behind Executive Producer Aaron Spelling's bungalow. His bungalow had belonged to child actor Shirley Temple whose curls my mother made me wear and that I cut off. The scale was right for the diminutive Aaron. His production offices were in two bungalows next to each other. In one lived *Mod Squad*, the other housed *The Rookies*—two new law enforcement series about young, good-looking, nice cops who had a different, more appropriate ways of dealing with the public. A new approach to law enforcement: acting human. And again, the show I was working on was a disruptive one with something to say. Our cops weren't in uniform and didn't ride in a squad car. They had a wood-paneled station wagon and were misfits, hippies who worked undercover. They were "black, white, and blonde," one woman and two men with equal billing and share of the scripts. The cast was Peggy Lipton, Michael Cole, and the amazing Clarence Williams III.

The Rookies had a black guy as well. Georg Stanford Brown

was a friend I'd made while working at Universal and one of the people Mark had distanced me from after we'd married. Georg was of Cuban heritage and was married to Tyne Daly, a white actor and the daughter of a famous television actor. He and his wife had featured in a magazine photo essay called, "Mr. and Mrs. Brown Go for a Walk." The photo essay showed them getting a lot of stares which ranged from surprise, curiosity, hostility and anger. Didn't see any smiles. We shared stories about the looks, comments and treatment we'd received as an interracial couple and had found a way to laugh about it.

Like *Trek*, *Mod Squad* had had an interracial kiss. Nichelle and Bill and Clarence and Peggy. Each time, though they were years apart, the producer still had to sell it to the networks. Again, it was no big deal in terms of audience reaction.

I loved that Clarence's character, Lincoln Hayes, was arrested in the Watts Revolt. We'd come to the screen world via the same event. And again, it was a revolt, not a riot. In a way it was like being back at *Trek*. The issues on screen had relevance to contemporary life. A positive black and female representation, a different way of handling conflict. Three equals. Linc's speech was emulated, as often happens with black speech. His "solid" and "keep the faith" were the "beam me up" of the day. He introduced "dig it" and "groovy" to cool kids.

Easy Rider, the BBS film that I'd loved, was groundbreaking in its depiction of the counterculture. *The Mod Squad* was out more than a year before the release of *Easy Rider* and was one of the earliest attempts to deal with the counterculture. As *Trek* showed a future way of dealing with difference, *Mod Squad* showed us contemporary lives with socially relevant drama.

The things we didn't talk about like child abuse and abortion. It admitted that domestic violence could happen to "nice" people, and that, amongst the honest and law abiding, there was protest. It admitted to police brutality and corruption, and the prevalence of drugs. We even learned new initials: PTSD.

There were two producers. Tony Barrett was the old man of the series. He had worked on so many shows that he had seen and done everything...several times. Tony had a treasure, a thick three-ring binder with the plot from every TV show he'd been involved with—the characters, act endings, all the actions and beats. One size that fit many different series. After all, instead of a single lead on *Mod Squad*, he had three different approaches and personalities and they made one complex human. Tony told me something that surprised me. He and Gene Coon had talked about me and Gene had told him that I was a hell of a good writer. Gene never said that to me.

The other producer, the one who'd hired me, was Sandor Stern, a former Canadian medical doctor, still relatively new in town. An uncle had told him that show business was great, and still he needed a job he could fall back on if it didn't work. Something substantial. Medicine fit.

After writing for a few television series like *Ironside*, he became a producer on *Mod Squad*. On the first day, I made the mistake of answering the phone, "Mr. Stern's office," and was quickly corrected. It was either Sandy Stern or Dr. Stern. At least I had a choice. There was usually a hesitation if I said Dr. Stern, with people wondering if they had the wrong extension; so "Sandy Stern's office" worked for both of us.

The associate producer, a very nice guy, was the son-in-law of a network exec. He was recently out of university and learning the business. His trajectory went something like this: for four episodes he was assistant to the producer and then the associate producer—the path I'd been longing for. In his favor, he recognized his privilege. He learned the job well and had, and I'm sure is still having, a successful career as a producer, writer and teacher. He got so good; he wrote a book to share his knowledge of screenwriting.

Clarence was a good actor. Like Ivan on *Hogan's Hero*, I think Clarence was serving his time and doing nothing to distinguish himself or stand out. Hiding behind the sunglasses until he could come out and actually act again.

My relationship with Sandy was good. He liked it when Francesca would stop by, back from Cannes or from having a fling with someone on their yacht or flown by private jet for a weekend with her favorite real-life gangster. She would leave and Sandy and I would look at each other, in unison, saying, "Our lives are so boring," and they were, in comparison with hers[50].

Sandy had a psychic come in to do readings and I couldn't resist. I asked her about my love life and she informed me that there I was on "a white wire"—that there wasn't a black man in my future. My next husband would come from a country starting with "A." I grabbed a gazetteer. Maybe Algeria, but I'd flunked Arabic. Still, my favorite film was *Battle of Algiers*, brilliantly directed by Gillo Pontecorvo and the music from Ennio Morricone, my favorite composer. I'd love the film so much I'd bought the screenplay book. When Stevie Wonder, who was dating my friend, asked my favorite book, I got him

---

50   you gotta read the book. The Chocolate Bunny by Francesca Emerson.

a copy to try on his new braille reader. I realized how much that film had influenced me, especially as a way to howl. To entertain and inform. To howl!

Sandy was pleased for me when I was short listed at The AFI and went for an interview for a producer fellowship. The whited-out application I'd gotten from Francesca had been successful that far. I made sure I ticked all the boxes, and when I walked out of the interview, I was pretty sure I'd sold them.

At *Mod Squad*, watching the young guy rise to associate producer, I felt frustrated with the work I was doing. I was desperate to get a chance to join that track. I was more than frustrated at the way the system would pick and choose, and people would fight to keep others out. Like the only black director I'd worked with.

Georg Olden was a revolutionary designer, the first African American to design a postage stamp and who'd won seven Clio Awards for design, as well as designing the statuette itself. In his early fifties, he'd been ready to take on Hollywood when we'd met on *Mod Squad*. He had the support of someone high in the network back in New York and his job had come ordered from the top. He was to be given a segment to direct and it was one of Sandy's, so I got to watch it play out. The first assistant director was totally pissed off. He wanted to direct and was standing in line, kissing up to producers, wanting his turn. That someone from outside had gotten in ahead of him pissed him off. He covered it well and smiled at Georg during the day then made fun of him when they wrapped and he came in to hang out with Sandy. Sandy was new and may have relied on the first AD's opinions and approval. One of the things Georg had shot was an interesting two-shot using an arm to frame it, almost "a peeking through the keyhole" point of view. They laughed behind his back and called it his armpit shot. It was interesting. He wasn't shooting the usual, wide-establishing shot and close-up reaction shots. He was trying to be inventive, creative and tell a unique story. Not in Hollywood you don't; the company wanted the standard master shot and cut-aways.

I hinted to him that things weren't what they seemed and offered suggestions of what he needed to be on the lookout for and to do. His response was dismissive. I was only a secretary, so what did I know? A few months after directing the episode, he moved to LA, certain he would find work, ready for a TV career. He couldn't get hired and found out he had a bad reputation. He came to me to check and I had to tell him what I'd tried to tell him. People had smiled in his face but his throat had been cut so slickly that he didn't know 'til he looked over his shoulder and his head fell off'. I thought it was good he was renting instead of buying. Sadly, Georg didn't have a fair go at Hollywood. His girlfriend shot and killed him before he'd cracked it.

56

I was accepted at the American Film Institute's center for advanced film studies. Wonder of wonders, I got one of the twenty two-year long fellowships they awarded. I was grateful to be one of the two blacks that were chosen each year. More than 2,000 people had applied, so even if it was a token spot, it was a thrill to win the chance to be there. I hadn't been picked for anything since the Betty Crocker Homemaker of the Year award, in high school my senior year. That surprised the hell out of the home economics teacher who'd given me a D and humiliated me in class when I answered red beans and rice to her asking the class what we'd had for dinner. "Two starches," she said, disdainfully ignorant of their plant protein. I had won the award for an essay on the housewife of the future. It didn't occur to me that I'd won a writing prize for a science fiction piece.

The AFI was my best chance to move into the spot I'd wanted. I had to stop waiting for it, hinting or asking the men for a chance. AFI would give me the credentials and show what I had. As much as I enjoyed working with Sandy, I gave him notice that I was out of there. His parting gift was a caricature of him—a mop of curly hair and happy eyes that said, "He who doth not surpass his master fails him."

Clarence, who never had much to say to me, shoved an envelope into my hand and said, "Don't you tell anyone... Get your kids some Christmas presents," and walked away... which contrasted with Michael or Peggy, who had also very publicly given gifts. There were several hundred dollars in the envelope. Christmas was taken care of. I happily hit my favorite spot, the dubbing stage, for one last time, swung by the editing suites and then I was gone. *Mod Squad* had been a job, I wanted a career. AFI could make that happen.

Greystone Mansion had been the suburban estate of the Doheny family. They called it "the farm." One story connected to it included a murder suicide. The journey was back through my old neighborhoods. West Blvd to San Vicente to Doheny Drive, then up through the hills of Beverly to Greystone.

In the Greystone parking lot above the mansion, I parked next to the same model BMW. Great! There was someone there with whom I'd shared cool taste in cars. I was hoping to fit in and stand out—to get the contacts and training to do what I wanted to do. It was costing me. For this opportunity I was living with my mom, on unemployment and accepting charity from my always supportive friend, Roz Heller, because this could help me break through the wall, ceiling—whatever it was. Looking down from the parking lot, I saw formal gardens, flagstones, and ponds. A magical place with a lush terrace from where on smog-free days, you could see the ocean and Catalina Island. It had a winding staircase and bathroom scales built into the floor. And the smell of passion...for making movies.

A big reason the fellowships were coveted and so highly competitive was because it wasn't an ordinary school. The AFI

Conservatory, a graduate level program, was becoming the most famous of all film schools in the United States, a special place to grow as filmmakers. AFI gave filmmakers support and actual experience in a cloistered environment. We made our films like any production company, hiring actors and equipment. Only we got special rates, special treatment and access. We were special! Prominent directors and actors dropped by, and some were invited guests who spoke with us, and some like Michael Winner, who hadn't yet made the *Death Wish* series and wasn't someone we admired, even invited themselves.

The European influence was strong from our Polish and Czech teachers. František Daniel had studied and worked in film in a Moscow, possibly still influenced by Eisenstein, the man who invented the film montage. He taught Milos Forman screenwriting and had produced *The Shop on Main* Street, which won Best Foreign Film Oscar in 1966. He taught us how to read a film, to understand all aspects of the craft—specially to develop the ability to improvise. And Roman Harte told stories of cinematographers in Poland who didn't touch a movie camera till they demonstrated lighting proficiency with a black-and-white still camera.

I could reach my goal from this hill. I'd get interned to a top TV show. I'd be able to view and participate in every step of the process, be privy to every decision. I'd be able to give input, and hopefully they'd give me a chance to carry out appropriate assignments. I was the only Producing Fellow, so I had no competition. But there was no producer's program.

"There was a problem with the producer's program last year and we've decided to cancel it." The AFI Admin didn't say exactly that. But yes, that's what it amounted to. The gossip was that the last producing fellow had been so shocked by the raw realness of the people and actions he'd seen that he'd quit the program, they'd cancelled it until they could rework it. This was a reversed "language on the dubbing stage situation." I knew what language the real world spoke. I could handle it. No, no. They especially didn't want a woman going into that environment. Again, a woman was deemed too delicate. I was told now I had to choose either cinematography, directing, or writing.

Sandy had replaced me. I didn't have a job to go back to. AFI was still a fantastic opportunity. Even though I couldn't do producing, I was at a fantastic film school, so might as well stay.

I had zero interest in cinematography. The thought of directing terrified me. Directors had bigger egos than I had. They were more confident. They weren't afraid to make snap decisions. They were able to instantly say what they wanted in a more direct way than I could manage. My decision making took more time and I was prone to overthink.

George Stevens, Jr., the AFI director, was biblical in his assertions of the director as the true author of the film, dismissing the important of the writer. The Auteur theory. No way, no choice. I couldn't handle directing. Translation: I was lacking in experience and confidence at that point.

The only choice was writing. It was an asset for a producer to be a good writer. I could live with it because one of the AFI perks was being able to ask to work with any professional in the industry. If I was going to have to do writing, I wanted to work with someone whose work had stirred emotion in me. Not necessarily because it was a black film like *Nothing but a Man* or Melvin's or one of the Blaxploitation films. They gave pride in seeing self-reflected, but it was not what I wanted. I wanted universal. Someone whose howl had awakened me to understand care and feel compassion about someone different than myself. Even better, something that stirred me to tears of laughter or sorrow. I didn't think I could write comedy, so it had to be sorrow. *Midnight Cowboy* was that film. I wanted Waldo Salt, the screenwriter, to mentor me. They had bragged they could put me with most anybody I wanted. When I told them who I wanted, they turned pale and ran away. They didn't, actually. They just gave me the run-around.

Someone who had been an insider explained what had happened. Waldo Salt was one of the people who was blacklisted during the HUAC,[51] era. (whitelisted is more accurate). Immediately, my request put me on the radar of the director and chairman of the board, gun lobbyist Charlton Heston. I felt I was in a right-wing hotbed. After all those years, the HUAC now had an effect on me. For the first time I was a target because of being a liberal in a conservative enclave. Roy Cohn was the success story at HUAC. It was he who'd taught Trump to lie extensively and to accuse others of his own dirty tricks. To delay, delay, delay.

Writer John Bloch came in to coach the writers. He was not Waldo Salt caliber. He had credits on twenty-five television shows. I knew and liked him. His wife, Ruth, I also liked. She had recently died, and he was having a life makeover. Teaching was part of it. He had broken my heart when he'd told the story of being in the shower when the telephone rang. Automatically, he called out: "Ruth! Hey, Hun, would you get that?" and the

---

51   The House Un-American Activities Committee.

realization that she would never do that again brought him to his knees. I felt that pain acutely. He started dating a young man and that seemed somehow wrong to me. I hated that. Like racism, systemic oppression included homophobia and had seeped in at a deeply unconscious level. I was confused with what he had seemed and what I then saw. But he was happy. Had he been bewitched? Mesmerized? Blinded, seduced? Where had I learned that? My "yes, but" attitude took a long time to shed. Gays and blacks were subjected to the same old images, attitudes, and beliefs that I was still unaware I held.

I made a short film about a young black girl who runs track and whose mom has a white husband and a new baby girl. It was about being estranged from her culture because she lived in the Valley where she rarely saw anyone who looked like her. The other project was a short script about taking revenge on a date-rapist. Talk about autobiographical and write what you know. It got me lots of strange looks from my classmates!

The good parts of being at AFI were meeting and mixing with filmmakers who would one day show up, and show off on the screen, and become well-known and regarded industry professionals. It was always a delight to run into cinematographer Fouad Said. I got a "one of us vibe" from him, even though he was from Egypt and not my hood. A minority in Hollywood, bright, knowledgeable in his arts, known for his excellent work and cute. He worked on *Across 110th Street* after developing what would be the Cinemobile when he was the cameraman on *I Spy*.

Fouad totally transformed studio filmmaking. With his mobile cine invention, he could take the equipment to the shooting location and save an enormous amount of money.

People were getting tired of seeing a stock shot followed by an interior shot. Audiences wanted realism and, rather than building an expensive fake, they got the real thing for $500 instead of building it for $40,000. With Cinemobile you got mobile access to the most advanced camera equipment in the world. It made low-budget films more accessible. And all black films were low-budget films. And profitable—until the fad moved on, killed by the belief that "there was limited audience for black films." It was said, "overseas markets definitely didn't want them." They made it come true. If there were no films, there was no audience. No blockbuster-budgeted black-themed films arrived for more than fifty years. *Black Panther* destroyed the overseas-sales myths. I was writing this on the day the film's lead, Chadwick Boseman, died. It was my fantasy that one day I would meet him. "Wakanda, Forever."

Suddenly AFI cancelled the Fellowships and imposed a fee on the merit-based scholarship that allowed me to study without financial pain. I loved AFI. With no income, I couldn't justify continuing. Other fellows, like Jon Avnet and Doe Mayer, had no problems with paying. Their last names told that story. Neither of my projects was finished to the level I was happy with. I buried them. My film studies were over. I had no choice.

I had gained a great film education, which made it so much harder to watch a bad film. František Daniel had been a great teacher. I'd already loved film, and he'd taught me how to read and understand it. We would watch a segment forward and backwards at full and at half speed with and without sound, breaking down the aspects: editing, sound, direction, camera movement, effects, visual and aural. Every little piece. It wrecked a lot of adequate films for me and made the joy from a well-crafted piece beyond measure. Exquisite little details made me delirious, like an Easter egg to a Marvel fan.

I left AFI after one final little howl. With no appointment I went into Stevens Jr.'s office for the last time. He was busy. When "the director is author of the film" finally looked up at me, I slapped a thick stack of paper on his desk. He looked down, it was obvious that the paper was all blank. "Shoot that!" I told him and walked out, leaving AFI thinking I'd gotten all I could from there. I was wrong: AFI had another gift for me. A very big one!

57

IVAN HAD FINISHED SHOOTING and editing *The Spook Who Sat by The Door* from one of my favorite books. He was a bit nervous about post-production. He asked me to give him a hand with *Spook*. I don't have to tell you; post-production is one of my favorite places to be. I was *thrilled*. Finally I wasn't a. sex target, I was a contributor. He accepted that I knew what I was doing, as I sat next to him with a note pad and pen, props which didn't get used. I wasn't taking down notes from him—I was whispering answers to his questions: What was going on with special effects, color corrections, or sound mixing. Suggesting options he had.

Herbie Hancock who would compose the music for the film came by while we were working, I attempted to impress him with my AFI back ground; but I didn't know how to pronounce film director Michelangelo Antonioni'. 's name, calling him "An-toe-ni-ni". Herbie corrected me, to my embarrassment. It wasn't to be my most embarrassing interaction with a black hero. The next for me would be much, much worse.

After *Spook* finished, I was looking for something else that would lead toward producing. The closest I came to a possibility was working with Godfrey Cambridge on a pilot called the *Furst Family*; but it didn't sell and now I was desperately needing a job.

Sandy Stern was producing *Doc Elliot* a new TV series and invited me to go back to work for him. He'd moved to the Burbank Studios on the Warner Brothers lot. Finally, I had crossed that last line and I was actually working in Burbank. I let go of my long-held 'black people don't work in Burbank' because it was where I found the best submarine sandwiches I'd ever had. I still made sure, just in case, that I was out by sundown[52]. It was summer so that wasn't hard.

I was working for Lorimar, the same production company that produced *The Waltons*, a hit TV series. Actor John Wayne's office was near ours. He walked past our front door with that funny, pigeon-toed, prissy walk and wearing a very tall cowboy hat, he paused, hawked up a loogie and spat it out at our front door. "Sandy," I asked, "do you think he knows we're here?" Sandy's Jewish. I'm black. Could be?

Sandy was glad to have me back. *Doc Elliot* was about a small-town medical doctor and, given Sandy's background, would seem on the surface to be easy. Besides being happy to return to work for Sandy, I was delighted that Ros Taylor was back in town.

★ ★ ★

The weirdest encounter brought Ros back. She had been living on a small, rural Florida property her grandmother

---

52 Sundown towns or suburbs are all white and practice excluding non-whites by local laws, intimidation or violence. They had signs posted that "colored people have to leave by sundown".

had left her, working in a small hair salon in an even smaller town where she accidently, magically met Flip Wilson, comic and TV star. Before she was a bunny, she had trained as a hairdresser and was in an adjoining room having lunch when she heard his voice. Impulsively, exuberantly, Ros sang out a welcome: "Is that my king?" "Is that my queen?" he responded and when Ros showed herself, he was very pleased at her petite perfection. He swept her up and back to his castle. Basically, when they saw each other, a connection was made. I understood that happening. And her cooking sealed the deal. She returned to LA, to a beachfront mansion in Malibu. His kids fell in love with her and her cooking and she fell in love with them. She was happy being at home looking after and feeding them. I hoped she had truly found her "king." Turned out he may have been her killer.

Ros sent the driver with the Rolls to pick me up so I could stay the weekend. We ended up in bed. With Flip. I wasn't that interested in Flip, nor he with me. I was happy to be with her. I had missed her so much and didn't dare examine that feeling. I was grateful to be spending time with her again. I loved the beach. The sunken living room and fireplaces plus the bathrooms were fantastic. The shower, sprays coming from every direction, were wonderful and I was envious of the heated-tiled bathroom floor. So that's what it meant to be rich.

Hanging out the following evening, with a few people, all of them paying tribute to Flip and anointing their noses from the large covered crystal bowl filled with cocaine, raiding the tall apothecary jar filled with joints rolled by Ros the perfect hostess.

I loved Flip's show. I hadn't been impressed by him in bed or in conversation. Watching him preening for the group,

I didn't like him much at all. He was strolling around in a beautiful cream silk embroidered kimono. I watched as he stretched out on the floor, on the thick carpet and I noticed on the back of his kimono, a dark line that curved with him. As he shifted, the dark stripe barely moved, and I could see it was a skid mark. Mr. Cool couldn't even wipe his butt clean.

But it was Mr. Can't-wipe-his-butt's chauffeur who drove me from Malibu to Burbank in Mr. Can't-wipe-his-butt's Rolls Silver Shadow. I was a little disappointed, I had hoped that it would be the Cornice, with license plates that said "Killer." Still, it was another super-cool, way-out-of-my-budget, once-in-a-lifetime-ever ride.

I wanted someone I knew to see me in it. There was a phone in the back to talk to the driver, and I grabbed it when we stopped at a red light. Next to the Rolls was one of the black-day players I'd known. He was in his reasonably late model Mercedes with the top down and trying to not be obviously sneaking a peek to see what big name was in the Rolls. I slid the window down and reached out the handset. "I think this call is for you." His jaw dropped and then he laughed. The light changed: "Do have your secretary send me an autograph," I called out to him as the Rolls glided away. We'd had a lovely moment. I had acknowledged I saw him and that he was doing well. It felt good. We were community.

58

A VISIT FROM AUTHOR and activist, James Baldwin lifted my spirit. We'd been introduced by Lincoln Kilpatrick, a NY actor. Baldwin was working nearby, on a film script about Malcolm X and stopped by to chat with me. What a sweet man! I had been shy when I'd met him with Lincoln. This was the first time I hadn't been nervous about talking to him. Sort of on my turf and I was safe. Baldwin approached me gently. He seemed so small and quiet and those eyes were tender. 'You knew Malcolm?"

"Yes, he was my friend."

"Mine too."

We were connected. He was unsure of this Hollywood world. He hadn't played here before, but he recognized the type of people. He was having troubles with the suits who still insisted on making black films from a white point of view. The usual with black people movies and most frustrating when it's someone or something you admired. James Baldwin was an icon. He was a deity. I could call him Jimmy. Wow! I shared Melvin's Columbia execs dinner party experience with him and my own BBS Harold Schneider story. We laughed that they wanted us back in the past. Those eye-rolling, teeth-chattering, ghost-fearing lackeys. I confessed to him my embarrassment at having a dearly loved uncle whose name was Willie and the taunts from the kids because of Willie Best, a black actor who worked with Bob Hope, The Marx Bros, Laurel and Hardy and 3 films with child star Shirley Temple in movies and had eye rolling, shuffling, parts in 118 films. I hid from Jimmy that, in those long-ago *Tarzan* movies on a Saturday afternoon, I'd wanted to be Jane, not one of those natives. I would have preferred Tarzan, but at least Jane had beautiful hair—as far as I could tell. Growing up, I didn't realize how rare it was for actors to be able to sneak a bit of real black into the scripts. How talented actors like Willie Best were to successfully portray those caricatures. I loved films and believed they were telling the truth. I know why I did think that!

At Burbank, the Lorimar folk were friendly and Earl Hamner, the Walton's creator, sounded like Wyatt Tee Walker. His voice melted me, even when he was saying goodnight to John-Boy on screen. Made me fall in like with him. It seemed returned. He always had a big smile when he saw me and made time to chat.

James Franciscus, the star of the *Doc Elliot* series, had helped disrupt the image of disability when his *Longstreet* series character challenged what we had been taught about blind and crippled people. Bruce Lee had appeared with him as his martial arts instructor and they'd been close. Because of that *Doc Elliot* shut down the day we got the news that Bruce Lee had died.

The people I worked with were fine. It was a boring show. Still, I could always learn something. I was always comfortable working with Sandy. Whatever feeling of "the two of us" was dispelled one day, and I woke up to my position in that universe.

Sandy was having a problem with the script. The motivation didn't work. The conflict didn't work. I thought I knew what was wrong. I had an idea and when I suggested it, it wasn't a way Sandy was used to thinking. He was thinking doctor-patient and I was thinking patient-doctor. The patient's justification, thoughts and needs would determine behavior. How they viewed the doctor's ability to satisfy their needs, to trust and believe he could. Sandy grabbed it. To me it was common sense. It motivated the character and it justified some good action.

Sandy was quickly on the phone to the network with the solution. When he swaggered back to my desk, I could tell by the smile on his face that they'd liked it. "They wanted to know what I'd been smoking," he chortled. "They love it!"

II'm pleased, then for some reason, I'm waiting for him to give me credit for my suggestion, to acknowledge my idea had helped him overcome the script problem. Nothing came. He's the writer, the producer, I'm the secretary and I ought to know that is my place.

I tell myself to stop thinking about being more, to stop thinking my contributions were valued, stop thinking I was a creative person. "You are a secretary, a black woman without a university degree, without relatives in the industry. You don't count and stop thinking you do". I was upset. A little bit of hope vanished.

If Sandy had acknowledged my idea, would that have sent me happily back to the plantation? Deep down, what was I? Maybe the world had been tantalizing me all this time? Just a joke? You can't join... You've been doing everything to qualify and there's no way you'd ever be let in. I was the house servant, the hired help, not a partner or collaborator. If I didn't change, things would never be any different.

★ ★ ★

Rosilyn Heller had grown even more powerful at Columbia. She had news—good news for me. There was a new women's group forming. It's called Women in Film. She is part of it and will let me know what's happening. I didn't intend to start hoping again, but Rich White Ladies had always been an untamable source of power when they put their mind to something. The women's movement had put aside the terror tactic they'd employed in gaining the vote and copied the Civil Rights movement that many of them had participated in. And more than that, their gains were visible. They were happening!

Everything I read about Tichi Wilkerson said she could be the one that would lead the breakthrough. I'd heard she had married her mom's boss, many years older than her, and gone to work at the powerful industry news publication he'd founded: The Hollywood Reporter.

Billy Wilkerson contributed to the "red scare" of the HUAC witch hunt that forced Waldo Salt and so many out of the industry or to hide behind pseudonyms. The existence of Hollywood was reflected from its pages and, when he died, she was ready and able to take over as the Hollywood Reporter's Publisher and Editor. Tichi was the RWL that could be the spearhead. A power player who had started a women's film association with the aim of getting women in front of and behind the camera, as well as across all levels of production.

I tried not to feel any hope, to not risk disappointment again. But the childhood myth rose up and awakened the stories I'd heard in the beauty shop: that a rich white lady said, a rich white lady fought, hired, bought, educated, helped. What I'd experienced with the librarian, nuns, in government jobs, saw them rising from the ranks. It was doable. And with them I could too.

Roz made sure I would be at the big meeting and took me. The excitement level was high. The speakers were focused and determined. Discussions broke out immediately after the talk finished. I wasn't good at chatting. As we shuffled from our seats, in my excitement I overcame my shyness, and started to chat to a woman. I was feeling the excitement, the hope and this was my chance to join with other women who had been denied. Women who loved film, who wanted to say something. I shared my Gene Coon "men would have to watch their language" story with her. She and I were in total agreement until I mentioned that being black made it even harder for me. Her words surprise me. "No," she tells me, "Being black doesn't matter; it's only because you're a woman." I don't believe what I'm hearing.

"Yes, it does,", is my schoolyard response.

"No, really it doesn't," she affirms from the same level. With great authority she continues, "It's the fact that you are a woman, not your color." I don't believe someone in this room would say that. This is a room of helpers, damn it! People who want to change things. I look to Roz, but she's surrounded by women.

Harlan Ellison had given me a copy of his book *I Have No Mouth, and I Must Scream*. And that was exactly how I felt

I started again. From the beginning. As we are women, we're both denied by the industry. Black or white. That we agreed on. But when I say again the factor of my skin needs to be acknowledged, she immediately disputes the validity that color is important. No, she argues it doesn't count; it's just being female. She's won't even acknowledge the possibility that it's a factor.

I was pissed off at my inability to explain intersectionality which I innately understood; but the action was not yet acknowledged and the word was not yet in existence. How to tell her she was making my color disappear, making me even more invisible? And, darn, I hated being told I was wrong about something I felt so strongly about and had experienced. Also politically, it was a disappointment because we were women who needed to stick together.

She was calling me a liar, denying my experience, my heritage, my oppression, generations of systemic discrimination. This was once again the white suffragettes giving into the southern white women. "For unity", putting the black suffragettes at the back of the parade, not letting them march together with the women they'd organized with from their state. She was going to make sure she benefited. The hell with us.

It feels like a bad movie where the friends turn out to be the ones behind the evil plot. I can tell that between this woman and me is a wall of prejudgment, which to me equals total powerlessness. My brain twists and turns looking for some incident amongst the many, something to share, to help her to understand.

"Yes but, yes but, I'm the only black woman on the studio

lot, the only woman who can't rent an apartment close by the studio." I was thoroughly pissed off now. She began to morph from she to them. I was the woman who got humiliated and terrified by police with hands near their guns for absolutely no reason. When she responded, "Yes, but," my hearing shut down. We were no longer discussing.

Fuck you! My fists assumed an Archie Moore position. We got closer to and more entrenched in our rightness, tempers coming to the boil. Our voices didn't gain in volume but had an impending violence—at least on my part. Caution asked me how would that look here in front of all these people?

Fuck all of you, I wanted to scream. "How fucking dare you," and my answer came back. "Because she can!"

Suddenly the room was no longer safe. I recognized she's no different than the men. She wasn't somehow one of my allies because she'd suffered the deficit of not being male. Her vagina was her primary identity. And equally her white skin.

She saw nothing but the gender discrimination. Anything else was disruptive, inconsequential or secondary. Anything which might rectify that inequality would lessen her chance, would weigh more heavily in my favor. That would be unfair. To her. Her attitude supported structural racism. A not racist rather than antiracist. [53]

And, there weren't that many blacks in the industry. A look around the room shows none. Don't need to fight for a few others, don't need slow the progress of many for a few. Put the black women in their place in the back of the march, just like the suffragettes.

---

53 Be Antiracist : A Journal for Awareness, Reflection and Action

Color overrides gender. I shut up, back up, and move away to join a conversation with Roz. The statistics say affirmative action has benefited white woman the most[54]. The whip is still the whip, only in a smaller hand.

It was too bad we hadn't connected. She was certainly skilled and capable. I understand she became influential in the industry. I hope she assisted, supported, and mentored lots of black women. I don't bother mentioning her name because I'm sure we had differing views of the encounter. Black and white women have had a problematic relationship, and It's sometimes a minefield for me today. Often it depends on what country the woman is from.

---

54 https://www.teenvogue.com/story/affirmative-action-who-benefits

59

I was still legally married to Mark Reese who had offered me a time-out. I agreed to go with him to Hong Kong for six weeks while he settled into a new job teaching at a university. I promised myself that, when I got back from Hong Kong, I'd re-evaluate and gather support for what I wanted to do. I had plans. I was going to learn how to sell my ideas. Do what David Rintels told us, slam my hand down on their desk and yell how it was the greatest and most bankable script ever written.

Gene Coon definitely had to help. He owed me for that dubbing stage-language-bullshit. I was going to ask the brothers that I knew in the industry for their help and definitely I needed to reintroduce myself to Clarence Avant and Ewart Abner.

Mark had gotten visas for the whole family, but Kandi balked at the vaccinations necessary for travels then. Kandi decided she's had enough and said, emphatically, "I am not no pin cushion. I am not going to no hongi kongi." She would stay with her father for the weeks I was going to be away.

My AFI connection surprise came from the black woman Fellow from the previous year. She was from Success Avenue, a street in Watts that we saw as a joke. She was nice. I liked her; but to me, she was a bit slow. I'm sure now that it was just my bias because she came from Watts, not the Westside like me. Back then I thought where you grew up made a difference.

She generously connected me with a company that was looking for black movie projects to invest in. They'd invested in her project and were looking for more. Their headhunter interviewed me on the telephone then I met with the company members at a Lebanese belly dance restaurant and later on their yacht.

On their yacht! I tried to act like I went on yachts frequently, while Mark and I worked in tandem to convince The Company guys that we are the people they wanted to invest in.

I figure it didn't hurt to take the white boy along, I'm black enough for both of us. We tell them about *BlackSmith*, the script Mark and I wrote about a drug trial in the black community. We have a shooting script; it's very low budget and it has solid attachments. I drop names, from MLK to MVP, Martin to Melvin. I do my best to impress them with my knowledge and background. Inflating my titles a little, but not exaggerating my passion. We stressed to the potential investors that our film is doable. The low-budget, I-have-friends, know-people, will-be-getting-all-the-freebies-I can. "We can possibly make it on $80K. They are so enthusiastic that they'll give us a check right there. Except it won't be $80K. They are going to mentor and manage the business with us, and they'll take back a retainer of 25%. Would I please give them a check for $20,000? I don't have that much in my account. Yes, but when the $80K clears it will be there.

All good. They hand me a check for $80,000, and I give

them one for $20,000. When I deposited the check, the receipt said my balance was $80,024.00.

Who would have thought the answer would come from such an unexpected source. They know that I am going to Hong Kong. That was no problem. It's part of a government incentive program for minority business investment. They'd be working on a management plan to assist me with all the technical and financial stuff and lots of paperwork. "It's the government" they shrug. I was only going to be in Hong Kong for six weeks to help Mark get settled. I'd come back full of ideas and enthusiasm.

The headhunter that initially interview us is excited but some of the things he says about their search for investments makes me wonder. Not enough to think any more about it.

★ ★ ★

The 1973 Writer's Strike was truly over. People were working again. Things were happening. People celebrating. Mark wanted us to go with him to a last party. It's okay with me because I needed to start networking seriously.

The party was in Bel Air. Richard Dreyfuss, who was about to be a star in *Jaws*, was in the pool playing with 28-month-old Malika, watched over by Mark when I recognize Leslie Uggams and sit down next to her. "Hi, Leslie. I'm a friend of Godfrey Cambridge." I let out my breath when she smiled and said hi. "That's his goddaughter." I indicate Malika, being entertained. We'd never met, but Godfrey was a friend of both of us, and that basically boiled down in Hollywood to being friends. To let her know she wouldn't be stuck with me and to signal I'm cool. I casually drop, "Be nice to spend the day here, but I gotta get home and pack." She looked politely interested. "I'm leaving soon; got a big packing job." Casually I volunteer as though she'd asked, "Going overseas. Heading into the sunset."

She looked mildly interested. "My husband's going to be teaching at a university." Curiously she responded. "Well don't go to Australia."

I don't get it. "No, I'm just going to Hong Kong."

I can't help myself. "But what's wrong with Australia?"

She told me that because they only wanted white people, even though she was married to an Australian. "Why," I asked. The answer turned into a wave of information.

Basically that, with a small population, they had protected themselves against a feared onslaught of Asians and other non-whites by restrictions on countries allowed in and strict skin color discrimination. The White Australia Policy. She said there's a new prime minister, Gough Whitlam and has heard that things were less restrictive than it had been, but racism was probably still around.

I take my eyes off Malika for a moment's processing. When I check as mothers do, Richard was gone; Mark was involved in a conversation, and Malika was sinking, going under the water. I screamed, Mark grabbed for her, and I'm poolside as he carried her over to me. She's been startled by his grab and looked about to cry.

I reached towards her, smiling at her, and I say, "Look at this nice towel I've got for you. I'm going to wrap you up, and we're going to find you some clothes. Would you like to wear the green shirt with the frog or...?" babbling as though it's all just fun, channeling what almost happened into normal so that she wouldn't be freaked. I wanted her associations with water, unlike my own, to be positive. It worked. It wasn't unnoticed by the people who'd heard my shout.

I hear a woman say, "What a bitch, acting like nothing happened." I don't stop to respond. Being subject to misbelief, to people's delusions is like producing. It's all about the choices you make. Your taste, your eye, voice. The hell with them! I didn't care what they thought.

* * *

I stayed at home that week, packing, saying good-bye, making arrangement to store the BMW while I'm gone. It wouldn't be that long. I had to catch up with Gene to update him. I'm going to need to let him know he's going to find me a new job with a producer track and confirm he's coming to our going-away party. Then on Wednesday he called me. I didn't like how he sounded. He's calling to let me know that he thought he had pneumonia, and he and Jackie and Kathleen won't be able to make it to the farewell party. That's okay. I tell him he'd better get well because I'm going to need his help. He's didn't seem certain. Business wasn't going all that well with the new projects. He'd had to borrow money from Jackie's mom. Good thing she liked him and she had a rich husband.

Two days later on Friday he called back, and the news wasn't good. It's not pneumonia; it's cancer. We'd have to see how that went. Sunday, two days later Jackie calls: Gene's gone! The cancer his first wife died from was likely the same cancer that took him. They had been in Las Vegas, guests at the nuclear testing site, observing the atomic bomb blast which could have been responsible for them both dying so young. It was his resolve that had taken him so fast. I knew it was what he wanted. He'd talked about his dad's lingering with his illness. I know he didn't want that. I think he willed himself to die.

I realized my good-bye was the last time I'd gone up Laurel Canyon to visit. He teased me about my weak jeans. I checked my butt, but he meant "genes" and told me Malika could use a bit more sun.

Soon after I hung up, Flip and Ros arrived for the bon voyage in the Corniche with his "Killer" license plates. He parked right in front of the house, and when he came in was immediately the target of all the male black actors at the party. Everyone wanted to be funnier than he was, some succeed. I laughed so hard I had to go outside. I laughed so hard my stomach hurt. I laughed so hard I cried, and I cried, and I cried. Semper Fi! Gene. Semper Fi, dearest Gene.

PART IV
I DISCOVER THE CHANGES THAT FILTERS MAKE

60

She just wouldn't stop screaming. Nothing is as crazy making as full volume shrieks from a super-hyper two-year-old.

Before flying, I'd gotten something from her doctor to help her sleep on the international flight we were about to take—a stopover in Japan before continuing on to Hong Kong. I'd given Malika the maximum drops and the doctor had promised, had *assured* me she would conk out. Actually, in my rush to settle her down as soon as we boarded the plane, I'd just used a spoon instead of the dropper and she might have gotten a tad more of the syrup than the doctor had suggested. It caused the opposite effect. What was on offer now was not the sleep that people on our late-night Seattle, Washington-to-Tokyo, Japan-long flight believed they were going to get.

Malika struggled away from me and from Mark to run down the aisle...again. And this time I did care what people were thinking about me. My scenario of serenely soaring through the silent skies was shattered. Guilt magnified the time. It felt like it took hours to calm her. I didn't tell anyone I'd accidently overdosed our child with a prescribed drug. I didn't act as if it bothered me. I was maintaining my cool, reminding myself that it would be okay. And totally filled with embarrassment they couldn't see. I was sure I was already negatively affecting the image of black mothers and refused to add to the blacks and drugs fallacies.

The toddler-wrangling continued. After another capture there was some residual wriggling from Malika; then soft sobs and hiccups signaled a slowdown. Mark calmed and encouraged her towards sleep while stealthily easing her into her seat. I was led down the aisle to a row in the back with empty seats. It was suggested I take a nap too.

The dream of a drama-free flight had been crushed and another blow was to follow. In Tokyo we stayed at the Imperial Hotel where I was disappointed that the Frank Lloyd Wright addition was gone. In the elevator Malika had diarrhea that ran everywhere. When we got to our room, I put her in the bathtub, shoes and all. Things got better. We discovered and loved buying beer from street vending machines. And the food. Oh, the food!

Hong Kong! The difference between the economies of the two China's was blatant. I began to discover the meaning of luxury at Hong Kong's Kai Tak airport when the chauffeur emerged from the hotel's Rolls Royce and gently relieved Mark of his IBM Selectric typewriter, the pride and inanimate love of his life. From all the hotels at the airport information center, Mark had chosen the Peninsula Hotel. He dismissed the budget-priced ones because none of them fit his idea of his new status as a visiting scholar. He felt that a hotel offering chauffeured Rolls Royce and Jaguars for their guests was perfectly appropriate and the university was paying for it. The Academic, a new Mark personality appeared. He became Professor Adam Beeler. It was the name of his grandfather and the university position held by his mother's brother. The cracks were apparent if I had chosen to examine his behavior more critically.

I was busy taking in the new experience. I'd gone east and west and north and south, but I hadn't left the North American continent. Barely explored it. I was truly overseas now.

The weather was hot and sticky and the coolness of the Rolls and the hotel were welcome. The Peninsula Hotel was located in Kowloon, the mainland China side of Hong Kong. the only way to get between the two was a boat. And the whole thing generally was Hong Kong but Hong Kong Island and Kowloon specifically. My first night was looking through the window toward Hong Kong Island. Rickshaws were lined up waiting for riders and everybody was Asian. Now I had definitely arrived at a place where no one in my family had gone before. And I was experiencing luxury and premium service.

The Peninsula was a welcoming place where we felt cared about, tended to, and catered for. I could see how rich people were willing to do what they did. Luxury, I discovered, wasn't things; it was a feeling. All your senses were satisfied. Your perceptions and sensory acuity saturated. An immersion, not a toe-dipping.

An attendant rushed to open our door when I got out of the elevator. The Welcome basket of goodies and wine would have been a meal if we hadn't ordered room service. There was a bidet and even a telephone in the huge bathroom.

High Tea at The Peninsula Hotel was a treat Malika loved! Every day that we stayed there, we went to the lobby where it was served. Because we were hotel guests, we were ushered in, avoiding the long line waiting.

When Mark's university learned where we were staying,

they freaked; we were soon in a more modest hotel. Darn! And now we had to look for an apartment.

I had thought the housing allowance generous until I saw the crowded, miniature, dark apartments with very high price tags. It was an expensive city. Even on Kowloon, the mainland side of Hong Kong. The apartments didn't fit us. The kitchen counters were way too low and not catered to our heights and sizes.

We selected an apartment in a huge complex—Mei Fu Sun Chuen in Lai Chi Kok, Kowloon. At the time it was the largest private housing estate in the world. 13,500 apartments housing up to 80,000 people. It was right on Lai Chi Kok Bay with a waterfront walkway and apartments with waterfront balconies.

At our end, across the street, was an amusement park that featured Chinese Opera, something I never learned to appreciate. That music, combined with the noise from the street, meant we had to immediately buy a stereo with headsets in order to sleep at all. I wasn't used to that level of noise. After a while I didn't pay any attention, but the heat was something I didn't get used to as easily.

Los Angeles was dry and Hong Kong, during typhoon season, was like lifting the lid on a tamale steamer and inescapable. You could weigh the air. One of my favorite outfits was a halter top with matching loose pants and jacket. Didn't need the jacket. I started living in halter tops my cousin June had made for me. They were a simple design, easy to duplicate, and didn't require much sewing.

★ ★ ★

Our balcony had a view of the bay and the wreckage of what

had been the largest passenger ship in the world at the time, the *Queen Elizabeth*. The previous year the vacant ship, waiting to be turned into a floating university, had caught fire and burnt. I felt like the ship looked. A stay-at-home mom was another fantasy that wasn't what I'd imagined. One more dream exposed as impossible. I was the first stay-at-home mom in my line since slavery. Dr. King had told me he didn't spank his kids. I was practicing that with some success. Failures regretted.

At two years old, Malika was going through changes in behavior, and she had no restraint in expressing desires for things off limits. I felt like her puppet. When she wanted to ride a trike, we'd get dressed for the outdoors, unlock two security doors, wait for the elevator, go to the podium level of the building… And after two minutes she wanted to go back home. My frustration grew. I didn't have the resources to cope and, for a guilty moment, I thought about tossing her from the balcony into the harbor just below.

In despair, I luckily found the answer in a book about toddlers. *"Remember, you are the adult"* the author cautioned me. Yes, I was! I needed to act like it. I was the adult and she was the child; so deal with it. And I did. I got a job which enabled me to hire an amah, a local woman, to look after Malika—and got the heck out of there, telling myself that my lack of child raising skills would be enriching for the child, because it gave Malika exposure to another language and foods. That was true, but the amah turned out to be someone who admired all things British and loved taking Malika back to the Peninsula Hotel for afternoon tea.

★ ★ ★

The job I'd scored was working postproduction on a hyper-low-budget film. Improbably, I'd run into a former AFI Fellow. The AFI connected us better than an audition, interview or resume. He was American, cool and smooth talking. One of those dream-weaving film producer/directors. The film had been shot MOS and absolutely needed me on the dubbing stage.

MOS (Mit Out Sound, or Minus Optical Stripe) meant it was a film shot with no synch sound recorded. The dialogue and music/effects were added in postproduction. Most early Italian films had been shot MOS. I'd heard it was because they had very noisy post-war cameras. A bonus was it allowed them to cast for looks and not worry about how or what language the actors spoke.

Meanwhile, in the low-budget dubbing suite, I got busy with the soundtrack. I loved adding layers to enhance the images. The equipment was primitive, even the sound effects were on records. I loved the challenge.

The director had a challenge of his own. He was coaching the actors and recording the dialogue. The movie was a *Butch Cassidy and the Sundance Kid* imitation. We were a mixed bunch. Butch was a Hebrew speaking Israeli; Sundance was Cantonese and the dialogue was English. Linda, in the production office, was a neighborly Canadian and we became friends.

Mark made friends with Jash Dahale, a university colleague, who was a very bright, soft-spoken Sikh and Elizabeth his equally bright and soft-spoken British wife. We'd met at our first university faculty banquet. I didn't understand why people suddenly began to rush out when the rice and the noodles I loved were served. They explained it was the polite thing to be too full—and show it, even if you loved and wanted the noodles. "I can't eat another bite" is something every cook loves to hear. Regretfully, we ran out too.

61

MARK, MALIKA AND I settled in. Three weeks in Hong Kong and I was comfortable with shopping every day for food. I was still bargaining and negotiating prices like a newbie but was getting better at it. I had started learning Cantonese, which made the locals I tried speaking to laugh a lot. Mark was having success teaching classes. Things were going smoothly. With the amah working out so well, Mark suggested I travel around a bit before heading back to the States. He'd care for Malika, reminding me that he was a feminist and a co-parent.

Linda, the Canadian, had been telling me stories of The Hippie Trail. She insisted they weren't tourists; they were travelers. They were different. What she described sounded like '60's people. My people!

Mark had been getting along very well and he hadn't mentioned Professor Adam Beeler again. Or becoming black. Maybe the identity thing had passed, said my fantasy that things between Mark and me might magically change by being away from the U.S.

I thought about it, debating whether it was ethical to use some of the film money to take a short trip. I didn't doubt that Malika would be safe with him. I was much more casual and trusting in my child than I had a right to be. The hippie 'everything will be cool'. I overthought it long enough for that last dream to get pooped on.

Mark invited students to a get-to-know-everyone party. He got to know one student very well. They were in the bedroom a very long time while I reassured her boyfriend that it was all innocent. It could have been. When he came out of the room, I realized Mark had come out just to get refreshments. I growled, "Screwing your student isn't ethical." He smirked. "Her boyfriend's my student—not her," and nonchalantly moved through the crowd and back into the bedroom, carrying two cold drinks. If the daggers I threw had substance, he would have been dead before he touched the door knob.

My RWL, perfect-hostess persona had been drug induced, a gift of the first Australians I'd met. I'd been wishing for a joint when Mark had brought them home and they had supplied the first weed I had in Asia.

As usual, the cannabis lifted my mood and there was something else. I felt in an altered state. My everything felt good! When the Aussies had arrived at the party early, I had a chance to find out more. Yes, a little something had been added to the weed. Heroin. I hadn't expected that. I was surprised that it could be smoked. The image I had was a spare-toothed, unkempt, skinny person with a needle in their arm or Rizzo from *Midnight Cowboy*.

Needles were a big no for me. The powder could also be snorted, and yes, they'd had some with them. I'd wanted to try it again. Had to. And it had made me a great hostess. I was a perfect hostess. When the party was finally over and the girl and her boyfriend were leaving with the others, my goodbye was friendly. I even invited them back, which Mark mockingly echoed. His barely veiled suggestion to "come anytime" lit my fuse.

An instant before my fury-fueled brick bounced off the door as Mark ducked behind it, back into *our* bedroom, which was now his "love nest." My ammunition dump was the materials for a partially assembled bookcase. He stuck his head out to offer his rationale. "We're separated; we aren't getting back together and you are leaving soon." Yep! He was totally right. I recognized how often this feeling had occurred. These feelings were coming from an old pattern. It was the "go away, come back" from my time with Jai. No punching, no black eye this time. Actually, I didn't want Mark. I was just pissed off.

At my passive-aggressive best, I chose the *"I'll* take poison and wait for *you* to die" option. In my new blue suede leather jacket, I took the elevator down to the harbor and walked along past the junks and the families living and working on board—and dumping their shit into the harbor.

I climbed over the railing at a dismantled pier. The thought of being helpless in water terrified me; so I doubt I was serious about drowning myself. Also, I saw turds floating in the water, fat ones, an audience of them. Then I noticed the other shit that was also floating there. Condoms, wrappers, dead rats. They really did shit in their living space. There was no way I was getting in that.

I'd taken my jacket off in preparation for my suicide and it fell in. I insisted that Mark climb down and rescue it. A minor payback. My new leather jacket spent the evening stinking in the bath tub. The jacket wasn't salvageable. Neither was my marriage. I was just biting off my nose to spite my face, not yet recognizing I didn't have to do that.

62

LIKE A *TREK* EPISODE, I was inhabited by a character who was changing the meanings of what I saw, giving me new filters, other points of view.

I discarded mental shackles in Hong Kong when I discovered I was a *gweilo*. It once meant "foreign devil," but the actual translation was "ghost person"—the way they saw the first white people. Then it became just a rude term used to reference any foreigner. (And it's now also a beer brand and a restaurant in Sydney.) In 1973, in Hong Kong, I knew I was one. All foreigners were. Europeans, Africans, SE Asians, including Indians, Polynesians, Micronesians and any other islanders and Antipodeans, and often, according to some unknown measure, sometimes overseas Chinese. Basically, we were all the same to them. We were other, just barely accepted as different. "You can't tell about them," a friend translated as the bus driver and a few passengers debated my gender. For the first time in my life, the discrimination wasn't about black skin. I had lots of company of every color and we were all *gweilos*.

I became closer friends with Linda and she agreed with Mark that I should have a look around. She was in Hong Kong just to earn money and get a new visa. She lived in Bali with a boyfriend who worked on an oil rig. The film was finished and her Indonesian visa had been renewed. She wanted me to visit her and see Bali.

What I knew about Bali was that "Bali Hi" was a song in the Rogers and Hammerstein musical *South Pacific* about a mystical island that was calling, "Come to me, come to me, your own special hopes, your own special dreams." I had been ten and impressionable and I'd fallen in love with the song. Juanita Hall had sung it for almost 2,000 performances on Broadway and became the first African American to win a Tony Award for best supporting actress.

I'd already had enough of Hong Kong. People laughed at my struggle to speak Cantonese. I did okay with survival needs. They could understand my Cantonese when I ask if they had my favorite Tsingtao beer and how many bottles I wanted. Perhaps it was the necessity of beer or need to make a phone call, but they always knew what I wanted. When I greeted my neighbors with a *"ne' ho ma"* in the morning or a "haven't seen you lately," they laughed. I thought it was derision, but later I reckoned it was just the sight of the big black woman trying to speak to them in their language. Or maybe I was fooling myself and asking if their cow had a twin sister. I could have used a *Trek* universal translator. They have them these days.

Hong Kong was too crowded and I didn't deal well with the rude people who would elbow me while walking down the jam-packed sidewalks or cut in front of me in the bus lines. I learned to walk with my elbows out and jab them before they jabbed me. I was a lot heavier and taller than most; so I sent a few people reeling. Malika was adaptable. I let her walk on her own without holding her hand. I could track her by people looking down to see what had just banged on their knee to get them out of the way.

My tits were eye level to many of the men and that was where their eyes stayed. I would sometimes duck down and make eye contact and make a point. The tits always won in the end.

★ ★ ★

While working on his film the director had laid out for me how he'd made his film on a budget similar to what had been invested for my film. Despite the fees I'd paid to the investor/advisors, making a film with the money we had left was possible. I could do that. I would produce. Tell a story that needed to be told. Then I heard from the investors. There had been some changes. We were no longer going to be a production company; we're going into business with Lord Drinkwater who was expanding his theatre chain to the States. I was told it's a fantastic opportunity. My company would buy in and I'd head up the black theater wing. After all, if you made films, they're no good without distribution.

It was an "act now" opportunity. They didn't let me have time to think it over. As quick as possible they wanted me to send them a check, the majority of the money, for the buy in. Less than $15,000 would be left.

I was devastated as my producing a film was blown out of the water but too deferential to suggest alternatives. I took what they put on the table and tried to have it make sense. I didn't think to offer anything different or put what I wanted out there. It *was* a great chance. It made sense because distribution was just another stepping stone to being able to produce. It would get me into the biz. I had to sell myself on the idea.

I agreed but sending a check was not possible. I explained that I transferred the money to a savings and loan so that it could earn interest while I was away. My contact went a bit crazy. He stopped short of calling me stupid, near enough that I felt his exasperation. I came up with a solution. I knew the manager of the black Savings & Loan where I'd deposited the money. She was a childhood friend and best friend of my cousin June. I called and managed to get her to release the money to them. The call had stirred up lots of questions. And suspicions. I made up my mind that before I went back, I was going to find that mystical island. Bali Hai was calling. I'd been in Hong Kong longer than I'd planned. I had a few weeks, before I absolutely had to be back in California. The breakup was complete, the marriage over and Malika would be well looked after for a quick trip.

I bought an orange backpack, a new ribbon for my Olivetti portable typewriter and moved from the apartment for an overnight stay at my first hostel. Because of the chronically congested Hong Kong traffic, I wanted to be closer to the airport. I didn't want to miss my flight because they didn't fly to Bali every day. I was going to join up with Linda in that magic place.

Once again, a *Trek* inspiration and a family pattern: I was leaving for a place that was unknown for a different experience, a different way of living. I was only going for a few weeks, and I knew someone who lived there. So, I knew the natives were peaceful.

63

When I arrived, my Canadian friend from Hong Kong Linda introduced me to the Mandara family matriarch. Ibu was a beautiful, graceful woman in an exquisite embroidered kebaya, the traditional top women wore with a sarong. I admired her shiny black hair. My mom would have loved her hair. It was *that* straight. Ibu managed the family's *losmen*, a cheap, basic accommodation. The bathroom had a squat toilet and a *mandi*, a tall concrete tub that held the water for bathing. There was a dipper for wetting and rinsing yourself.

Linda had stayed across from the Mandara's on Kuta Beach's main road in their old house before she had her own. It was a traditional dwelling and had been divided into two rooms. I moved into the front-facing room with a large porch. It was walled off from the barely used road and had a large courtyard with a giant pomelo tree, a kind of sweet grapefruit that triggered my love of tropical fruit. Ah, mangosteen!

I discovered hallucinogenic mushrooms the night I arrived. After I ate them, I wandered alone on a beach in the blackest night I'd ever experienced. The most illumination besides the moon and stars was a candle in the only *losmen* on the beach. I confronted fear and terror in the blackness. Something gave me comfort and courage, some soft inner illumination. I was able to relax and just be. I was without depression for many weeks after. I recognized the connection at some stage, gave credit and hoped I'd still be around when they were finally decriminalized—or even better, legalized. Psilocybin mushroom are decriminalized in Oregon and Maine at this time. I hope it reaches Sydney.

In Bali my cannabis rolling skills improved. I learned to roll a decent joint. My rollies evened out from the early "python after a large meal" shape to a slim, easy drawing smoke. I had lots of practice. It took a while to roll a five-paper joint. The weed was so good I decided to share. Some of it got through in the mail and I became a legend back in LA.

Linda introduced me to her friends. They were people who had lived in Bali and Ubud for years. I got a rare treat when we loaded into a jeep to visit their friends, dancers and artists and carvers in Ubud and other villages. We were invited to dinner with a radical dancer who choreographed new dances as well as performing the classics. We were invited to a Hindu-Balinese tooth-filing ceremony, a rite of passage the Mapandes or Metatah undergone at adolescence, partly to improve or to trim any unattractive fanged teeth. Symbolically, it was to balance an individual's personality. I loved that toddlers were carried constantly by someone in the family. What love, what smiles, what beauty! The mixing was noticeable. Australian girls and Balinese boys. Black. White, Purple or Pink doesn't matter in bed with the lights out. The parts universally fit. Our friend Katut was building a residence on Poppy's Lane his Australian girlfriend always next to him.

One thing was disturbing. The Balinese women cautioned

me about the sun I was luxuriating in. kulit hitam, kulit hitam, black skin, they warned. Like the Chinese women I'd met in Hong Kong they were also concerned about being too dark. I wonder who taught them that? My mother had suffered from colorism. She was the darkest child of a mother, who was the darkest child of a father, who was the product of the white slave owner. My mother had favored my lightest daughters and was never able to get along with my darker daughter whose daughter was even darker and who my mother never liked or accepted. I wondered if she had married my dad because he was so light. There was no doubt that her last husband was her ideal. He had fair skin and blue eyes and had passed for white during WWII because the job had required a white person.

★ ★ ★

Some "traveler not tourist" traits were respect, kindness and value for the culture, the people and the environment, both physical and spiritual and necessary. Squatting truly was the best way to evacuate. I learned to squat. I learned to squat and be comfortable. I learned to squat and be comfortable and read the newspaper. I picked up other things. I left a bit of food on my plate for the gods and to show the person who had provided it that I had had enough.

I love picking up the local interpretation of universal gestures. I learned that a few words in Bahasa, were appreciated. I used the word *"permisi"* a lot and added *"pak"* (sir) and *"ibu"* (ma'am) to it. Respect and courtesy went a long way, and the effort to say a few words even further. *Permisi*, permission, is important in any language. I'd start a sentence with it and then switch to English. No one was laughing. One word built on another. I began to trust myself. Fractured phrases were appreciated. That gave me confidence and soon I was almost singing *terima kasih* (thank you.) It felt good. I added more words, and it became *terima kasih banyak sekali* (thank you very much). I could say the response too: *sama sama*. *Di sini* (here) and *Di sana* (there), along with *Apa* (what) added a new dimension to my ability to communicate.

I moved off the main street to a newly built two-room *losmen* on Poppy's Lane. It was a narrow trail down to the beach, parallel to the main road.

I could still stand in the middle of the main road and have a conversation, but Kuta felt crowded. I moved about half a mile down the beach to Legion. There were only two *losmen* there and one food stall on the unpaved, pot-holed road connecting Legion to Kuta. Beyond Legion there was only forest and the rumor of a resort, like the exclusive ones on the rich, tourist side of Bali. Outside my room past the grass was an empty beach. Cows ate the grass and blue meanie mushrooms grew there. The woman at the food stall cooked them for me. I happily settled in.

64

CHANGE ARRIVED WHILE I was sitting on that beach one day, in awe of life, breathing, and glad to be alive in such a beautiful place. It was empty except for a woman walking down the beach with a basket of mangos and a bearded young man who caught up with her. He came over to me, offering a lovely smile. "Would you like a mango?"

His name was Manfred. He was in his twenties, didn't speak much English and was avoiding the draft in Germany. He lived in Australia worked for a printer and had a small t-shirt business. Although Leslie had told me about Australia, it was now on my radar.

Also, I'd met Aussies. Sandra was elegant and sophisticated and I enjoyed spending time with her. There were a lot of Australians around. When it was a loud and often drunk, male Ocker Aussie[55], she would pretend not to speak English. Susan was from New Zealand "a Kiwi" and I couldn't tell their accents apart. Susan was my kind of crazy-curious who explored drugs, people, and food. She is also a talented photographer. The Swiss and Germans were cool, the French

---

55   image

suspect and the Americans few. I met some Brits, even one who had distant ties to royalty. "About 30 people would have to die for me to get the crown," he'd joked. That group didn't brag — only when writing down their address was something sometimes disclosed.

Linda was going to Australia. Going there "on a run" she'd called it and shared her plans to smuggle hash into Australia. To an audience of close friends, she demonstrated the concealment cleverly built into her tourist outfit. I was impressed. The pack of joints I'd smuggled from Mexico didn't compare. Her co-smuggler was a real-life Beauregard and I'd slept with him just because of the way he looked, the life he lived, and his *Gone with the Wind* name. He lived in a traditional house that was on the beach. Everyone knew it was the most expensive accommodation around and that the guys who lived there were drug dealers.

We had a party to send them off to Australia. News of their arrest and incarceration got back to us pretty quick and wasn't much of a surprise.

★ ★ ★

In Bali I was only reachable via Post Restante, the international General Delivery. Paperwork from the financial partners arrived and piled up. All of the documents required an affirmation that all details were correct and needed to be sworn to. They wanted them signed immediately and returned. I couldn't sign papers or swear unless it was true. The papers didn't reflect the experience I'd had with the talent-scout person who'd signed me up—or the with the principals. I think they were counting on what they thought I was.

I found out from one of my new friends that there was no Lord Drinkwater. It had all been BS. All the fragments were there. Tells. Significant disclosures I'd heard and not questioned or understood the importance of. The questions that were brushed aside. It had been confided that a competitor for the funding I got was just out of jail and wasn't terribly bright. I'd dismissed the significance of that consideration as well as the changes from film production to development and distribution. Of course, the exchange of checks at the very beginning had been weird. I had just wanted it all to be true. It was their panic over my transferring the money out of the easily accessible checking account that was truly disturbing to me and awakening. Underneath, and I hadn't recognized it at the time, was a deep-seated reaction that they were implying that I wasn't competent. That my putting the money in a place to earn instead of it just sitting in the checking account had been a bad decision. I wouldn't have admitted I was reacting to a slur on my competency. If I had, I'm sure I would have called it something else. But that was the motivator to gather up all the pieces, had a good look and recognize it was a con in the guise of helping minority businesses.

I needed legal advice. My high school friend, Johnnie Cochran, was now famous and busy with important things. I didn't want to ask him. The only other lawyer I knew besides him was a guy at Desilu, a studio attorney I'd gotten friendly with when I was the floater. I hesitated, remembering I'd heard gossip. I needed to be sure that he was the right person to advise me. You didn't mess with Uncle Sam. I found a phone.

Over a not-very-clear connection that screeched and crackled, I briefly told the whole story to the studio lawyer. He assured me he could handle it all, the company, the government. He told me to send the thousands that were still left, and he'd look after everything. It didn't feel right. They'd been taking from me and now this guy wanted the rest!

The hell with everything. Now that I'd got started, I wasn't gonna stop. I was going to use whatever money was left to find a suitable way to carry out my original intention of making a film. Screw them all! I would pay myself a salary of $200 a week to look for a project. I was still gonna howl!

Since I was going on the hippie trail, I scored a copy of *Asia On The Cheap*, the first Lonely Planet guidebook. It told me enough that I also got a 10,000USD cashier's check to show at border crossings in countries that were leery of hippies. It was proof that I was a hippie with money to spend.

It was January 1974 before I was confident and ready to leave. Manfred had moved in with me and his English had improved beyond his original asking if I'd wanted a mango. The better his English, the less my interest. I was moving on. I called up my sadness face at leaving him, jumped on a train and leaned back in my seat, exhaling. Jakarta, Ibu Kota, new adventures and new lovers were ahead. I felt positive I'd enjoy them.

On the Hippie Trail, we were part of an alternative form of tourism, which prolonged the stay by travelling as cheaply as possible, getting a sense of and connection to the people of the land and learning by observing and interacting. And doing drugs to experiment and explore. Just for fun.

In Jakarta I would have gotten visas for Singapore and Malaysia and transferred the S&L balance back to my Bank of America account. Marines were security at American Embassies and when I started a conversation with one of them, I had a revelation. The Marines were at every embassy and they usually included at least one black one. Yes! From then on, no matter which country, when I hit the capital, I'd head for the Embassy and ask the first Jarhead I saw, "where's the black one?" I'd get information from them. Where to get my hair cut, where to eat, where the happenings were. The brothers couldn't figure me out. I wasn't on vacation. I wasn't on business. What the hell was I doing? Why was I there? I was on a seek-and-discover mission. Whatever it was I'd recognize it.

In Singapore, I had a Singapore Sling at Raffles Hotel. The bartender, pleased I'd come so far for the signature drink, poured me a comp. I was wowed by the beautiful kathoey, who glamorized Bugis Street. I defied the local laws and stayed in an illegal hostel and then headed for Malaysia where I had my first run in with the moral authority due to my tits showing.

It was another learning experience. A never-gone before place. The three-piece pants outfit that showed my boobs and belly that I thought of as my dress-up outfit wasn't appropriate in a conservative Asian-Muslim country. The Malaysian immigration official couldn't bear to look at me and he turned his head away as he told me, "Cover yourself". The white guy behind me said, "That's a pity. That's the way we like them." In Malacca, my first stop in Malaysia, my learning was reinforced when an old man tried to grab my tit and I had to chase him away. This wasn't Hong Kong where they just stared and didn't touch. I got out the long-sleeved shirts, put on my worn jeans, and covered my hair. I shared a cab to Kuala Lumpur, the capitol. In the cab I realized that it might not have been smart to share it with five men to save a few dollars. I wasn't in Bali anymore.

65

I grew up thinking what I did was what everyone did. That the United States was the standard. I'd been groomed by the "whytophiles." Now I was learning about different values and rules that weren't covered in their travel guides, and certainly weren't taught at home. But some things are universal.

Siva was a beautiful, deep-black Indian-Malay man who preferred being called Mike and showed me Penang. As a local, he was happy to be seen with me and took me around—even to an opium den where I just looked. I had been given opium for Bali belly and ended up vomiting off the back of a Chinese junk. Luckily, out the window was straight down into the water and no one got splattered. Too much like heroin which I liked too much. I did have a tiny bit of medicinal opium tucked somewhere in my backpack. I'd kept it in case I got that sick again.

Siva got a little too restrictive and too bossy and I got seduced by a Scottish brogue. He was also called Mike. I didn't bother to tell the first Mike he'd been replaced. I just wasn't available to him. One night shortly after Mike-the-Scot had dropped me off at my cheap hotel in a non-tourist part of town, I didn't hesitate to open the door when the voice responded with, "Mike." But when I opened it, there was Siva, the other-Mike, and he was pissed off. I was pretty visible and my change of partners hadn't gone unnoticed. I'd caused him to lose face, and he wasn't having that.

I couldn't get out! The hotel was locked at night. There was a folding steel gate and men guarded the door. I didn't speak the language. The people who could open the door or help were his friends.

Siva's face scared the heck out of me and I was calculating defensive actions, seduction or escape. His voice was cold and clear: "You're leaving on the early train." He was only getting rid of me. Thank goodness. I started packing. I didn't fancy hanging around there any longer. There was no way I could sleep. I was grateful for the experience and recalled a happy story we had had, as a way of sort of saying sorry. I must have caused him a lot of embarrassment. I hadn't thought; I hadn't cared. He stayed stony faced! After I'd packed the orange backpack, not daring to sleep, I sat up till we left in the morning.

There was heavy traffic. His friend with the taxi was a little late, and we missed the train. There was no going back. Siva wanted me gone. He had the driver race the train. We beat it to the next station and I was offloaded. It wasn't to be the first time I missed my transportation or needed to get out of town quickly. It reinforced Ms. Onita again. *Black, white, purple, or pink, mens is mens.* People were people. Nobody liked feeling played. I needed to be clear that like, Mr. Natural, I was just passing through.

★ ★ ★

Thailand was my new paradise. I got the night ferry to Koh Samui. It was welcoming and almost tourist free. Monks were inviting travelers to stay at the monasteries. I saw only one car while I was there. The food was great and cheap, as was the accommodation and I decompressed, at peace on the empty beaches. I was offered a cup of tea, simmering on the fire at a roadside stall. I turned it down because I don't like drinking hot things. A small crowd gathered, staring at me. Black women were a rarity. When I reached for the chilies to put on my food, murmurs of dissent came from the group. I was sure I'd eaten them before; they weren't that hot. I was used to hot Mexican food. My experience was that these were manageably hot.

One bite and I knew these chilies weren't *those* chilies. These chilies were hot-hot, not fun-hot. The expectant looks around me dictated my reaction. Discreetly sucking in some cooling air, I casually scooped up another sprinkling of chilies and added them to my dish. The gasps were audible. Looking as relaxed as I could under the circumstances, I continued, painfully eating the food. The woman with the tea wasn't fooled and handed me the cup of boiling hot tea I'd refused. I took it with gratitude and sipped. It cooled my mouth, I swear. Another lesson learned: locals knew dangers you might not perceive. Listen to them. Try not to lose face or cause them to. Respect the culture.

★   ★   ★

Susan, my Kiwi (New Zealand) friend, was ahead of me on the trail somewhere. We caught up a couple of times. Sitting on a beach, a kid came up to me and said with absolute certainty,

"Ande, Susan's looking for you." It was like she had lookouts. We ran into each other without help at the Bangkok main post office while I was checking Post Restante. I always let family know where I was heading next so they could stay in touch. Susan introduced me to Bangkok's Hippie Hilton—the Malaysia Hotel. I settled in and made it home.

We had a lot to debrief since we'd last seen each other a few weeks before. She had met up with an Australian friend, John, who was an artist and addict. Heroin was his drug of choice. I was amazed that he was quite productive. He made beautiful art. John was creative and prolific, dispelling another heroin belief I'd held. I thought shooting up meant nodding off, like Lee Morgan with Art Blakey's Jazz Messengers who I'd flirted with. Now I got used to watching people shoot up. It was addictive, but darn, with proper medical supervision and care, it was certainly manageable and it was their choice.

I satisfied myself with weed. A karambit, a carved Thai knife, a dresser drawer and a few Buddha sticks. Turn the drawer bottom up and chop the Buddha sticks on it with the knife. Buddha sticks were the most potent Indica strain I'd ever smoked. The bud was wrapped around a bamboo sliver and tied. In Australia they were called Thai sticks or "tied sticks" by those who misheard. To me the best was some Lao weed that I'd scored in Bali and mailed some to friends in LA. I had a small amount of it left that travelled everywhere with me, across all the borders. It was legendary weed—smell, taste, and effect. Buddha sticks were the next best. By now I had mastered the four-paper joint. Firm and slender, elegant and potent and much complimented and smoked.

The Marine I met at the embassy in Bangkok turned me on

to a soul food restaurant where there were lots more black men. There was a US airbase in Udon Thani. When I went to Laos to renew my Thai visa, I could pass through on my way. I didn't want to renew it in Malaysia, didn't want any chance of running into Siva. Besides there was a barber there who cut black hair.

Vientiane, Laos, on the other side of the Mekong River, had the best coffee I'd ever had, very cheap weed that was sold openly in the markets and I met couple of guys from the States. They were very friendly and invited me to their house. They wanted to get to know me—probably to figure out why I was in the area. I think they were CIA. I reckoned I'd had a file with *somebody* since my days with Malcolm.

I realized why we were still fighting an unwinnable, immoral war when I checked out their comfortable accommodation. I saw the adoration and affection from the fawning Lao women they shared it with: paradise and pussy. It was these guys wallowing in a suburban replica with a barbecue, beer and beautiful women satisfying all their needs. They didn't want the war to be over. They would find and support any efforts to keep the need for them to be there.

There in Laos I saw the Vietnam war from a distance. Then it got closer. War was more visible one night, coming home when we ran into a bunch of guys in that well-reported black pajama combat garb. They pointed some very big automatic weapons at us. Time to get back across the muddy Mekong.

★ ★ ★ ★

Back in Udon I had some grits and buttermilk biscuits for breakfast and got a good haircut. And I had new red denim traveling clothes made. I put on the jeans. Then I walked around, sat and bent and stretched and when there was a little bit of give, I had them made tighter. I had no extra weight on my body for the first time in years. The matching red denim jacket had Mr. Natural embroidered on the back, a long, flowing white beard and his slogan "just passin' thru". It was all topped by a big red denim cap. I liked wearing the denim with a low-cut yellow t-shirt and no bra. I still had the same pair of travelling jeans. Before I left Udon, I got the tailor to make a leather cut-out of a dragon to patch a hole in the butt of my jeans. I thought the message obvious though not true.

★ ★ ★

1. *Me and friends about to drive around Bali to visit their friends.*
2. *Me and Malika.*
3. *You could have a conversation in the middle of the main street in Kuta beach in 1973.*
4. *Mei Fu Sun Chuen where we lived in Hong Kong.*
5. *Me and Manfred, Darwin Hospital.*
6. *Young love, the parts fit. Doesn't matter if you're black, white, purple, or pink.*
7. *Manfred.*
8. *Malika.*

I sent Mark money to bring Malika to see me in Bangkok. He was now Swami Anan Dharam. Professor Adam Beeler was back as well. Perhaps the newest identity showed his growing spirituality. He was meditating and he had a guru. No, I was wrong. His identity was more fragile than I realized. Mark and John, the artist, got along well at the Malaysia. I'd forgotten his persuasion worked on men as well and I didn't realize Mark was cooking up something.

Malika was a delight: fearless and imaginative and stubborn. She wanted frills, and I wanted her to wear hiking boots and jeans. I remembered to be an adult, aware and appreciative of her needs. She got ruffles. We got hugs. She and Mark went back to Hong Kong and I was back on the Hippie Trail. Nepal, India and Goa were next.

The end of the Hippie Trail for me turned out to be Nepal. Kathmandu didn't start too well. The immigration officer not only singled me out, but he also made me change currencies and when I came back with that done, he sent me to the end of the line.

For the first time in months, I had a throwback feeling. He was as dark as I was so it couldn't be my color. I was completely covered, wearing long sleeves, so I wasn't immodest. I became convinced it had to be because of my ethnicity. For some reason, he didn't like Black Americans. What else could it be? That was the only thing that differentiated me from every other single non-citizen in the queue.

Finally, I was the last person. Everyone else had been swept away by ravenous modes of transportation. Then I imagined the worse possible outcome. The official either knew what I was carrying or he would search my backpack for drugs. My confidence was shaken: I had my special Lao weed stash and the illusive dab of medicinal opium somewhere lost in my writing and paperwork, I needed to find and throw them away. I'll make sure that I did. I was holding my breath and that made my fear look more like anger. Good! I was both. He finished flipping curiously through my passport, which now had additions, fold-out pages of passport stamps, proof of where I'd been. I was about to pull out my aces, the American Express card and the cashier's check, when without searching my backpack, he returned my documents and smiling warmly, asked, "Would you have dinner with me tonight?"

Onita's Law again. *Black, white, purple, or pink, mens is mens*. I gave him a sarcastic look. He wasn't getting anything from me, not even a word and I swept off to find some way of getting somewhere.

I no longer had the company of the hippie travelers. I was alone and I'd had enough hassle. I missed the protection of the herd. On my own I made it to the guidebook-recommended lodging I'd picked.

When I checked in, I saw that that wouldn't work. I needed an upgrade. It was too cheap, a bit too basic for the moment. I'd been spoiled in Malaysia and I needed a little comfort. I got a bit of advice, found new place and started to breathe again.

This town wasn't like any place I'd been before. There were more flies, for one thing. That pulsing, iridescent buzzing ball close up was a melon covered with flies. It was back to open sewers again and I was alone. I knew no *words*. I knew no one. I needed to go to the embassy.

I was settling in as well as I could, spreading a batik from Bali over the pillow, putting my lantern in an easily accessible place. I was hanging up things and making my room home when I got a visitor. Someone was waiting to see me.

I'd only given the usual Poste Restante for Kathmandu; I hadn't told anyone my exact location. I didn't know anyone. I didn't even know in advance that I would be at this hotel. No one...except the immigration officer.

Yep, the power of the badge. The man had had no difficulty tracking me down. "Would you have dinner with me now?" This time I considered. There was a monologue going on inside me. All his crimes. Another voice interrupted: Who better to give me local, insider info, to tell or show me what-ifs? I juggled responses. A good practice because it makes sure there's a conversation and that makes better decisions. My yes was more likely because of his smile, and his eyes, and because he'd be interesting to know. He was darn lucky that I was saying yes.

His name was Nardev if I remember correctly. I knew he had lived in Hong Kong because that became a starting point. He had served in the British Army as a member of the Gurkha Brigade, the most skilled and fierce warriors in the world. When he gave me a large chunk of very, very good hash, I caved into a feeling that I was going to enjoy staying in Kathmandu for a while. We went to dinner and parted with fond looks, without touching, taking it slow and easy.

* * * *

The next day before I had gotten to the embassy and talked to the Marine, I was scrambling to get back to Hong Kong and incredibly grateful I had Nardev with me who knew how things worked.

The first place we went had been the telephone exchange so I could check in and see how Malika was. John, Susan's Bangkok artist friend, answered Mark's phone. He had come to Hong Kong, bringing Buddha sticks for Mark to sell. Instead, Mark had smoked too many and had a total breakdown. Abruptly, everything was up-ended. Nardev became my support, my lifeline, my protector and my personal shopper.

Mark had had delusions that Malika was a goddess he served. He was saving the planets from destruction by sheer mental power. And when the goddess had gone missing from the apartment he'd moved into after I'd left, he'd unleashed the fire hose in the hallway of the high-rise. He had figured that if he turned on the fire hose, the water would attract other people, and they could help him find the goddess. Instead they had turned off the water and called the police.

When the police had arrived, they'd discovered the Buddha sticks, located the goddess and arrested Mark. When they'd attempted to take him to jail, his behavior had changed their minds and, instead he was taken to a mental hospital and placed in a locked ward. Malika had been taken to an orphanage. One good thing—Josh, Mark's university co-worker, had removed her from the orphanage without permission and over staff objections. The mild, soft-spoken Sikh had just picked her up and walked out with her as the staff got out of the way. His family were family to her.

For Malika and for Mark, I needed to be in Hong Kong as fast as possible. Flights from Kathmandu were infrequent to anywhere other than India. Union of Burma Airways had the first flight to Hong Kong. It was leaving in a day and had an overnight stop in Bangkok. When I got to the airport in

Kathmandu, I had a shock. In most countries your baggage was examined when you arrived. Here in the home of excellent hash it was closely inspected on leaving. I hadn't hidden my stash. I was terrified until Nardev, out of uniform, greeted me to say goodbye. He was still looking after me. He walked me past the inspections to the boarding gate. I promised I would be back. I remember his smile. Somewhere, I have a photo of him taken out in the country, mountains behind him, smiling at me. I'm grateful for his kindness and great hash.

★ ★ ★

Remembering the stares I'd gotten in Hong Kong, I changed into my red denim and the low-cut t-shirt with no bra the next morning before boarding the plane. A little distraction helped because I still had my special weed that I'd stashed. Knowing women were usually averse to the sight, I tucked a sanitary pad with blood on it between my legs with my stash tightly compressed and wrapped, inserted inside the pad.

In Hong Kong, when the immigration officer asked me to step out of line, I was ready to show the Am-Ex and check. I needed to get a handle on things as quickly as possible and my focus was totally on seeing Malika. Instead, I was taken to a room where my orange backpack was being examined by a senior border official. I knew where I'd hidden the weed, the opium location was a question mark. I couldn't remember where it was, just that it was in there somewhere. I had planned on throwing it away and hadn't seen it when I'd looked and then I'd forgotten about it. I'd be okay as long as I kept my clothes on.

I was taken to another room with a woman who indicated she would be doing a search. I was getting worried. She motioned for me to unfasten my tight pants, and peel them down to around my ankles. That wasn't enough. I was instructed to pull down my underwear. What I didn't want to happen was happening. It was time for the performance of my life because it was about to get deep, so I pulled out my best effort, the Oscar-winning moment. I pushed my undies down, muffled a shriek and turned my head jerking them back up, my face showing revulsion. My stash-pad only needed to be flashed quickly. The blood was dry, but given women's attitudes to their period back then, combined with my shriek and look on my face, for the instant it was sighted, it would've looked fresh. The search was over, and they hadn't found a thing. Where was the damn opium, though?

Back in the first room, I was with the senior officer who hadn't yet given up, despite the body search not giving me away. He had good instincts. He was examining my karambit, my Thai chopping knife. I thought of how much cannabis, how many Buddha sticks I'd chopped with that knife; it must have had traces of resin on the edge. And... where the heck was the opium? Then a funny thought occurred. I didn't know where the opium was, and he didn't know that was cannabis resin on my knife. Either one could land me in jail. The thought that he didn't know and I did seem hilarious, and the laughter that was threatening to weasel out of me started to turn into a smirk. That was a dangerous face to show to a man with his experience; so I channeled it into wronged victim, growing hysterical mother and loyal wife being unfairly prevented from comforting her family members. Tears and snot and outrage.

That wasn't the only time. Until we were all secure, I code-switched and switched identities as necessary. That safety equipment was in black kids by first grade. We might have skated through kindergarten but, by first grade when the shit went down, it's automatically activated. In an echo of Brer Rabbit, the trickster, we do, say, or act as we need to get thrown back into the briar patch. It's a valuable ability and there was shame in how, and when, we've used it sometimes. If you're honest, solid in what you're doing, you won't feel shame. I can't claim it as my creation; it was more like something that came through me that I trusted enough to guide me past the danger filter. I was always grateful later when I was a mediator and facilitator. The perfect thing came out of my mouth sometimes, and I didn't know where it had come from—a higher power, my guardian angel—just that it was what was needed to help everyone involved.

After I made sure Malika was okay, I went to the psychiatric hospital. Mark was in a locked ward and I had to wait, then follow the institutional protocols. Mark wasn't in a straitjacket or anything and seemed in good spirits. Almost as though it was of his choosing. He pointed to the TV where a rerun of *The Rookies* was playing with Cantonese-dubbed voices. Our friend Georg Stanford Brown on screen. "Georg has been sending me messages. He told me you would come and get me out of here."

Mark spun his story. His revelations that Malika was a goddess, how she went missing and how he turned on the fire hose in the apartment building to get help finding her, the mistake the police had made in arresting a spiritual man. His special powers had directed them to take him to a place of safety instead of jail. Now he needed to go to India and be with the Master, be with Bhagwan Shree Rajneesh, who was in Poona. He didn't want to go back to the States.

Mark had changed more than apartments. He had a new woman. Dealing with his girlfriend was touchy. I was the ex-wife and I was truly pleased he'd found a new love and was no competition. I spent the night at the apartment she shared with her brother, making friends, engaging in girl-talk and picking her brain to see how she could help. Her brother worked in a consular role and I needed all the help I could get.

While I was there, I came upon a strange scene. She was in her brother's bedroom with the door open. Her large breasts were bare and she seemed to be getting clothing advice on the blouses she held in front of them. What was even more peculiar was that the brother was naked in bed, his naked girlfriend in cowgirl position, grinding away while he squeezed the girlfriend's breasts with his eyes on his sister's. This was truly some place I knew existed but had never thought I'd see in real life. Strange, and for me, new life forms. *Trek* never tried a show like that.

Manfred called from Australia. He wanted me to come there. I told him I had my child with me now. I wouldn't go anywhere without her. He said no. No kid. I said, "Okay. No, Manfred." He had been reliable and a support. I remembered the day an unannounced period had soaked through my jeans. There had been nothing we could do; so he'd put his arm in mine and we'd just carried on walking down the street. He was responsible and no BS, but he also had the sense to quickly change his mind. He promised to help and shelter us both. He would be back in Bali soon. Hopefully we'd meet there.

My tasks were clear. The targets were the university, the

hospital director, the police and the airline. I would need all my code-switching ability. Heightened, even!

The university had a travel agent who would issue me a return ticket and, since I wasn't going back to California, it was of no use. It would not be refundable, at least not to me. I whipped out my Am Ex and bought tickets back to California for the three of us. Then I insisted the university reimburse me. I told them I'd spent all my money on buying the tickets. They didn't like it. I upped the requests, and just in case he'd be able to work again someday, I wanted them to provide him with a non-damaging work reference to indicate his duties had proved satisfactory. They wouldn't want his illness to affect their reputation. I was a beast. If I couldn't get over or go around, I went through them. Something I'd never been able to do for myself.

The university reimbursed me. I used the university money to pay American Express for tickets to Bali and Poona and Am Ex refunded the tickets to California. I bought one for John back to Bangkok. Now that I had the tickets covered, I had to get Mark out of the locked ward and released from the psych hospital for at least twenty-four hours before he was to fly or else the airline required me to provide a doctor or nurse to accompany him on the plane.

The mental hospital was a tough one. Psych doctors are used to people putting on an act so I kept it as close to the truth as possible. I did want him to be with his family—the family at the ashram in Poona. With the head doctor I went where necessary, from demanding advocate to frail, weeping wife. Finally, I discovered the key. The hospital had a responsibility of care for Mark. And his going to jail was not caring for him.

I had to ensure he wouldn't be arrested when the hospital released him.

That made the final task handling the police. Getting them to drop charges, so the psych hospital could let him out at least the day before the flight without fear of arrest, was played like a seduction. I teased and raged, belittled and built up. I made fun of the Clint Eastwood-looking Brit who was in charge of Mark's case. I laughed at his short pants and long socks. When was he going to have long pants like a real grown up? I badgered and bullied, demanded and insisted. I rationalized and justified. And they dropped the charges.

My mother had been the first person contacted when he was arrested. Mark's mother hadn't wanted to have anything to do with him. She even left Malika out of her will when she'd died. Mom sold my BMW and used the money to send my cousin June over to help. She sold the car for about half the valued amount. "It was only a small car, but the guy who bought it seemed very happy," she explained.

Hong Kong was a fearful and strange place for June, and there wasn't much she could do. But Hong Kong was a place I could read and respond to. One night the taxi driver was going the wrong way for our destination. He went into the Walled City area that I'd never go into during the day—much less late at night. We avoided a potential problem by jumping out of the cab when it stopped for a moment and ran down a very dark garbage-strewn, rodent-heaven lane. Maybe it was a shortcut the driver was trying, and we ran away without paying. We found another cab which we paid for and made it home.

June got lost while travelling alone on the train to the New Territories and she got braver and stronger. She ate chicken feet for the first time. She went where she'd never gone before and was proud of herself. She's a Booker too.

★ ★ ★

Another first was my "Mr. Woo", the cute Chinese guy I was about to have sex with. I was in Woo's apartment. We'd connected, and was I about to check out and again verify Onita's Law. *Black, white, purple or pink, mens is mens.* I was tired and stressed and in need of some serious relief. I'd held grudges against the Hong Kongese and what to me was rudeness, but I was ready to make peace.

A storm had been hanging around, lights went out, and things got a little weird. Bolts of lightning hurled around the building and thunder so near it shook the door. I felt a wildness and a desire to shake off the past. To show my true self. I would face him completely bare, just me, who I was. For the first and only time I was unself-conscious and totally accepting of my body. Thunder boomed, the building shook, and when I took the bracelets from my wrists and bared my neck I had nothing to hide behind. it was my choice. I loved and accepted me. I was ready to explore limits. A flash of lightening showed he was ready too.

At the same time we realized some of the noise wasn't coming from the storm. Someone was pounding on his door. Torn, but not able to ignore it, he went to check. Just like Dr. King, had been surprised at my blushing. I was surprised when Woo went white. It was his girlfriend at the door, a flight attendant. The storm had cancelled her flight. the lights came back on. I was a bit pissed and didn't hurry putting my clothes on while he made excuses through the closed door. He was going to get his ass kicked because of this. The woman he loved wouldn't understand it was just pussy. I'd never been big on monogamy. But I'd never faced a woman whose man I was having sex with. He stalled and I had most of my clothes on by the time he opened the door— I had to put back a few things under her ferocious gaze. I'd never faced a woman who knew for sure I was having or attempting to have sex with her man. When I looked at her, trying to keep up the façade that I had just dropped by rather than just put on my clothes, I could see she was checking me out, judging my worth, comparing her value and the one thing I didn't get was concern about my skin.

She wasn't giving me the side-eye because I was black, she was hatin on me because I was a bitch who was after her man. And before she could do or say anything, embracing my inner *gweilo*, I got the hell out.

66

With the charges dropped, Mark would be released from the hospital the day before we flew out. He could fly without an attendant.

When Mark was released, it was completely done. We were all leaving Hong Kong. I even managed an overnight stay at the Peninsula Hotel. Once more the luxury of our first night. Despite the changes we'd been through nothing had changed at the Peninsula. They put us in the same room as on our original stay, and the basket of goodies and very welcoming smiles were there. I had earned it!

The next day Mark was off to the airport with a ticket to India while I tidied up the loose ends. We had kept the fiction that I was taking my sick husband back to the US to the bosom of the family that would facilitate his recovery. What was real was I'd had seen John off back to Bangkok with some money and Mark's plane had already left.

Mark's illusion was he was a professor and swami who had received divine revelations and he was heading for India to share them at the ashram of his guru Rajneesh. My illusion was that I was heading back to Bali to Manfred's arms. He had promised to look after me. What was real was I was in a

Peninsula Hotel's Jaguar, at a standstill in the congested Hong Kong traffic with the clock moving toward take-off time. Sure as shit the airline check-in counter was closed when we got there. No one was around.

I had told lies. I'd promised a reunion in "the States" to Mark's girlfriend, but I hadn't said which country. To the psych doc I'd promised a California hospital report and to the police—oh shit, the police. There wouldn't be another Bali flight for two days. I closed my eyes tight. No, no, no! Not after all that. Now I had to leave.

When I opened my eyes, the airline check-in counter was still closed, the boarding gate still abandoned. I was too late. I was probably going to jail and Malika back to the orphanage. When I looked up to the universe for help, I saw the airline office. I had to get out today. Desperate, running, and backpack banging with Malika in one hand, her suitcase the other. I had nothing to lose. I was at the airline office in a flash. I had to leave now. I had to get away.

Whatever it was that I'd said or done, I was grateful to whomever or whatever was guiding me, when Malika and I, my orange backpack, her little backpack, and my typewriter, were loaded into a station wagon and driven out onto the tarmac where the already-pushed-back plane was about to head for the runway. A ramp came down and we were loaded in. The plane took off and I could breathe again.

When I got to Bali, Mrs. Mandara and family had moved off the main street. They had opened a small hotel near the airport. The old house was still there and it was available, both sides. Malika and I moved in.

The pomelo tree was full of ripe yellow balls. My hands

were stripping away the peels when Manfred appeared. We embraced and I relaxed into the safety of his arms. I felt his interest shift. Malika had come to investigate and once they made eye contact, they were friends. I felt confident that he would look after us. "Set us down." And he did.

Back in Bali after less than a year, I was amazed at the changes. Some of the same people were around. My friends Erna and Arno were still there resisting the Swiss winter. But Kuta had changed.

I had read Huxley's *Island* and felt the resemblance of his island Palau to Bali. Traffic had increased moderately on the Kuta main street. You could still hold a conversation in the middle of the road, but it might be interrupted. Poppy's Lane was wider and the road to Legion was now paved. The warm splash-able rain puddles I purposely rode the bike thru were no longer there, and a hotel resort was being built where there had been a forest.

You can't go back to perfection, to paradise. Every time I hear someone raving about what a paradise Bali is, it's hard to stop myself saying you shoulda been there when…

Manfred had friends in Central Java in Magelang. They were working on the restoration of a nineth-century Buddhist temple, Borobudur, the world's largest Buddhist temple. We went to visit them. We stayed only a week and I was glad when we left. Everyone spoke German and I was left out. I started feeling inadequate. And very tired Manfred made the case for checking out Australia. He had a place for us there. I didn't have the energy to insist on Europe. We bought tickets for Australia. My farewell gift was a tour, in English of the restoration, a magic sunrise personal tour of the temple. The whole place opened just for me, the Central Dome surrounded by seventy-two Buddha statues, each inside a stupa, the rising sun throwing shadows and light. Reflecting, refracting. What a joy! It was the last time I felt good for a while. I'd managed to pick up a bug at one of those roadside food stalls. A virus was making itself at home in my liver.

★ ★ ★

The trip to Australia was uneventful except during a stop at the airport in Timor where I was asked if I'd give up Malika's seat. Of course not. I didn't realize that people were evacuating the small country, that an invasion was about to occur. The Portuguese were leaving. Indonesia was taking over and stopping the independence movement. A bit more information, more knowledge on my part, and I'd have been willing to give up the seat.

67

I had arrived in Australia at Darwin Airport and I didn't want to. It showed. The doctor at the airport trying to verify Malika's smallpox vaccination looked about to have a heart attack. I challenged every word he said. Not giving an inch. Red-faced and puffing, I could tell he wasn't used to being confronted. I acted as though the White Australia Policy was still being enforced. It was like I was fighting for my rights against the "Klingons." I was letting white Australia know in case they thought I would take shit from them.

The Darwin beaches were beautiful and so were the people. An amazing assortment of skin and hair tones, features revealing a mixture of origins. The kids with India's deep, dark skin tones and Scandinavia's pale blond hair were especially striking. This was someplace I'd definitely never been before. The sunsets called out wonder and gratitude and a certainty there existed a Creator of Awe!

Manfred had warned that I wouldn't have a connection with the original owners of the land because they looked different. That was *his* thinking. The only difference between me and them was the many tribal languages that intimidated me. The sounds were not familiar. And I didn't know a way in. Timidly, I shrank away from direct contact. And okay, I admit the deep-black skin of the blond children was a look I hadn't seen before. But humans share features. I'd recognized a family resemblance or two in the places I'd been.

My social skills were lacking. Where was my Kiwi friend Susan when I needed her? She actually wasn't that far away. Susan was living with and photographing indigenous groups living in the central desert. Maybe even close by. I didn't yet get Australia's vast distances.

I looked at these black people as closely as I dared. We had a connection. Where was it? Manfred was wrong. Bali had taken a while, but I had connected there. Then my eyes turned yellow, my pee turned brown and bubbly and soon I watched the First People from the infectious disease ward of Darwin Hospital. I'd picked up hepatitis A.

The Darwin Hospital was shaped like my high school with triangles of grass between solo storied spokes. Manfred and Malika visited outside my window. She wasn't allowed in at all and he only in protective clothing. I could see extended family groups of *"blakfullas"*[56] sitting on the ground outside other windows, visiting, laughing. And seeing that, I felt an at home likeness, a kinship. We gathered around like that too. I also saw and heard harsh-voiced, white-women workers, nurses, or whatever aggressively shooing the families away with angry gestures, as though the visitors were an annoying flock of chickens. I didn't appreciate that!

When I was well, I went to the Star Theatre, an open-air cinema in town. There I saw black folks sitting in groups on

---

56 That's how many First People say it in Aus.

the cement instead of in seats. That recalled segregated seating, and knowing no better, I assumed they were forced to sit on the ground against their will. I was wrong, but my structural thinking said roof and chairs were better. Everything I knew about the First People had been from the media. Not much of it laudable. From what I'd read, they were a useless bunch. Just like the popular media said about us back home.

I saw the Harry Belafonte and Sidney Poitier film *Buck and the Preacher* at the Star Theatre. Sitting in the covered dress circle seats, I watched those black faces on screen making these black faces in the audience laugh. I made a promise to make them a film full of love, laughter, and positive images of themselves. I made a promise to let them howl.

I was getting restless. Darwin then was boring and full of drunks. I was happy to be a drunk but I wasn't allowed to drink because of the Hep A. Darwin was very expensive. All food had to come by train and road train[57] from Adelaide. It wasn't just not very fresh it was very expensive. Steve and Lisa, Manfred's friends and work mates were a relief. They were British and drove a Moke, my new favorite car at the time. Bright and full of life, I liked them both. Still do. Manfred's English had become fluent and idiomatic. He had lots of words, and I wasn't interested in any of them.

---

57 A road train consists of from two to a record breaking twenty-one semi-trailers hauled by a prime mover.

68

MALIKA AND I HEADED for Sydney. To save paying full fair for her, I claimed she's only two and carried her wrapped in a blanket. I wasn't yet back at full strength and I struggled. I also carried the one thing that occupied her when I needed to rest: a television set gifted by a friend that said, "Return to Radio Rentals." I almost didn't make it when we changed for the Sydney plane in Adelaide. Malika was three and a half and heavy. So was the TV.

In Sydney we got into a taxi and I told the driver we wanted to live at the beach. There are a lot of beaches in Sydney, over a hundred, including 70 surf beaches. He realized I wasn't from there. Luckily, he was typical of many Australians I would meet, full of questions about all things 'Afro-American' and 'willing to give it a go'. We started at the beach closest to the airport and then made our way north. I comfortably answered his questions, dropped in a few names, (I can't help it. There have been so many incredible people in my life). Bill Russell got his attention. He knew a lot about black people. I answered his questions and enjoyed his thirst but I was starting to get a bigger picture. I had to reevaluate the situation. I liked what I saw but nothing felt like the place I wanted. The ride could be expensive. Before I finished running through the options, definitely couldn't do a runner like Hong Kong, he flipped off the meter. "Let's find you a place to live." The move was so casual that it seemed natural that he would do that. Our conversation and trip continued.

The beaches go on forever. From the road the ocean is beautiful, the shorelines hilly or flat, covered, sometimes sparsely, with people, trees, or with apartments. He was selling the merits of the city to me. I was just as full of questions about him. His background. How he got there. He's a mongrel, he told me, meaning his family background was a mixture of cultures. He could only trace the Irish. When we got to Bondi Beach, everything felt right. Hills bracketed the beach and the center sloped gently with shops and restaurants on flat streets. This was where I wanted to live. He found a motel for us. There was a vacancy and we were all set. He left satisfied. His ancestors hadn't been treated any better than the original inhabitants, he explained, "but overall, it's not a bad place." I doubt his ancestors had been killed and the kids taken away from home. I got what he meant, though. He thought I was gonna like it there. The nicest person I'd met in the city was a white Australian that I'd been warned would be racist. What an unexpected welcome to country from one of the bandits. Yes, I was gonna like Sydney. Inconsistent, like me.

★ ★ ★

Peter, a guy I'd met at the Malaysia Hotel, sounded glad to hear from me. He invited me to come to his place. He was just a bus ride away in Paddington, a gentrifying area.

Peter's big sister was an old-school protective Italian. The family had bought several houses in the area, and the one where Peter lived had been turned into studio apartments. When he suggested there's one that would suit Malika and me, she wanted to know for how long. She was suspicious and questioned me about my background. I hadn't ever thought of him as other than a friend. She must have agreed and Malika and I moved to Paddington.

I was back "in the world." On the street, foot traffic streamed around me like a swift river around a rock. I was still moving at a taking-in-the-wonders pace. Linda, my Hong Kong/Bali friend was in Sydney and introduced me around. She was out on bail, still facing drug import charges.

She was living in a share house with Elaine, a woman from Florida with two children who were a little bit older than Malika. She was one of many school teachers, brought over to deal with an explosion of students.

Elaine still had a softly southern accent and she attached to me immediately. She quickly assured me she was not racist, and went on to tell me how she was raised by a wonderful black woman she'd loved, who worked for her family. The woman had always used the back door and had not been allowed to sit in the front seat of the car. Not realizing the racism that her story implied, Elaine guiltily confessed that she felt blacks were better than whites and transferred those feelings to me. I'd found a friend for life.

Linda was still super cool and she took me to Martin's, a private club walking distance from Peter's place in Paddington. It was on Oxford Street along the Gay Golden Mile of clubs, bars and restaurants. Martin's was like the Australian Candy

Store. Martin himself stood outside and only let in people he was in a mood for. There were no guarantees of getting in. Each time I approached his Alfred Hitchcock profile, I wondered if I'd be admitted without Linda. One night while trying to be cool and get in, I reminded him of Linda, who I'd come there with. He said to me in Hitchcockian, "Oh, yes—your friend! The one who thinks she's a legend." I was admissible on my own, for who I was.

* * *

Australians seemed to like African Americans. I realized that I was heir to unearned approval. I represented everything good they had heard and admired about African Americans—"Afro Americans," they called me. They automatically assumed I could sing, dance and play basketball, and my hair was so interesting they reached for it, fingers already grabbing as they asked permission to touch it.

I didn't sing, didn't dance that well and hadn't played basketball since high school. If you weren't fucking me, keep your hand out of my hair, and besides, I no longer felt like the African American representative. I was only me, and whatever I did, I did. If someone wanted to stamp my actions on millions of other black folks, that's their problem. I wasn't playing the represent game anymore. I felt responsible to, not responsible for. Besides everywhere I looked it was white. No black people behind counters, driving buses, selling suits, sweeping, floors, or carrying briefcases. I was in a white, white world.

When it looked like I might hang around for a while, I knew I wanted to live in Bondi. And it must have view of the beach and be in a quiet area that would suit Malika. Also, it needed to be cheap. The investment money needed to last for a while, Australia was looking like where I needed to be.

I found the perfect place. Only one apartment in the building was occupied. The building was scheduled to be torn down and townhouses built, then permission had been denied and I had my choice of flats. I settled into a ground floor apartment with a narrow patio opening from the living room and one of the bedrooms. Ken and Sue were my only neighbors. Soon there were visitors, I was meeting people.

The beach and the kid's ocean pool were clearly visible from the apartment and Malika was free to roam the neighborhood with notice. It gave her an independence she was capable of and liked. There was only a short dead-end street to cross to get to the green-grocer and the milk bar. She was almost four and could handle some errands, and I learned to tell her *to-mah-to*s instead of *to-may-to*s if I didn't want her coming back with potatoes. She didn't have permission to cross the busy main street but she did anyway. I found out when I checked on her. I wasn't surprised. The cake shop was on that side of the street. Her declaration of independence also failed when she departed the children's area to go to the main part of the beach. She said she felt a sense of freedom as she spread her towel on a space of her own choosing. Then almost immediately her peace was interrupted by, "Malika, your mother wants you."

Manfred arrived soon after we moved in. We didn't last long together. The spark was gone. When he was comfortably off, with a successful business and several homes twenty-five years later he tried again it was still gone. I'd discovered to be set down wasn't enough. He was still Malika's "Mumford," though and we stayed friends. I liked, trusted and respected him; the romance was finished, but the connection wasn't.

Then Steve and Lisa arrived and moved in with Malika and me and we were like a family. Steve was an artist and they were both bright. I enjoyed that ideas bounced when they were around.

69

Life at the beach was great but my visa was about to expire. Manfred, along with Steve and Lisa, agree to look after Malika while I left the country to renew it and I'd take care of her resident status later. I'd have to go either to Papua New Guinea or New Zealand. Both were about the same distance and costs. New Zealand, I'd heard, was nice enough—a bit bland, a smaller Australia without the snakes, spiders and wild things that would kill you. Dickie, a barrister friend of Lisa's from Darwin, was going to PNG. He was going to hitchhike to Cairns and fly from there. I could travel with him. That sounded like more fun. He and I could connect in Brisbane, which gave me a chance to see a couple of places I'd heard about. Mullumbimby, I'd been told, was Australia's hippie capital. It would become one of my favorite places later. At that time I just saw a boringly small farm town and I got on the next train to Brisbane.

It was another of those instant, immediate connections: Dickie turned out to be simply the best lover I'd ever had. I couldn't get enough or stifle my vocal appreciation, which embarrassed him in his friends shared house, full of POSH Poms where we crashed for a few nights. He was also intelligent, imaginative and articulate. A perfect travelling partner. A travelling companion with benefits!

We started hitchhiking from Brisbane. At first, we weren't getting any rides. I was slim again and people would think they were seeing two guys, one white and a black one with a close-cut afro and they would pass us by. I changed into a halter top that barely contained my tits and a low-waisted skirt, leaving as much flesh bare as possible. We got rides after that and even had a couple people ask me to leave Dickie and go with them. Some who gave us rides had been like the cab driver in Sydney—curious about meeting a mythic Afro American, filled with questions, and often, surprisingly knowledgeable about heroes like Paul Robeson and Jack Johnson. We did accept an invite to spend the night with some young people in Bundaberg. They were amazed that I'd gotten a bit sunburnt, hitch hiking so long in the sun. They didn't understand why I was peeling; so I had to say clearly, "It's skin, not leather, and it burns."

A woman at the post office turned her back on me when I stepped up to the counter and ignored me to start a conversation with her work mate about dinner plans. It surprised the shit out of them when I demanded, in Yank style, to see the manager and ordered him to do something about their pathetic level and standard of service. I left no doubt what I thought about them, their intelligence, and ability. They obviously hadn't been spoken to like that before, and their dropped jaws let in a few of the flies that I noticed were omnipresent. Not as many as Kathmandu, but plenty enough that many locals talked with their teeth together—on top of the accent that made understanding them difficult.

★ ★ ★

This was my welcome to Far North Queensland (FNQ), called the Deep North to the US's Deep South because of its racist history and connections. It was where they took most of the people stolen from the Pacific islands within ransacking range. There was a traditional connection between South Africa, FNQ and Mississippi. They shared close ties and laws to suppress blacks. In Australia they called their slavery "black-birding." When the practice ended, many of those who'd been stolen and their descendants were arbitrarily gathered up and dropped off willy-nilly on any islands, regardless of where they had originally come.

We arrived in Cairns in a Mercedes Benz with a guy from Sydney who was having a lifestyle change. We stopped at a pub to buy him a thanks and good-luck beer. The woman behind the bar stared icily at me before saying, "We don't serve your color here." It was so unexpected I stopped breathing for a moment. Then I slowly started to respond and lost it! With my voice rising incrementally in volume and pitch, I said, "What color do you serve?" And for a moment I went patriotic: "How about red, white, and blue?" Then I went loco and had a fit on them, yelling, "Sue them, Dickie. You're my lawyer sue them!". I created such a fuss they tried to serve me the beer. I told them where to shove it, and, recognizing I wasn't in Kansas anymore, looked around for the Klan. This was the Australia I had expected. This was the one I'd been warned about.

Dickie and I spent a few noisy nights in Cairns and when we arrived into Port Moresby, I was doubly satisfied. It was the first black country I'd ever been in. Looking out the plane window at the airport, I could see no white people at all. Blacks doing everything. It was a proud moment.

Where we stayed was filled with expatriates, Australian government staff and various contractors, all still carrying a colonial mentality. They didn't care much for me and Dickie as a couple. Dickie was the second son of a second son. He wouldn't inherit a lot, but he had gotten a very upper-class upbringing and schooling. His accent was undeniably posh.

Dickie and I didn't stay long in the city. It was a depressing, dangerous and uninteresting city. PNG was going to be independent soon. It had a lot to overcome: a second-class country's oversight, Missionary influence, wartime occupation, patriarchy, inter-tribal hostility and the oppression of the women. Around Mt. Hagan a frequent sight was a bare-breasted woman with her overloaded *billum*,[58] the strap digging into her forehead, her back bent beneath the weight of its load, while the male with her walked ahead, armed with a thin stick. Since I felt Australia was a British copycat nation, their stewardship of the black nation seemed to me an example of underdevelopment, insufficient education and potential indigenous leadership so starved for the spoils of government, they had no appetite to nourish their people. The one good thing was that I met Shireen Malamoo, a politically charged South Sea Islander/Aboriginal woman who lived in FNQ. It was my luck that she happened to be in PNG, or my stay in Australia might have been different.

In PNG Dickie and I ticked off our to-do list: visited towns, engaged with people, bought a couple of pieces of art from a student exhibition at the university that featured a rising artist, Mathias Kauage and I renewed my Australian visa. We

---

58 A woven very expandable carry bag.

flew back to Cairns, home of gold top mushrooms, staying long enough for me to sample them. As usual they lifted the depression that kept returning, despite Dickie's gift of good sex.

The tropical sun hadn't reached full force, and we were walking to the railway station for the early train to Brisbane when a car swerved from the opposite side of the street. It screeched to a stop in front of us, blocking the sidewalk. All four doors flew open and four big guys jumped out with hands on guns. Who else but the cops? I dropped my bags and held my hands down and away from my body. One of the guys looked at me approvingly. "This happen to you before?" I responded with a head shake, then: "No. I watch television."

They searched our bags and then Dickie. From the back seat of their car, his untanned white ass mooned me as they made it a serious search. That was just too far for Dickie, and in his barrister's voice, he demanded, "Take us to the watch house or let us go." I didn't know but guessed that meant take us in and book us or let us go. Then this unimposing, sparsely bearded, long-haired, love-bead wearing, skinny guy continued, his commanding tones carrying an unexpected authority: "I'm a barrister and fully prepared to lodge a complaint." The cops loaded back into the car and peeled off so fast I barely had time to shout, "Any chance of a lift?" They were in such a hurry they left a generously sized cannabis bud in his backpack. Evidence for the arrest they had planned. We burnt the evidence with friends later.

70

BACK IN SYDNEY I connected with Nellie Enares, Shireen's friend who was also from FNQ. That made a BIG difference in my life. Hanging out with a person who looked like me and had a similar perspective was a relief. She lived just up the road in Bondi with two kids, Emelda and Tony who were near Malika's age. Nellie helped me find a place in the black community. She told me that there was going to be a Roberta Flack concert for "us." It was going to be in Redfern, a place I'd heard about it, mostly in the same ways people back home had talked about Watts—a black area of town with high arrest and low incomes. Redfern was the traditional home of the Eora people in the first city settled by the British.

Redfern had a black theatre and a lot of creativity was going on just like in Watts where The Watts Writers Workshop had created a new art form called Rhythm and Poetry. Some claim it as an ancestor of rap.

First Nations people in Australia found a role model in the African American civil rights movement, and young leaders like Charles Perkins, a Sydney University student, led their Freedom Rides. I was surprised to find they had been given the vote barely a dozen years before and were yet to graduate any doctors or lawyers. The Black Panthers had many admirers, and a local chapter was founded by Denis Walker, the son of Oodgeroo Noonuccal, a noted poet and political activist, who was the first black poet to be widely published. Sol Belear had also worked with the Panthers in the US and brought back their ideas. His brother Bob later became one of the first lawyers and the first appointed First Nations judge.

Nellie wasn't able go to the Roberta Flack concert, so she gave me the details and a friend drove me to Redfern. I was happy to say goodbye to him and to be with black folks. I had gotten tired of Aussies being so excited to meet me because they'd never met a black person before. When I'd challenge that black people had lived in Australia before their ancestors had come and stolen it, they would respond, "But they're different." I got so tired of "wypipo." One new friend earnestly told me how hard they had tried to make contact. They had called a black organization and requested a couple to come to dinner at their house. It hadn't worked, he'd told me disappointedly. They had tried. I was so tired of explaining to them, of interpreting. I needed to breathe.

National Black Theatre Redfern was influenced by Amiri Baraka's Black Arts Movement, born in New York, which had attracted several local black activists to New York. I had a closer connect with The National Black Theatre Redfern than I knew. Artist and activist Bob Maza had worked and studied at the National Black Theatre of Harlem, founded by Godfrey Cambridge's ex-wife, Dr. Barbara Ann Teer. The alimony Godfrey had complained about paying Barbara Ann enabled her to keep the theatre afloat in the early days. In a way Godfrey's alimony had created a new home for me in Australia.

That evening at Black Theatre I was rapt! What a delight to be with a bunch of black people speaking English. At least by now I had gotten used to the Australian accent but could not yet differentiate it from a New Zealand, a kiwi accent. "Where you from?" was a common first question in the community. Although the settlers had called all black people Aboriginal, they weren't one group. There were more than five hundred clans or nations—or "mobs" colloquially. They are the world's oldest surviving culture. Often lumped in with them were the descendants of the black-birded Torres Strait Islanders and South Sea Islanders.

As usual I drifted toward the disrupters. Having had friends like Martin, Malcolm, and Maulana Karenga, why should I change? Roberta Sykes, "Bobbi," I met first. She wore a big Afro that caused the press and The Australian Security Intelligence Organization (ASIO) to label her "The Australian Angela Davis." We bonded immediately. Smart, sassy, eidetic memory, unbeatable in an argument and she loved to dance. She became my main running buddy, as well as main competitor in the search for the scarce black men in Sydney.

Carole Johnson, a fellow African American, was quiet but just as militant. She was a dancer from New York and her background was Julliard and making things happen. Carole was not a big talker; she's a doer of the highest order. In New York her ability to bring arts to people was demonstrated by her creation of Dance Mobile, a mobile dance performance theatre. She was a soloist with the political-cultural provocateur, Eleo Pomare Dance Company and had already added her support and choreography skills to the growing voice of acknowledgement of the rights of the original inhabitants.

The Pomare company on tour in Australia had threatened to cancel their show unless the theatre facilities were improved and seats were made available for First Nations people. When we met, Carole had already started organizing community dance support for a major political action in Canberra, the Australian capital. At The Tent Embassy she demonstrated using dance as protest and with community support, Carole was invited back to Australia by the national arts agency, The Australia Council for the Arts, as a paid arts advisor.

I don't know how Roberta Flack knew about Redfern, but she changed my life. Not only did I have the joy of her performance but new friends I'd met there. I'm forever grateful.

★ ★ ★

In May 1975, autumn was ending, and I was about to face my first Sydney winter. Living at the beach and seeing surfers everyday kept fooling me into believing summer would last forever. I loved living at Bondi. I could watch Malika walk home from the Bondi Pavilion Daycare Centre. There was another black child Deni, she became friends with. Deni's mother, Marsha Hines, an African American singer, was Australia's Queen of The Pops.

As was common I had no telephone. I rang from the public telephone up the street and was lucky to have such good access to communication. To have a phone installed would cost a lot and take at least six months. "Are you on the phone?" was a common question.

I reconnected with Sandra, my Bali friend, and she started

to introduce me to local film folks. One new friend was David Huggett, a film editor whose work I admired. With my social circle expanded, and with such a good location, I was having lots of visitors at my place. My hippie friends, my sorta straight friends and my black friends all got along. More than one beneficial connection was made. All the stores, food and everything else, closed at noon on Saturday. I cooked at lot. I felt I always had to have lots to eat around in case people dropped by. Mom had always said to feed folks. Soon, the pounds I had lost were looking for me, aided by my using a knife and fork again, instead of chopsticks.

* * *

Carole involved me in her work with the Australia Council and introduced me to Chicka Dixon, the only black man on staff there. The Aboriginal Arts Board was a black body with a white head. Another black man involved was a consultant, Brian Syron, a no-shit-taking, extremely competent and creative artist. He shared with me his story of his youth, a young man in trouble who got his life back together and became a model and actor. How he snuck away from Australia, pretending not to be First Nation in order to get a passport without permission. How he worked for fashion houses in Europe and continued on to study acting in New York, where he was the first Australian accepted into Stella Adler's studio and became her senior teacher. Then he said one day he looked into a mirror and it reflected back to him the face of an ancestor, a warrior. He knew that was a sign it was time to go home, to pass on to his people what he had learned. Brian was another disrupter. With the mainstream western acting techniques that needed to be incorporated and adapted for the nuances of the Aboriginal Islander communities he was uniquely able to accommodate the needs of the community.

Brian and Carole had plans for an intensive theater workshop that would last six weeks involving First Nations people from the entire country including Islanders. It would take place at Black Theatre Redfern.

The workshop would include acting, speech, writing, a traditional language taught by song and conversation and a traditional and contemporary dance spectrum. It would be an intensive course with classes held five days a week, twelve hours each day, for the first four weeks with everyone participating in every class during that time. The last two weeks they would separate into the discipline of their choice and concentrate their energy on preparing for a closing performance. The hope was that the initial six-week workshop would nurture interest and demonstrate the need for the establishment of a permanent course or school to continue the process. It was a hard sell. It had never been done there. Even some liberals feared that the project was overly ambitious. Dancers, yes, but future administrators, choreographers, playwrights, directors?

71

To set the six-week training workshop in motion, Carole and Brian devised mini-workshops to be conducted in three capital cities prior to the full workshop. They were held in Sydney, Brisbane, and Melbourne. Because the tutors for the workshops would be travelling from city to city, the mini-workshops were occasionally referred to as the Travelling Theatre Workshops.

The instructors had a unique task — they were bringing live theater and training directly into Aboriginal and Islander communities. At that time there were no established systems of teaching that incorporated the nuances of Australian Aboriginal — or Islander-temperament, character, language or expression.

There were many talented artists in the communities we went to. You don't need degrees to be creative. And you didn't need to know something to teach it, which I found out when Carole made me the playwriting teacher. I taught playwriting, sneaking peeks from a book on Playwriting by Lajos Egri. The three mini-workshops accomplished several significant objectives. They provided quality training outside of Sydney, gave a realistic picture of what was involved in performing arts, created a preliminary formula for future support and successfully networked and promoted trust and good feelings about the upcoming six-week workshop.

Each trip was only three days. It took a while to get familiar with the participants. Learning from them. Codeswitching me to them, them to me, until we got more us. Getting their humor was a gift!

The six-week workshop at Black Theatre Redfern was going to be brilliant and needed to be documented. I <u>had</u> to make a movie, both to complete my mission and also to justify taking and spending the money from those con men. It made sense so I put the idea of documenting the event on the table.

Carole and Brian liked my idea of making a film about the workshop; we worked out a budget and they wouldn't have to pay me a salary. YES! I would also keep my promise to make a film for the people sitting on the ground in the Darwin cinema (which I knew by now were there by choice). I felt this opportunity was probably the reason I was guided to Australia. I was in the right place and at the right time. I would make the most of my opportunity.

The film was funded by the Australia Council, it wasn't a big-budget Hollywood film, shooting thousands of feet of film. Everything would be tight. I gathered the people who would help me make it happen. Sandra's friend, David Huggett, was the first person on my crew. I loved his editing. What I'd seen him do in a commercial running on local TV was what I wanted—lots of tiny cuts perfectly in synch with the music. He had a sense of rhythm, which was good because there would be dance. David suggested Robert, a sound recordist that he knew. Robert would do the job at a good price. I was putting together my film crew. For *my* film! At last!

Micha Nussinov was Israeli, a Sabra, and like me, new to Australia. London Film School trained, he showed me some of his camera work and we clicked. I needed a director and when I asked around, I found there were no black ones that anyone knew or could recommend in Sydney. But there turned out to be one, a Melbourne guy who had made a documentary. Except for his film, films made about black people had been made by white people. In every film I watched, my feelings were that they were depicted as noble savages or victims fighting the system. It looked like I was going to have to direct and that scared me. I was confident only about producing. It was either I direct or a white guy. I tried another option: co-direct. I chose a white guy with film experience, whom I'd met through an indigenous friend, to be my co-director. He was part of the movement, he assured me. Now I had my team, just the four of us.

I was due to start the shoot on Friday the 13th. *Great* date! Whatever! I was ready to work. I was happy. I'd gotten my chance.

Except there was a drastic change in my life. Mark, Malika's dad, suddenly appeared in Sydney with no warning. Mark gleefully told me how he'd gotten my address from my mother in Los Angeles and discovered he also had a current American Express account in very good standing. The card was in his name since we were still legally married. He'd gotten a replacement card and used it to buy new clothes, luggage, and a ticket to Australia with no intention or the ability to pay for them.

I warned my friends. Seriously instructing Susan, Bobbi and Sandra, warning them about his influence. Warning them not to have anything to do with him. He was too convincing and not to be trusted. All in vain.

Sandra eventually found out why I warned them when she took a road trip with him in her convertible MG and he insisted she wear her clothes inside out to deflect the evil-spear vibes the people in the hills around Mullumbimby were hurling at them. Susan found out why when he dropped by to visit and she introduced him to the couple she was sharing the house with. Susan and the husband went down to the wine cellar. It was an extensive collection of wines and it took a while. When they returned with the bottles, Mark and the wife were upstairs in bed.

Bobbi found out why when she saw the crazy in his eyes and felt threatened at his sudden changes of mood. She was sensitive to dangerous men. I learned why later.

I tried to ignore Mark. I made it clear he couldn't live with me. He met a woman and moved in with her. I hoped he would be out of my hair as I got busy with film preparations. I could feel old reactions, old patterns emerging. The relationship I had started became a problem.

* * *

When I met Chris, he was painting his living room, and the white in his hair that I'd mistaken for gray was paint. He was much younger than I'd realized and incredibly good looking. I loved his smile. It was a done deal when I learned the classic FX Holden parked outside his door was his. I was in love… with the car. Chris had just broken up with his girlfriend who lived across the street.

"Go away, come back" was a previous behavior pattern, and having not done it for so long, it threatened to regrow. I had a chance to produce a film, to howl. It was all on me, so of course, I managed to get in my way. To complicate things. Did I really want to be concurrently managing suicide thoughts, and provoking situations so that I could more easily fail? With no one standing in my way, self-sabotage was all that was left to get past. What would Kirk do? What would Gene L. do? Then, of course, things got worse.

72

THE FIRST DAY OF filming started off with a fight with Mark; me throwing a glass of orange juice at him, it breaking against his face. The theater was locked and we didn't get set up until almost lunch. All day there were technical problems.

We were supposed to be co-directing but my co-director quickly took over, making decisions without consulting with me, decisions I didn't agree with. I managed not to say anything; just watched and listened. Very soon I was disturbed. We definitely were not heading in the same direction. I gathered myself and corrected his approach. He didn't like it. He talked a good game but his subconscious was betraying him. He was no different in his attitudes than many others I'd met. He didn't get what my intentions were and I had to stop him. He didn't take it well and walked out. I kept going and didn't miss a beat. Darn, I was directing, after all. Good or bad, we would have footage in the can.

I finished the day better than I'd started, and when we went for dinner that night. I felt in charge and was treated like that was true. I was shooting only one day a week, but I was teaching playwriting every day. The people who turned up for the class were some of my favorites. Maureen Watson, a Murri (Qld) Elder who was attending the workshop with two of her sons, Michael and Johnny Bales. Jack Davis, who was already a professional writer. Aileen "Bunji" Corpus was an actor who had appeared in the ABC program comedy sketch series *Basically Black*. Ros Forgan was typical of the time, a young woman who had been removed from her mother, a "stolen generation" child. She had been adopted by a white family and raised as a white person. She was interacting with indigenous people for the first time, learning about her culture and participating in the dance.

* * *

1. Brian Syron directing two of his actors
2. Me in Papua New Guinea wearing dog teeth currency
3. Aileen Bunji Corpus at Black Theatre
4. Wayne Nichol and Cheryl Stone
5. The view from the porch, the beach and Bondi Pavilion.
6. Sunday brunch on the porch.
7. A smiling Bobbi Sykes
8. Ralph Rigby, Lillian Crombie and Rosilyn Watson
9. Me and Mal arrive in Sydney.

Mark, if it was possible, became more and more erratic. He was fearful and protective, and I didn't have any idea of the threats he sensed, was responding to or wanting to protect me from. I was concerned about him being around Malika. He was spending time with Justine, a girl who lived in a big-shared house. She seemed nice and I'd been to the house. The people who lived there were like her, young and pursuing a radically different lifestyle than their parents. She treated Mark as though he was normal. He wasn't. This was reinforced when I got word that Mark had gone to Sandra's, and she had to call to police to get him to leave.

I was trying to get to know some of the people in the workshop. Having them over for dinner seemed a good idea. Mark barged in, saying he'd finished with Justine, made himself at home for a moment and then tried to make it *his* home. I wasn't expecting him to visit; much less move in. I wasn't having him back in my life. He had a major freak out, throwing things and making threats and becoming more and more of a problem.

★ ★ ★

I'd given up on my "not working out" relationship because Chris was vacillating between me and his ex. He was the one doing the "go away, come back" thing to me. I was depressed and suicide thoughts were back. It was crazy! I was actually doing what I wanted. I was carrying out a project I loved and doing what I'd promised. There was nothing in the way. Except me! I could obsess over what was going wrong and let it take me down, strip me, rob me. Sink me. It wouldn't be the first time I'd given up, that I quit. No! Time to be like

Spock in Doomsday and rethink, start over with what I had to do, one step at a time. I had responsibilities and I had made promises. I keep agreements!

I kept going. But it was hard. There was nothing at all except crying for a long, long time & sleeping pills. I took two & gave the rest to my neighbor, Ken, for safe keeping. I didn't like having the temptation around.

While I was mourning my lost relationship, my neighbors decided I needed a dose of sex to fix me. Sue insisted I try Ken, her partner. She thought it would do me good. More than good, it was great. The climax to the climax was the vase of flowers that rocked off the headboard of the bed and covered us in cool water and rose petals. I wanted more. Sadly, it was a one-time only offer. Oh, well. Ken won Outstanding Performance in a solo episode....

★ ★ ★

From my first couple of meetings with the guy from the Arts Council who was administering the film budget, I could tell something was going on. The first warning was that he kept moving his chair closer and closer to me while "showing me the book", the record of expenditures. I was within budget. There was no problem.

The Arts guy, had sort of a strange vibe. After the chair thing, I invited him to lunch to check him out. At the restaurant when the food was served, we both reached for the fish sauce or something, and our hands touched. A spark arced between our fingers that was so violent it hurt! I almost cowered in my chair. Well, maybe not that bad—noticeable, though. I think maybe the universe was telling me to stay away from him. Danger. I was being warned. For some reason I needed to avoid him. I told myself; there was something about his chin, something about him.

Filming had mostly gone fine. We had only had six shooting days and there had been problems with the last one. The camera and the sound recorder had to be in synch. Most of the footage we shot that day wasn't. I had interviewed Brian Styron on camera and the interview felt stiff and without warmth. Not what I wanted to project. But this was something I could fix in the editing room. No worries, mate. I was getting a bit more Aussie.

★ ★ ★

At a club I'd met a man from Brisbane whose name I couldn't remember and I discovered that he'd left me a present. I was a week overdue on my visa and a week overdue on my period. Soon I would have to make a decision about an abortion. Again.

The pregnancy hormones dumped depression and loads of guilt on me. Malika wanted a little brother or sister. I didn't want to do pregnancy again. I had no job prospects and I didn't have enough money to support us for much longer.

On top of that I got the news that Mark was in jail for assaulting a woman. When I went to Long Bay Prison to visit him, he wanted me to understand he was there because he was trying to help. "It's all a mistake". He'd been in Rushcutters Bay Park meditating, healing the park from the negative energy of the million-dollar yachts parked nearby. He and a girl had started talking. After hearing her story, he'd tried to heal her by banishing the influence he'd sensed preying upon her from a sexually abusive stepfather. He told me I shouldn't worry about him. He was okay and understood his circumstances. He had recognized that it was **he** who'd come to save the world, not his goddess child.

Mark's family ties came into play this time. The American Consulate visited him. Mark was released on bail, and suddenly he was gone. He'd somehow gotten a new passport and a ticket and slipped out of the country. I was safe because he wouldn't be able to get another visa; it's never wise to re-enter a country from which you've done a runner. That was my only visit to Long Bay Jail, though, but would not be my only husband to occupy a cell there.

I'd started itching. Mark had been sleeping in my bed when I wasn't around and he'd left me scabies. Malika got them, and when Manfred wondered where he'd picked them up, I was silent. Couldn't bear the shame of admitting I was now the kid my mother told me not to play with. I had to do all the annoying things to get rid of them. Taking all the bedding to the laundromat. I'd rather have scabies than Mark. I was glad Mark was gone but soon I had to deal with the other problem.

* * *

A decision had to be made about the pregnancy. There was a yes-no argument raging in my head. A knockdown, drag-out fight with "no" threatening suicide and "yes" believing it. Couldn't face the baby thing again. The responsibility, the fear, the tiredness, the weight. No. Not again, not ever again. I didn't think I was very good at the job. I was better at mothering men than children who needed it.

I kept breaking dates with the Arts guy—not sure why—and after another cancellation, he came to my house with a gift he had made for me. He brought Australia's favorite dessert, a Pavlova, which was well received by the friends that were hanging around that day. He had changed; something was different. It was the beard; the weak chin had disappeared and there was a different air about him. My friend Steve eyed his moves and started calling him my Pav-lover. When I started to cut into the fluffy white confection, Steve jokingly placed the Arts guy's hand over mine, mimicking a wedding cake cutting. I don't know what happened; I found myself cowering in my closet. They told me I went pale and ran out of the room. Something was happening. Whatever he did I felt like a mouse being stalked by a cat thing. No matter how I twisted and hid and demurred, I was afraid the Arts guy would pounce. I made excuses and put-up barriers.

Pregnancy terminations were legal in Australia. I got a referral from the Aboriginal Medical Service. I was proud to attend a clinic staffed by black people. I went to the termination interview and was then scheduled. I was dropped off in the morning. Intake was smooth. I'd also asked the Medical Service to include a tubal ligation on the termination referral. My tubes were to be disconnected so that there could not be another pregnancy no matter the power of the sperm and the willingness of the egg; they would have no chance of meeting or getting involved.

I'd had two abortions and two children in four years at twenty-two and despite my best efforts, I found myself pregnant again and again. Nothing I had tried worked. That plug thing, like an early IUD, made me smell but didn't stop me getting pregnant. I found myself one night in a back yard, off a dark alley where I'd been dropped, looking for the woman who claimed that her Creole family in Louisiana had taught her well. Even their dogs didn't stay pregnant. I didn't hesitate but handing over the money meant there would be a lot of sacrifices, more beans to eat.

The woman took the catheter tube I'd brought with me, picked up a metal coat hanger, and started untwisting it as I turned my back on her young male helper to take off my panties. Then I lay down on a cot covered by an old, tattered blanket and spread my thighs. The young man moved in I think for a close look, then I see a small lamp with a bare globe in his hand. He was the illumination.

I watched while she inserted the straightened coat hanger into the tube. And then into me. My doctor had had problems inserting my birth control plug; he'd said I had a skittish cervix that moved away when touched. It wasn't any better behaved with the woman. The young man moved closer to shed light, but he got too close and the bare bulb came in contact with my inner thigh. It burned me. She started to get frustrated when finally, she got it in, perhaps a bit too far in. Blood gushed out; I was sure I was going to die! The bleeding slowed. The catheter stayed in. Air would go up the catheter and out the small hole at the end and those air bubbles inside my uterus would cause the miscarriage. I hoped the cabbie that took me home didn't notice a possible small puddle I might have left behind. I wiggled around, hoping my skirt and coat would soak up the blood that I was grateful was still flowing. *With that much blood, it should work. Please, God, let it work. Please,* I thought to myself.

At home I'd stuffed a sheet between my legs to contain

the blood that was still flowing when I went for a wee. When I took it away to sit down, something small dropped out of me, attached by a kind of string. I couldn't stop the scream. Frantically dropping onto the toilet, I went crazy, bouncing as hard as I could on the toilet seat, trying to break the attachment almost hysterical. Wanting it gone, wanting it gone. I don't remember the ambulance; I heard a siren, but I don't remember who called it or how I got there, but soon there were white men in white clothes in a white room looming over me, demanding that I tell them who had butchered me. I was terrified they would recognize the round red circle on the inside of my thigh as a burn. I denied it, because there was no way I was giving up the people from that little back room off that alley. No one should have to go through that! No one should have to risk their lives! Legal abortion, and a woman's choice, her control over her body is a right I still fight for.

As I waited at the abortion clinic I was parched. I'd had no fluid since midnight and enviously watched the women leave the room for the procedure. I wished they'd hurry up. Then all the other women were gone and I was still there. *What the fuck?* It was afternoon by then and I was thirsty and pissed off. The smiling doctor came and said, "We're ready for you now."

"What took so long?" I had to know.

"We had to get some information from the intake nurse and she had already left. We had to wait for her to get home." I was totally confused. What info? I'd been there. Wasn't it something I could have told them? No, it must have been something technical.

I couldn't help myself. I could smell racism. So many small things are buried so deeply. They are like air, unnoticeable, and they still influenced behaviors. I had to ask! "What did you need to know?"

"Your referral said tubal ligation and we needed to check with intake that it was correct."

"I was here. You could have asked me." And I think he realized the assumptions that he had made: couldn't speak English, was too dumb to understand, response not trustworthy. Whatever it was, it was based on my color and my referral from a black organization. His attempted explanation was that they didn't want to be accused of genocidal actions. My response was the same. "I was here. Why didn't you ask me?"

Some ideas have been reinforced for multiple generations and were so implanted, their presence was accepted and gave no warning of how they limit. I had identical knee surgeries and you could tell the difference between the work of the POC and a self-disclosed supremacist. They saw me differently. Systemic racism has no boundaries and isn't bound by intelligence or education. It's permeable. Wonder who taught them?

We finished shooting and moved into the editing room. The editor, my friend David, was located in North Sydney at Kiwi Editing. Since Kiwi was a shoe polish and also a slang for a New Zealander. Their logo was a shoe polish can with a Kiwi on it and the slogan, "Finishing with polish".

I had to get David used to a new way of working. Most editors got the script and the footage and made an assemblage, the rough cut of all the pieces put together. Then the director or producer viewed it and made any changes. Not this time! I was there from day one of the cutting and David had never worked that way before. Because I had the structure in my head, I had to tell him where all the pieces fitted. I'd got a bonus with one of the students, Andrew Jackomos, who had some film school experience at NYU. He shot some stunning closeups.

David and I had lots of fights and good creative battles. It was hard to explain to him what I was doing. For example, I refused to let him cut from a shot with the person's head down. I had to explain the subconscious feeling that the image of a black man with his head bowed took to whatever shot was next.

We had finished editing 10 minutes of film, when it looked as though Malika had the measles. After a hell of a week, Malika sick, me working late, the police were at my door looking for weed. They arrive when I had a house full of people. The straightest, most conservative person I knew happened to be there and answered the door. He closed it and came to me with the news: "Ande, the police are here and insisting they need to come inside to talk." I ran to the back door, hurled the bong as far as I could, grabbed a glass of wine and, slopping it, lurched the door open enough to refuse their request to enter. I staggered slightly as I came out and closed the door firmly behind me. I explained that it was a work and social event, and my employer was there, and they just couldn't come in. Patty, my new, loud, Ocker next door neighbor, stuck her head out of her door to see what was going on and I manufactured an event. I started hurling abuse at her for calling the police. Of course, she started yelling abuse back at me, and the cops soon left this "neighbors' dispute." They said they'd be back. I wasn't sure they wouldn't come back and dumped my half pound of weed, which would have lasted me forever, into the toilet. Weed was very hard to flush. Even harder to replace.

★ ★ ★

Flat assed sick on my back, I was feeling worse than hepatitis or the Bali ball breaker and worried about money; but we at least had 30 minutes of film cut.

The days in the editing room were alike. Absolute heaven! David would pick me up and we'd spend the day in the edit suite. It was difficult to explain what I was doing and he would question my decisions. I had the structure in my head. Introduction, familiarity, involvement. David still hated that I wouldn't cut away on a person whose head was down. The transitions had to have energy. There were little things he didn't understand. He needed František Daniel's AFI lessons.

We had a rough-cut screening and I was disappointed with the first reaction from the audience; but I knew the film was good. We took a break for sunrise and drove with blankets down to Milson's Point and watched the sun come up. We slept together that night. Good. If only I didn't have to go back to the States. Money and visa were running out. Time to plan for the future. Mike (the Scot from Penang) was still in touch. He wanted me to come to Perth, said he'd buy me a house.

No doubt about it, I was gaining weight. No more walking long distances, carrying a heavy backpack. No more eating healthy food. I'd eaten mostly vegetable dishes with small amounts of meat and fresh fruit while I was in Asia. Now it was big chunks of meat and lots of sugary things and bread, bread, bread.

We had a very good reception at the next screening with a full house there. Two weeks later we finished the fine cut. Cutting a dance sequence was the last problem we had. David really stretched out on that. He exceeded himself.

Finally, it felt like the film had come together. I stopped

bitching and moaning. All the pieces were where they fit best. It satisfied my soul. The doubts were still poking up. Was it a piece of shit or a good job? I was bouncing back and forth, uncertain, unsure, afraid I'd screwed up (much like writing this book at this point).

★ ★ ★

I think I knew that David had invited a director friend, to have a look at the film. David had worked with several directors. Of all of them it was this director's films I liked best. When he dropped by the edit suite, I was trying to be cool. I thanked him for coming to watch our piece of shit. He shot back he wasn't interested in a piece of shit and I hotly informed him it wasn't a piece of shit— it was a good film.

Great start! And it was. Saying the film was a piece of shit and then supporting it was my first overt taking ownership, taking responsibility for what it was. It represented my choices. The ingredients I'd chosen, the way I chose to put them together. My taste, my recipe. And I hoped like heck he would like it.

I slid into seat in front of the flat bed editing table when David's unexpectedly left the room to take a call from his mum in New Zealand. Watching from behind me, the director started commenting on the film. I quickly noticed that he was identifying even what I'd attempted even if I'd not accomplished it. He even got the seriousness that showed under the jokes. Soon I was fighting tears at his understanding and sensitivity. I did love filmmaking and appreciated those that delighted in a well-made film. Those who could read the film. Since David didn't always understand what I was trying for, sometimes I just did it his way. Years later he apologized for some of the cuts he'd insisted on making when the film was chosen for restoration and honored by the Australian Sound and Film Archives.

David's Friend understood. He was reading my mind—or at least my film. I wish we could have worked together. I'd never felt so connected to someone on a head as well as heart level. No one. Ever. It had always just been physical. But he actually got me, who I was inside, my need to howl. He had been leaning back against the wall, watching the monitor from behind me. "When do they lose?" he asked. I turned to face him: "Not in this film!"

The film ended with upraised hands and triumphant smiles. I stood, and when I turned to look at him, my body continued into his arms. I must have floated there. I don't remember walking. We kissed and continued kissing as we went down the stairs out of the building. I felt like I would gladly walk off the edge of the earth with him. It would be a wonderful adventure! There were stars out there for us to dance on. That night my brain and fear weren't in control. My instinct and my core, my heart and my gut, and probably my guardian angel were and they were congruent. It was the kind of moment you want to last forever.

But I couldn't believe it was real! I couldn't believe I was good enough for him. Within a month I was engaged to someone everything was warning me not to go near.

★ ★ ★

The Arts guy had kept up the pressure. It was a lot of pressure. He rationally countered all my deflections and excuses, not accepting any rejection. Finally it was just that I didn't want to. That was all I had left. I caved. It was like getting raped again. I know it seems far-fetched, but both times there was minimal or no physical force. I didn't—just didn't—fight for myself. I froze and let it happen. Freeze goes with fight and flight. I'm sure other women blame themselves for that seeming acquiescence. I would have to justify what had happened, convince myself that it was what I wanted, that I cared about him and I fell back on another old pattern: "someone to set you down."

73

Finally, I was satisfied that I'd done my best with the editing and moved on to the rest of the post production. I was there for every minute of the mix, the place where Gene Coon had said I couldn't be: no one watched their language and no one was uncomfortable. I was respected, as it was clear I knew what I wanted and loved the process. We laughed a lot; so it was fun too. I got on so well with the guys that the lab made a tiny mistake in the grading and insisted on doing a second print. I had two copies and I only had to pay for one. Yes! The budget couldn't have handled paying for two.

Now the screenings seriously started. I'd invited any of the workshop participants in town to come, look and make comments. The group gave their approval. They laughed in all the right places and when I thought they were too quiet, I saw they were engrossed, not bored. Bobbi came and gave me her approval. That meant a lot.

I was spending lots of time with my friend Bobbi. The support from another black woman helped. She was smart and she thought I was too. She invited me to go on the road with her while she did her health department job. Bobbi insisted I see something of the country outside of Darwin and Sydney and hauled me away with her to visit clients—First Nations people who live in country NSW. It was different. I'd never seen anyone cooking on a wood stove that also heated the water for bathing. The people were welcoming and I appreciated their sense of humor, much like black people at home. Even though Bobbi wasn't First Nations she identified with and shared their unequal access. Her father was rumored to be a black WW II serviceman. All I know is the Australian women's avid acceptance of black serviceman caused a fight between white and black soldiers. The Battle of Brisbane[59] lasted 10 nights.

On a long drive on two-lane highways, there was a tendency to fill the silence, connect dots, and share dark places. On the Waterfall Way, the scenic road home, we drove into a dense, dark fog. We were going from the tablelands down miles and miles of steep, winding, narrow roads with killer drop-off cliffs to the ocean. The last 50 kms of Waterfall Way, curved the steepest through National Parks and tiny towns. With the sun setting, there was no way we could continue driving in the fog.

We found a safe place to pull off. To fill the space, Bobbi started to talk. As it got darker, I was glad I couldn't see her face when the conversation veered into an even darker place. I wouldn't have been able to stand seeing her pain as she told me about being pack-raped and beaten. How her girlfriend had left her alone at a dance. There had been poor transportation; so she accepted the generous offer of a ride. Once she was in the car, the presumed occupants exchanged places with strangers. It was too late to get out as the doors slammed, tires spun and the car headed in the opposite direction from her destination. Her pleas were answered with a blow. When she regained

---

59 https://en.m.wikipedia.org

consciousness, she was already being stripped. Brutal rapes followed, accompanied by laughter. Her life barely spared; she was discarded near a roadside. She had to beg for help from a reluctant passerby., and the police couldn't care at all.

Bobbi's white mother refused to let the police off the hook. She didn't accept their lack of interest. At the trial months later, one of the men couldn't resist asking for a peek at the baby born from the attack. Just couldn't resist seeing if it was his son. She made me promise I'd never tell another person. I carried her pain for years until she shared it in her books. I was in awe of the woman she had become.

Food was my comfort and I was unable to sleep. I thought we'd eaten all the food but I found one last candy bar in the bag and ate it without waking her. When Bobbi looked for it in the morning light, I had to admit I'd sneaked it. She never let me forget, and her "just like you ate the last candy bar" became a tag line that always made us laugh.

Gough Whitlam, the Labor Prime Minister had presided over a reimagined Australia. He had brought in universal health care, abolished university fees, raised wages, promoted multi-culturalism, gave traditional land title to First Nations people, granted independence to Papua New Guinea. He gave generous government support to the arts and a livable amount to the unemployment. The "tall poppy" syndrome (getting put down for standing out) was demolished and standing out congratulated. It became appreciated just how excellent Australia was and people weren't afraid to claim it. Australian ex-pats were coming home, new people were migrating from "the colored countries" and we were all proud to be Australian. Australia was to be a different place.

* * *

Then on November 11, 1975 the Governor-General dismissed Whitlam and appointed opposition leader Malcolm Fraser. Suspiciously, the U.S. was conducting military maneuvers around Australia at the time of the Whitlam government sacking.

My working visa had expired. I hadn't gotten a job and my money was almost gone. It was time to head back to California and I was a bit frightened. I didn't know if I ever wanted to live in the States again. Mom told me she'd been contacted by the FBI. They wanted to talk to me. I had never signed the papers for the money I'd received from the film people. It was something I would have to face when I got back. Malika and I were set to share a cabin on a freighter with Steve and Lisa and stay with them for a while in the UK. I had deluded myself into the romance with the Arts guy. He made sure he met every need, catered to my every whim. Made me believe that he was there for me in every way. He told me his sad stories and I felt protective towards him. I was leaving the poor guy who needed me. I entered the clinging 'how can I leave you' stage.

Telegram: bad news. Massive heart attack. Mom was in intensive care. The slow boat home with Steve and Lisa that we had booked was off. I needed to go home immediately.

The Arts guy reminded me that I had once jokingly asked him to marry me. Even if I was joking, he wasn't. He would fix everything, take care of me, make things work. It was seductive. Since it was Christmas holidays time Malika could stay and go on holiday with him, his kids and his ex-wife. I would go to LA and come back and stay in Australia. He would find a house for to move in together.

He suggested that Tom, who was dating Carole and loved my beach flat could take it over. I wouldn't have to move out. He'd help packing up my personal thing. He would handle everything. I felt looked after, taken care of. I was being groomed.

Malika headed off for camping on the south coast at the beach and I booked the cheapest return ticket for the shortest possible stay

LA was scary. Mom "Ande what have you done this time. Why is the FBI looking for you?" was the first thing Roz Heller asked when I joined her in Malibu. Nice when your best friend assumes the worse. Being wanted by the FBI was a hard thing to explain to her and to Ivan.

I made sure mom was ok. She'd been released from the hospital but looking after her mother was to

I headed back to Australia as soon as I could. Before I left, I filed for a divorce from Mark. Sorta handy to have if thinking about getting married again.

I was flying as cheaply as possible on a super budget airline. I had a few days stopover in Noumea. Using my Lonely Planet guide book, I found a brothel that rented cheap rooms to tourists. A good thing I was going to be a kept woman. I was broke and unemployed.

When I returned to Sydney, I was greeted at the airport by the Arts guy with a bunch of roses and an envelope filled with cash. He was demonstrating that he would look after me and my child.

We had a big party to announce that The Arts guy and I

were officially a couple and living together. I was oblivious that my 5-year-old daughter was being skillfully stalked and groomed by the man I'd sold us to. Today, she's pleased that when you google Richard Peter Maddox (The Arts guy's legal name), her accusations and his conviction and imprisonment show up as well as his achievements. She tells her story better than anyone else. Read about this mighty woman and the women she springs from in her book, "Five Women [60]".

★ ★ ★

David and I screened the film, *Tjintu Pakani* (Sunrise... Awakening), for the press. Praise was coming from all points, making it hard for me to keep tearing it apart and discounting it. So I tried paranoia: "Why are they saying such good things about my film? I may have to take responsibility and admit I made a good film."

Maybe I thought that hearing good things would jinx the project. The old feelings of not being good enough, was still hanging around. My mother's exhortation that I needed "to be the best dish washer in the world".

I started to work on a film script. The title was "Warning: Sisterhood is Powerful." I wanted to write something empowering for women that inspired and supported them.

The Filmmakers Co-op on St Peter's Lane became my hangout. I'd found a great group of white women filmmakers all of whom were political and aware of systemic oppression. One, Martha Ansara, from New York, later worked with Essie Coffey, a Muruwari woman, who directed the first film made

---

60 5 Women http://www.malikaelizabeth.com

by a First Nations woman and co-founder of the Western Aboriginal Legal Service.

Writing was still painful. I was feeling a failure one night, totally hopeless as a writer. My Sisterhood script had been assigned an assessor to help. I was feeling as though I hadn't taken advantage of whatever talent I'd had and now it had evaporated. The previous week I'd been feeling miserable about something else. Maybe it was because if I didn't find the misery, I might be finding myself very happy. On the surface nothing was wrong, but that which I created in my head. Real things were going on but I was oblivious.

Finally! The Sydney Film Festival! My film was entered into the Australian film competition. Three of the films in the documentary category were about indigenous people. I watched the other two. One was a very moving work filled with social issues. The other was breathtakingly filmed. Both very worthy, excellent, relevant work. I didn't think I had much of a chance. After watching their films, I left before the judge's decision. I couldn't bear to be inside when they announced the winner. I was sitting out in front when one of the guys that I vaguely knew from the Filmmakers co-op came up to the car where I was waiting for the bad news. "What are you doing out here? You should be inside. You won!"

I caught my breath, stopping whatever I was about to say changing directions! "That's cruel. How could you say that to me?

He looked at me in disbelief. "I'm not teasing. You won!

Here's a couple of reviews for Tjintu-Pakani. I still prefer to let others talk about my work.

The review from the feminist magazine, *Womanspeak*, reviewed by filmmaker Margo Oliver:

"It's a stunning film on many accounts: A documentary that doesn't seem to be alienated from the people it is observing. The camerawork is superb and the editing spot on... I think the film is a must for anyone interested in the situation of urban blacks in the use of theatre and dance to do far more than keep people entertained and amused or in the art of documentary filmmaking."

From the biggest newspaper, Murdoch's 'The Australian' review by film critic Mike Harris:

"It is an amazing and inspiring film showing how a group of Aboriginals assemble a show incorporating playlets, music and dance. A sophisticated updating of the old Warner Bros. "Putting on a Show Movie". Ande Reese has created a narrative flow in the cutting and editing that creates an uncanny sense of familiarity with the people in her film. A feeling that increases with each successive sequence. The actors grow not only as actors, but more importantly as people. It's a beautifully handled and restrained example of observation. It's a joyous picture with some wonderfully human moments that are immediately identifiable for any audience. An exultant film that deserves to be seen by the widest possible audience."

OTHER HOWLS AND HOWLERS

AFTERWARDS AFTERWORDS

I WASN'T FINISHED. I went after the Australian Broadcasting Corporation, the national broadcaster, to buy and show the film. I was aggressive as I had never ever been before and wouldn't take no. They agreed to air it if I made it a half hour, (from 47 minutes) I chopped out a few chunks. It was painful; but we didn't have the money to re-edit. When the film aired, finally I felt I'd done what I promised.

Our pebble had started a ripple. Brian Syron's Black Theatre workshop students began to appear in "Wanden Valley" and on "Ramsey St," the locations of the most popular Australian TV shows of the day: *Neighbors* and *A Country Practice*. Michael and Maureen Watson and Lilian Crombie would become professional actors and Johnny Bales a radio broadcaster. Aileen Corpus continued to act and later became a well-known artist.

The dance class from the film became a school, the Aboriginal Islander Skills Development Scheme, the covert name for Careers in Dance with its wider intent of bringing Australian Indigenous culture to the world while preserving its roots and passing it on. Dance was a part of the culture and an approved career; but ideas of choreographers, administrators and ethnographers and a direct worldwide culture transfer was pretty farfetched — "overly ambitious" said the assessors of the funding sources. It was Carole Johnson's intent for those things to happen, and they did! It became incorporated as NAISDA (National Aboriginal Islander Skills Development Association) and is now the oldest dance school in New South Wales helmed by a former student. it is turning out professional dancers, choreographers, dance ethnologist, administrator, and producers. Its student performing wing, *Aboriginal/Islander Dance Theatre*, morphed into the professional international Bangarra Dance Theatre, envisioned and launched by Carole and driven to its current prominence by former students. I was thrilled when they let me choose the name for the company. Bangarra means to make fire and they are a hot dance company. Bangarra Dance Theatre was the first overseas company to perform in New York after 9/11.

Jack Davis, one of the writing students from the workshop, became famous. He took my meager writing tips and his great talent forging plays that toured the world featuring First Nations actors.

Andrew Jackomos, displayed talent with the beautiful, telling, close-up shots he contributed to the film. He went on to the Australian Film Television Radio School but after that I could find no evidence of his involvement in film. High achievements, extremely high. Yes! Just not in film. It was the 1990's before black director and producers appeared in those production roles.

Andrew became the inaugural Commissioner for Aboriginal Children and Young People in Victoria, responsible for the most vulnerable in the areas of child protection, youth justice and homelessness as well as taking on other innovative and high-profile positions.

Maroochy Barambah (Yvette Isaacs), one of the students in the film says she thinks she wants to do singing. In 1993 she became the first Australian to perform at the United Nations in New York in honour of the International Year for the World's Indigenous Peoples.

* * *

One family stands firmly at the center of that creative revolution. The Bostocks! Euphemia, Gerry, and Lester were at the beginning of black growth of dance, art, theatre and film. Their contribution is unmeasurable!

* * *

My good friend Bobbi, Dr Roberta Sykes, became the first black Australian woman to earn a doctorate from Harvard. Her successful writing and lecturing career ended when Bobbi had a stroke and didn't receive treatment early enough. She was impaired by both the stroke and an internet that, at the time, required a telephone line which wasn't available in the nursing home she was shuffled into. She was cut off from the world in a facility where her active brain was constrained and her body maltreated.

* * *

My Sydney Film Festival win wasn't enough for my mom. She expected that the film would be screened worldwide. "But mum it was rejected by the Melbourne Film festival." Okay, it screened in Paris, London, and New York; but I still wasn't the best in the world not even at dishwashing.

★ ★ ★

Returning to California meant the FBI had to be dealt with. The film money I had taken scared me the most but ended up the easiest to deal with. Ivan terrified me when he prophesied that I'd get hit, that I would be killed for taking off with the "investors'" money. Taking his words to heart as usual, I started to quake at any knock on the door. My paranoia and depression grew until I found myself with a pile of pills in my lap, about to swallow the lot. I realized I had to see a lawyer and face the terror of what "could happen." My choice was a lawyer who grew up in Watts and had been a Rhodes Scholar. When I told him the story, he couldn't contain his laughter and practically had to pick himself up off the floor. He said it was such a good story that he'd check it out for me and not to worry about the cost. I was extremely relieved when I found the scam had been uncovered and investigated and I had not been indicted and faced no charges.

★ ★ ★

Back in Australia I was tired of dealing with my hair, sick of asking "Do you know how to cut my kind of hair?" There were no black beauty shops. I decided to have dredlocs. This took my "Hair War" with mom to our biggest battle. I didn't know anyone who had dredlocs. I had the barber take off all my hair in order to "dred from the roots", like the song said. I didn't know any other way. Worse than back in the day, this change freaked out my mother. With no hair I looked very masculine to her.

What finally slipped out was that she was fearful I was gay and expressing it through my lack of hair. My sexuality was none of her business. Of course, I attacked. She was trying to explain and justify the reason my hair was wrong and would give "people" ideas when she gave away her big secret. She had found a female close to her in bed with their best friend, pleasuring each other.

In a few years, I had locs past my shoulders which made her happy. To mom, long hair was as good as straight hair. As my hair got longer, our relationship improved; but the biggest change was when conflict resolution training entered my life.

We had had a few disputes going on at the dance school and I called the Conflict Resolution Network (CRN) for some help. They suggested I take one of their courses and see if I could make workplace improvements on my own. I was challenged by the course, irritated by the trainer and ready to walk away. I couldn't. It was the second meeting of the class when I got a glimpse of its value. I'd come home from work and found my daughter Malika watching TV instead of studying. After words and her bedroom door slamming, I thought for a while about what I'd learned that day and tried it out. 'I' worked! With changing the point from you to I, I'd found a way of asking for what I wanted without blame or justification and expectations, a way of speaking that was more easily heard and responded to. I was a convert!

At work there were things there that needed changing. It was time for me to go. I trained a team to take over the publicity and a plan for long-term, corporate sector fund raising. It was the Aboriginal Islander not the African American dance school and I wanted to get out of their way. It was scary to leave. I needed to support my daughter and me and my skill set didn't fit any job I saw advertised. I could envisage being in one of the nearby hotels, pushing a laundry trolley and asking if they wanted their linen changed. At least Australia was generous with unemployment support.

Then I saw an ad for enrollment in a mediation training with one of the prominent family counselling agencies. Mediation was something I'd learned about on *Star Trek*. At that time, you had to be a lawyer to be a mediator in the real world and so that idea went into my basket of "would be great but not possible." I had enough money to pay for the first half of the training.

I'd started using the CRN manual as a volunteer conflict resolution trainer and my conflict resolution trainer, who had become a good friend, let me tag along with her to pick up training pointers. With her mentorship I developed my own clients. My first group I taught sitting down with the Manual in my lap, just like I had at Black Theatre.

When the second part of the mediation course started, I was allowed to continue without paying. They thought I was going to be good at it. I was! I had also become good at teaching the conflict resolution course as well and was invited to be one of their six CRN master trainers who taught other trainers.

Teaching meant knowing the material, but it didn't promise

family peace or a conflict-free life. I heard the other trainers complain. Teaching it didn't make conflicts go away. It did challenge me. If I was going to teach, I was going to have to walk the talk to earn respect from myself. My oldest and more deeply disturbing and infringing conflict was the war with my mother. I made up my mind it would end. I started from a new belief: She had done the best she could.

When the mediation course ended, I was asked to help teach the next course. They were right: I was good at it! I was soon a much in demand consultant, flying in the pointy end of the plane all over the country. What mediation and conflict resolution gave me, though, was something much more important than the airline upgrades. Using those skills, I was able to end the hair war.

It took a couple of years before the war was over and peace declared. The first sign was when my mother used the word "option." The shift was obvious when she told me about the difficulties of her next-door neighbor. The neighbor's favorite son had died, and she didn't like the wife of her remaining son. Mum looked at me and said, "You know, she'd rather be right than happy." When my jaw dropped at hearing something I'd taught and repeated so often around her, she said, "You're not the only one learning new things."

I was proud of myself that she was doing so well and was surprised when she called me out. "When I come to visit, you leave town," she said to me as I packed to leave soon after she'd arrived. I caught myself, started to—tried to—deny that it was true; but it was. The family habit of holding onto resentments hadn't passed me by. I took a while to finally work through the buried anger.

I was laughing with her one day, joking that I been damaged growing up, moaning that she forgot to put treats in my lunch box in primary school, when I remembered I'd reacted angrily, stealing money from her purse, and buying treats for the whole class. I remembered the sneaky things I'd done. My part in keeping our war going. As I apologized for the rotten things I'd said and done, silently adding the things I'd thought and not said my laughter turned to tears at all the needless battles and bad feelings. Time wasted. Mom wrapped her arms around me. She held me tight, cradled me, due to Malika's influence, I'm sure. It sure wasn't the previous lean in, A hug and there was no back patting. As she hugged me there were tears on my face and I held her closer than ever before. She said "I always knew I'd get my baby back." It had only taken me 50 years.

MY TAKEAWAYS

I'VE BEEN TOLD THAT it would be good to say what I feel I've learned from contact with such incredible people and I dared to wonder if they might have learned from me. I asked Gwen Green, who knew Martin better than most people, why she thought he encouraged me to hang around. Her thoughtful response churned a while and she responded, "You asked good questions."

I have a fantasy that when Martin and Malcolm met that one time, one of them said to the other, "Ande told me about you," and the other's response was: "She told me about you too." And they would've laughed and been at ease with each other and would have made plans to work together when they could.

Okay, that wasn't likely; but it's my fantasy. And in my 80s, here is what I've learned and where I learned it:

★ ★ ★

Gene Coon: Drug use by adults should not be criminal. The last 20 years in Portugal has proven that.

★ ★ ★

Spock & Allan Parker: Be aware of prematurely extrapolated conclusions.

★ ★ ★

The Great Bird of the Galaxy (Gene R): You can go from the front to the back, but you can't go from the back to the front.

★ ★ ★

George Takei: If you judge a drink (or person) by its color, you can wreck yourself.

★ ★ ★

Nichelle Nichols & Ricardo Montalban: Carry yourself to Represent!

★ ★ ★

Martin Luther King, Jr: Generosity.

★ ★ ★

Malcolm X: "A chicken born in an oven ain't a biscuit."

★ ★ ★

Bill Russell: Deliver more than you say.

Melvin van Peebles: Look at yourself! See how beautiful you are!

* * *

D'Urville Martin showed me a life lived exuberantly and artistically. I still aspire to emulate D'Ur who died on his way to another party. Also, his was the funniest funeral I've ever been to.

* * *

My mom, Olivia: told me that love is absolutely the most important practice, and baby steps are enough when they head in the right direction. Malika, my youngest modeled resilience. She doesn't bounce back. She bounces forward with laughter and love. Paula, my oldest, demonstrates forgiveness, kindness and service. Daughter Kandis, is my life long creative impulse.

* * *

I never met Marvin Gaye or Tupac, but their songs, "What's Going On?" and "Changes" are the guides for my final years. My necessity: Gratitude. Practice this mindfully and it might stop you wanting to kill yourself.

No matter where you learned it, take responsibility for your words and actions. Check yourself! Love yourself and your planet. One person can howl!

ACKNOWLEDGEMENTS

Timothy Barrett: Every time I told him a story, he said "you gotta write it". He got me telling stories on stage and now, finally, written down. Thank you isn't enough for holding and warming my hand for the last 15 years. There is no better friend than Franny. Francesca Emerson has provided friendship, support, encouragement and hugged me and wiped away my tears when it all became too much for over 50 years.

My companions on this journey were Ben Pritchard who was joined by master Star Trek fact checkers Michael Kmet and Maurice Molyneaux. The three stayed with me the whole way through the first draft.

Polishing is about smoothing the rough edges, rubbing things the wrong way. There were a few tight lipped "it's your book" moments. Here are the boots on the ground folk, the friends that got commas corrected and thoughts made clear: Fiverr's Vanessadreme and ckkorfo, coached me past my self limits and modest goals. Don Ellison, Tjaye Jefferson were first to read the whole draft, and gave me a whole lot to think about. Barbara Cleary and Marta Houske read it, made comments and caught errors and omissions, plus supported and encouraged me. Shelley Feinman brought the litmus test to the final draft. It passed. It's me. Editorial efforts were complemented by Tim Kliendienst of Alphabet studio who designed and generously donated a book cover that took my breath away. Zac Campbell, a brilliant portraitist did the author photograph and created 4 collages to help tell the story.

Carole Johnson and Dr Vanessa Lee-AhMat originally proposed the book idea and Robin Henderson promised me I'd finished it. When I finished writing what I thought was the final draft Rob Edwards started the book on the publishing road when he convinced Allan Parker, James Hamilton, David Elliott and Chris Powell to also put in money in to help it along.

The ability to keep going two years after I thought I'd finished the book is due to friends like my bravehearted Lion, Lionel Bawden, If you're one of the people who heard me cry, held my hand or assured me I could do it, please raise your hand. Allan Parker! Thank you for getting me here!

All my bodily fears of "please don't let me die before I finish" were managed by an astounding cast of specialists: Cardio, and Kidney, Hematology, Mental, Dental and more, all coordinated by the better than marvelous Dr Helena who I can't thank enough.

And thank you for reading. I am grateful.

I was born in a place to which I had no spiritual connection. This place, this land I live and love on, the place this book was written, is Eora land. It was occupied but has never been ceded. Listen to these people. Howl together with them if you can.

Voice • Treaty • Truth

ood-product-compliance